Why Baptize Infants?

A study of the biblical, traditional and theological evidence

by

ARTHUR S. YATES

With Foreword by

DR GÜNTHER GASSMANN
A Director of the World Council of Churches

The Canterbury Press
Norwich

First published 1993 by The Canterbury Press Norwich
(a publishing imprint of Hymns Ancient & Modern Limited
a registered charity)
St Mary's Works, St Mary's Plain,
Norwich, Norfolk, NR3 3BH

A catalogue record for this book is available
from the British Library

ISBN 1-85311-061-2

*Typeset by Cambridge Composing (UK) Ltd
and printed in Great Britain by
St Edmundsbury Press Limited
Bury St Edmunds, Suffolk*

TO

ALL WHO BELIEVE

IN BAPTISM

Foreword

From the beginning of the ecumenical discussion on those controversial issues which have contributed to the divisions among Christians, the sacrament of baptism occupied an important place on the agenda. Since then we have come a long way in common study, better mutual understanding and convergence of formerly contradictory positions. With this went the growing recognition that the one baptism into the Church of Christ (and not into our respective denominations or traditions) is a fundamental expression of the unity given in Christ. The 1982 Lima document on *Baptism, Eucharist and Ministry* has formulated the achieved convergence and the common affirmation of the significance of baptism for Christian unity. The consequence of this ecumenical development must be the mutual recognition of baptism between the different churches, and this has been already achieved in many instances.

It is in this ecumenical context that I welcome very much this book by Dr Yates. It provides an exegetical, historical and theological investigation which cannot be undertaken in ecumenical texts in the same way. And it considers the issue of baptism in a horizon that is much wider than the ecumenical debate with its focus on those issues which are controversial between the churches. The book, therefore, provides the comprehensive framework in which the ecumenical debate must be set. For this service I am deeply grateful, and I hope that Dr Yates' book will render a contribution to our mutual recognition of baptism as the free and unmerited act of the Triune God by which we become his children, united with God and united with one another.

Geneva, September 1992 GÜNTHER GASSMANN
Director of the Commission on Faith and Order, WCC

Contents

Preface

In my contacts with students and colleagues, no question seems to have been discussed more often than 'Why baptize infants?' This book is for those who wish seriously to consider the evidence which has given rise to so much questioning, even dissension, in the past and in the present. The reader is also invited to focus on future prospects for an observance of baptism that would be widely accepted ecumenically.

These pages are not written with any personal axe to grind; nor do they represent any pressure group. There is no special pleading here for any particular denominational position. This book is an enquiry – not a declaration. It seeks to fulfil the sub-title by offering an objective study of the biblical, traditional and theological aspects of Christian initiation, with particular attention to the pressing and timely concern regarding infant baptism.

Here an attempt is made to cover the relevant issues as deeply and as comprehensively as the various aspects of the subject require. The debatable relationship between infant baptism and confirmation is considered in the larger setting of ecumenism. In this connection, I am much indebted to the co-operation of the mainstream churches – Roman Catholic, Anglican and the Free Churches – and to the British and World Council of Churches.

My indebtedness to other writers is plain on nearly every page and I take this opportunity to express my gratitude. In expressing this indebtedness one is reminded of the limits of originality. We soon move out of the sphere in which we may be credited with some specialism. This study is mainly an attempt to bring together for a given purpose the relevant baptismal beliefs and liturgical practices of various writers and theologians from apostolic times to the present day.

On a more personal note, I must express my appreciation of the encouragement given, as in the past, by Dr George Carey, Archbishop of Canterbury. I must also acknowledge the help given by the Rt Revd Christopher Budd, Roman Catholic Bishop of Plymouth, and by Sister Julie Ann Donnelly, SND, in supplying information on the current Roman Catholic position with regard to entry into the Church. I am also grateful to Dr Günther Gassmann, a Director of the World Council of Churches, for the information he supplied during my research. He has added to this kindness by writing his relevant and knowledgeable Foreword. I greatly value his personal commendation of this book. I also appreciate the interest and co-operation of the Revd Dr Colin Davey, the Co-ordinating Secretary for Church Life of the Council of Churches for Britain and Ireland. For the present position of the Free Churches regarding initiation, I am much indebted to the Revd Dr Derek Tidball, formerly President of the Baptist Union; the Revd Jonathan Kerry, of the Methodist Church; and the Revd Dr Bernard Thorogood, General Secretary of the United Reformed Church. The belief and practice of the Church of Scotland regarding Infant Baptism and Confirmation were made clear by the Revd D. M. Beckett, Secretary of the Panel of Doctrine, and by the Revd D. G. Hamilton, of the Education Department.

The Revd Dr Paul Avis, Vicar of Stoke Canon, and Mr Kerry critically read the typescript and made valuable suggestions, which I have been glad to act upon. I am very grateful for all the help given in the typing and checking of the manuscript by Mrs Dominie Burns, a task carried out most competently and cheerfully.

I was greatly helped by having the use of the copying facilities at St Andrew's parish office in Plymouth, facilities kindly placed at my disposal by Prebendary John Watson. I must also acknowledge the unfailing interest and encouragement, during four years research, given by my family – Margaret, Rachel and Jonathan – who readily understood even when I worked during 'unsocial hours'. Finally, I must thank my publishers, especially Mr Kenneth Baker, for all their smooth efficiency and for making this writer's involvement such a pleasant experience.

ARTHUR S. YATES

CHAPTER ONE

The Aim and Scope of this Enquiry

It all began in responding to an invitation to write an article on the subject of 'Infant Baptism in the Early Church' for a Symposium on Christian Initiation. The evidence and the ideas that emerged developed along lines beyond the limits of that article, and so this book began to take shape.

Looking ahead to the following chapters, we face first the pressing question as to where the authority for the administration of infant baptism is to be found. Is it in Scripture, or is it in Tradition, or is it in both? There is surely no theological sphere in which the problem of authority is more vital. On this issue, theologians and churches do not answer with one voice. Some Christians look for the validity of the rite in the New Testament and would question the authenticity of any baptismal belief or practice which had no warrant in Scripture. Others give credence to traditional beliefs and practices even though they do not appear to have any firm or evident support in the Bible.

It is essential, therefore, that we should attempt to assess the relative importance of the evidence offered by Scripture and by Tradition. We must also consider which of these authorities has the prior claim or the greater weight, especially if the teaching and practice of these two sources appear to contradict rather than confirm each other. The question of authority presents one of the fundamental problems of theology. It is a basic issue in nearly every religious enquiry. Not least does this apply to a study of infant baptism.

We shall then turn our attention, in the following chapter, to the New Testament. Is infant baptism to be found there? Scholars are not agreed as to the answer. Some theologians see indications that the rite was practised in Apostolic times. Others draw the opposite conclusion. Most scholars, however, would seem to agree that whatever evidence there may be is slender – at the most indirect or inexplicit.

We shall then move on to the years immediately following New Testament times. Are there any traces of infant baptism in the first two centuries? Here is another area of disagreement – scholars taking up opposite positions. As we look at the diverse ways in which some writers interpret the evidence of the sources, we realize how difficult it is to discover objective truth and meaning in history. The relevance of hermeneutics is very apparent.

One thing is certain. From the third century onwards infant baptism was established and was practised in ever-widening circles. It was becoming the universal custom. We shall try to discover the reasons for this development. In later chapters, we shall trace the progress of the rite, and the perils that sometimes beset its observance or non-observance, up to and during the Reformation and beyond.

As we shall see, little effort seems generally to have been made to adapt the adult form of the baptismal ritual to the immaturity and unresponsiveness of infants. Indeed, we shall observe how the rite became increasingly more elaborate and consequently more remote and unintelligible as far as infant involvement was concerned.

However thorough and sound an enquiry may be into the historical evidence for or against the practice of infant baptism, it is clear that historical research by itself is not enough. There are also Biblical, Theological and Psychological factors to be taken into account and to these we turn our attention on later pages. It has been said that 'the historian is driven to lay down his pen, not because he is defeated, not because his material has proved incapable of historical treatment, but because . . . he is faced by the problem of theology.'[1]

We must look, therefore, at some of the theological aspects of this enquiry. Infant baptism is regarded by many people as the Christian rite which corresponds to the Jewish rite of circumcision. This suggested correlation calls for careful examination, which we shall undertake later in this book.

The relationship of 'original sin' to infant baptism has often engaged the attention of theologians over the centuries. As some of us have sensed from experience, belief in this inherited 'taint' or 'guilt' seems perhaps unwittingly to underlie the wish, even anxiety, on the part of some parents who press for a baby to be baptized – a baby who is seriously ill or who has been born prematurely. As one writer puts it: 'There are still some mothers who fear lest an unbaptized child should die and be deprived of the glories of heaven, but their number must be diminishing rapidly; and there are few theologians now who would want to argue seriously that the future of such a child was in jeopardy'.[2]

There is no doubt, however, particularly in the early centuries and in the Medieval Church, that the theory of 'original sin' wielded a great influence upon the rite of baptism. Its relevance and force are easy to appreciate. The link between 'original sin' and infant baptism has an obvious rationale. If baptism must include remission of sins, what sins have infants committed? Incapable of sinning on their own account, they must have inherited their sinful condition – a condition which endangers their eternal destiny. Remission of sin and assurance of heaven only baptism can achieve for the 'innocent' infant. Note should be taken of the converse to this explanation – a sort of circular reasoning. Infant baptism, once established, could find justification for its perpetuation by reference to 'original sin'. We shall need to look at this doctrine from a biological and theological point of view in a later chapter.

Certain beliefs regarding the relationship of divine grace to the baptism of children are held to be partly responsible for what is called 'indiscriminate baptism'. It was this situation which prompted Emil Brunner to wonder what being baptized as infants meant to people who neither knew nor cared whether or not they had been baptized.[3] As long ago as 1926, Charles Gore, a supporter of infant baptism, went so far as to say that the indiscriminate use of the rite had been a 'real disaster'[4]

Such critical and challenging observations as these by Brunner and Gore direct our attention all the more seriously to the important issue as to whether grace operates effectively and beneficially without any conscious participation or active involvement on the part of the person being baptized. This is clearly one of the most vital considerations in the theology of infant baptism – vital both for Christians who accept that sacramental grace operates fully and effectively in the baptism of infants and those who interpret the activity of grace in quite a different light. It need hardly be said that this aspect of baptismal theology calls for the close study which we shall attempt to give it in chapter nine.

In initiating or perpetuating the baptism of infants did the Early Church err in that, by so doing, they neglected the place of a personal experience of repentance and faith – features which are widely recognised as prerequisites of baptism? Some believe that the answer should be in the affirmative, if we accept the priority of

Scripture over Tradition. On the other hand, should we give credence to the view that repentance and faith can be held vicariously on behalf of the child by other people – parents or sponsors or the Church? These are very significant questions to which we shall give careful attention.

There is also another issue that has exercised – and still exercises – the minds of many Christians and Churches. It is the relationship between infant baptism and what has become known as 'Confirmation' – the latter obviously brought about by the establishment of the former. There is some truth in the well-known comment that Confirmation is 'a rite in search of a theology'. We shall try to determine what each is designed to achieve and what is the relationship between them. The reunion of baptism and confirmation would seem to commend itself to many schools of thought and Christian persuasion. Should they be reunited at the infant stage, as in the Orthodox churches, or at the adult stage, somewhat comparable to 'believers' baptism'? If the latter, then we would have gone back to a situation similar to that which seems to have existed in the Primitive church before infant baptism was separately established and widely practised.

We must also bear in mind that infant baptism is a theological subject of great significance and difficulty for the Ecumenical Movement – as the Reports issued by various commissions on Baptism and Confirmation make plain. A resolution of the problems that attach to these rites would make a significant contribution to the unity of the churches. In this connection we are much indebted to all the mainstream Denominations for the recent authoritative statements which they have sent to us for this study.

This material will assist us as we consider, on later pages, the possibility in the future of a unified form or mutual recognition of Christian initiation – set in an ecumenical framework, based on principles satisfactory from the point of view of Scripture and Tradition and in keeping with the contemporary situation. 'Perchance to dream!'. Perhaps we may be permitted this vision of what might be, despite the difficulties that would need to be resolved. 'Faith is the assurance of things hoped for, the conviction of things not seen.'

CHAPTER TWO

By what Authority – Scripture or Tradition?

Any enquiry into the doctrine and practice of infant baptism inevitably raises questions about Scripture and Tradition. As we said in the previous chapter, these two sources of authority and influence will underlie our discussion of baptism throughout this book. Both these spheres are involved in considering the meaning and validity of the sacrament. It is necessary, therefore, in this chapter that we should look at the nature and relationship of Scripture and Tradition as seen in the past and in the present. We shall then be better placed to understand and interpret the various aspects of Christian initiation on later pages.

The Edinburgh Conference in 1937 on 'Faith and Order' defined tradition as 'the living stream of the Church's life' – a definition regarded as reflecting the influence of the Eastern Orthodox Church. Baptists generally seem to emphasize Scripture at the expense of tradition. But this cannot be said of Stephen Winward, a Baptist minister, who states that the apostolic tradition was much wider than the New Testament writings and as there was continuity in, and development of, the Church, it is reasonable assume that it was conveyed in other ways. Winward is not alone in drawing attention to those Christians who, failing to appreciate tradition, 'jump from the Scripture to the present day as if nothing of value has been preserved or transmitted in the intervening centuries.'[1]

The idea of doctrinal development is traceable at various points in Church history. John Macquarrie, for instance, sees the influence of Vincent of Lérins' 'dynamic understanding of tradition' reflected in 'the image of the flowing stream' in Vatican II and also expressed in this statement of the Constitution: 'There is a growth in the understanding of the realities of the words that have been handed down; for, as the centuries succeed one another, the Church constantly moved forward toward the fulness of divine truth until the words of God reach their complete fulfilment in her.'[2]

The attitude of Jesus to tradition is not invariably the same. At times he commended it, at other times he condemned it. In the first three gospels, Christ is portrayed in his relationship to tradition as being both reverential and critical, conservative and progressive. St Matthew's Gospel presents Jesus as a supporter of tradition, though sometimes critical of those who teach or transmit it. He made it clear that oral tradition was subordinate to the authority of the Jewish Scripture – presumably 'the law and the prophets' (Matt. 5.17) in the Old Testament. He apparently condemned any traditional practices in which there was excessive ceremonial or any weakness in the moral and intellectual content. (Mark 7. 1–8).

It is believed that the ancient Catholic tradition can be traced back from the ecumenical councils, through the sub-apostolic writers, to the New Testament and to an acceptance of the natural meaning of 2 Thessalonians 2.15: 'So then, brethren, stand firm and hold to the traditions (*τας παραδοσεις*) which you were taught by us, either by word or mouth or by letter'.

Paul's indebtedness to tradition is clearly indicated in connection with two very important events. In both, the apostle uses two words which signify the 'receiving' and the 'passing on' of a tradition – 'I received (*παρέλαβον*) and 'I delivered' (*παρέδωκα*).

The first event concerns the sacrament of the Eucharist in 1 Cor. XI. It is the earliest account of the Last Supper. The consensus of scholarly opinion seems to be that the apostle did not receive the revelation direct from the risen Christ, but from some traditional information transmitted orally or in writing by one or more eyewitnesses. Dom Gregory Dix, who lays great emphasis on tradition, says that eucharistic worship from the outset was based, not on Scripture, but solely on tradition.[3] The other event, well established in Christian tradition, is the resurrection of Christ in 1. Cor. XV. Paul writes: 'I delivered (*παρέδωκα*) to you as of first importance what I also received (*παρέλαβον*), that Christ died for our sins in accordance with the scriptures, that he was buried, that he was raised on the third day in accordance with the scriptures.'

It would appear that Jesus did not expect Jewish tradition to last. But did he plan to establish a new tradition – an original deposit of permanent value, a deposit his disciples would preserve and pass on to their successors as leaders in a future church, 'the ecclesia', the new Israel of God? In reply, it is suggested that Christian tradition consists of a deposit of faith (depositum fidei) which Jesus formed partly from Jewish sources and partly consisting of what the risen Lord revealed to his apostles during the 'great forty days' (Acts 1.3) concerning 'the kingdom of God'. This Catholic belief holds that Christ revealed to the disciples the chief Christian doctrines and the sacraments of salvation. These apostles were the nucleus of the church, built on St Peter (Matt. 16) and were assured that the Holy Spirit would guide them into all the truth (John 16.13). It was held that Jesus committed the preserving of this deposit to the twelve apostles and through them to their successors, the bishops of the church.

The New Testament grew out of tradition – out of the experience and thought of the community of the resurrection, of which the apostles were the founder members. As F. W. Dillistone puts it: 'A tradition grew and developed in history, a tradition which included the belief, the worship, the way of life of a community and from this tradition came the succession of writings which were ultimately gathered together into the Canon of Holy Scripture.'[4]

The peril of persecution from outside the church was matched by the challenge of Gnosticism from within. But it is an 'ill wind that blows no good'. The church encountered in Gnosticism for the first time the idea of an unwritten tradition as an authority for doctrine. This made the church re-examine its faith and reinforce its links with the apostolic tradition – a tradition already appearing in written form, first in the letters of St Paul, the indomitable missionary to the Gentile world, and then the Gospels. This written tradition – our New Testament – rooted in the apostles' faith and authority, together with the apostolic succession of bishops, proved to be the best answer to the heretical writings of the Gnostics and their spurious claim of a 'secret tradition' going back exclusively to the apostles.

Gregory Dix makes an interesting and distinctive contribution to the subject of tradition in his book, 'The Theology of Confirmation in Relation to Baptism' – his Oxford lecture – at which we shall look more closely in a later chapter. He claims that some two or three decades before the New Testament was written there existed the early liturgical practice of the churches and the comments upon this of early Christian writers.

He goes on to say that this liturgical evidence ought to be treated as absolutely primary, since it was to some extent formative of Christian theological thought before the New Testament documents were canonized. He claims that there is available another source of information on the original and authentic apostolic interpretation of Christianity, which the Scriptures presuppose and which must be used in the interpretation of the scriptures. What Dix does not seem to make clear is how we gain access to this unobtrusive evidence.

It is widely held that the apostolic tradition has gathered additional elements of belief and practice in the process of being handed down from one generation to another. Indeed, the New Testament authors themselves were not passive. In writing the epistles and gospels, they interpreted and commented upon their material, as our Form and Redaction Critics make clear. Dr Kelly says that 'the New Testament is a thoroughly propagandist miscellany, written "from faith to faith",' and that the Gospels 'are carefully elaborated expositions of certain dogmatic beliefs about Jesus.'[5]

Yet, in recognizing the personal involvement of those who wrote the Scriptures, we must not overlook the widespread belief among the early Fathers – a belief that has echoed down the ages – that 'all scripture is inspired by God' (2 Tim. 3.16) and that 'men moved by the Holy Spirit spoke from God.' (2 Pet. 1.21).

When disagreement arose about the content of the apostolic tradition, the church convened an ecumenical council in order to determine what was the original deposit of faith. These councils played an increasingly important role from the middle of the third century onwards. Their aim was, not to add new doctrine, but to support and to define the faith once delivered to the saints. Kelly points to the growing awareness of the magisterial authority of the Catholic church and the increasing recognition of the Roman church in particular as the custodian and mouthpiece of the apostolic tradition.[6]

Dr G. L. Prestige says that while suspicion of antique survivals may be justified, the rolling stone of tradition may gather valuable moss. 'An accretion, enlargement, confirmation of the faith is to be expected and welcomed in the process of transmitting the truth.' But while development in the tradition is to be expected, one must distinguish between the original deposit once delivered to the saints (1 Tim. 6.20; Jude 3) and 'the fully formulated conclusions of theology . . . deduced from the primary data.' Prestige illustrates this by pointing out that, while the Nicene creed may simply summarize what the Gospels contain, the two are not the same. 'The one represents the evidence, the other records the verdict.' It needs to be added that it is always possible to check the evidence afresh and, if there is sufficient justification, to offer a different verdict or interpretation.[7]

In the course of nineteen centuries, observes John Macquarrie, the tradition has thrown up many false and misleading developments. That is why we need to keep going back to the origins to ensure that the tradition remains true to them.[8] According to Daniel Jenkins, Catholicism would not welcome such a policy of re-examining the original evidence lest it jeopardized the faithful transmission of the depositum fidei. He says that this Catholic concern is due to a failure to interpret tradition in terms of 'the living stream of the Church's life.'[9]

A serious situation developed for the early church when the 'heretic', as well as the orthodox theologian, proved how ably he could 'cite Scripture for his purpose'. Another authority beside the Bible was therefore needed. It was now emphasized that only the orthodox church and its theologians were spiritually competent to interpret the sacred writings, to identify true tradition and to refute the false exposition of the heretics.

As St Vincent of Lérins says, Scripture is 'sufficient and more than sufficient', but in view of diverse interpretations, we need the guidance of church tradition. Vincent approves the development of doctrine provided that, like the growth of our bodies, the growth of doctrine can be traced to at least an embryonic form in Scripture.[10]

John of Damascus (c.675–c.749) – the last of the great eastern Fathers – calls the Bible 'the divine tradition' and holds that scripture is the only source of revelation and warns against extra-Biblical doctrines.[11] With the main subject of this book in mind, one is prompted to ask: 'Would the early Fathers have regarded infant baptism as an extra-biblical doctrine?' It is a question we shall attempt to answer on later pages.

Irenaeus's contention that only those in the episcopal succession are the true interpreters of the Bible[12] is endorsed with 'characteristically augmented vehemence' by Tertullian, whom Prestige further describes as 'an ardent flame of cultivated energy from Roman Africa'![13] According to this bishop of Carthage, heretics have neither the right nor the equipment with which to interpret the Scriptures.[14] We have good reason to reflect that things have not changed very much over the centuries when we consider Tertullian's insistence on a canon of interpretation in order to guard against individual excesses in the exposition of Scripture. Hermeneutics are seldom superfluous.

Basil the Great, a Cappadocian Father in the fourth century and leader of Monasticism in the east, refers to a number of 'unwritten customs', including the sign of the cross, turning east in prayer, the blessing of the water and the oil for baptism, the liturgical prayers of consecration, the baptismal creed and the use of chrism.[15] Basil concedes that none of these has scriptural warrant, but he makes the questionable claim that they go back to the apostles. Perhaps he believed that the church which had produced the New Testament could legitimately initiate a custom in line with apostolic tradition – a belief not easily resisted on purely rational grounds.

As Lampe makes clear, unwritten tradition is also the source of many liturgical practices solely on the authority of church custom including: baptismal renunciation; threefold immersion with credal response; the administration of milk and honey; early celebrations; observance of martyrs' anniversaries; standing for Sunday prayer; the feast from Easter to Pentecost and the sign of the cross.[16]

An obvious fact needs to be borne in mind, namely, that the church existed, worshipped, baptized, broke bread, before the New Testament was written. The sacramental ritual had roots and meaning in the Hebrew Scriptures – the Passover helped to shape and signify the Eucharist and the allegorical use of the Red Sea and Noah to typify baptism. These elements in the Primitive Church preceded the writings of the apostolic tradition of doctrine.

Certain events in the history of the church clearly show that the theory of how truth is communicated through Scripture and tradition is one thing, the reception of that truth in personal experience is quite another. The problem is most pressing in those situations about which Scripture is silent – as in the case of infant baptism – and where tradition is unclear.

Such a situation was doubtless in St Vincent's mind when he claimed that church authority was added to scriptural authority in order to provide a true interpretation in the midst of diversity. It therefore follows 'that the line of prophetic and apostolic interpretation should be guided according to the norm of the sense of the universal church.' This norm, according to Vincent, is: 'What has been believed everywhere, always, by all' (*quod ubique, quod semper, quod ab omnibus creditum est.*).[17]

Commenting on this ancient formula, John Macquarrie says that it 'cannot be set aside without abandoning the community itself.'[18] Is Macquarrie's statement inherently true or logically defensible? Truth does not always line up with the big battalions. The 'heretic' may prove to be a Joan of Arc and the rebellious monk a Luther. Ultimate victory may await the 'godly remnant'. Macquarrie seems to be on surer ground when he says that 'each generation must appropriate the tradition and . . . interpret the ancient formula . . . into its own categories of thought . . . Such re-interpretation is needed if the tradition is to be carried on . . . as a living and growing tradition.'[19]

The Reformation

The Reformation was a new day in the developing self-consciousness, not only of the European States, but also of the Christian believer. It began as a reassertion of the rights of the individual. The protest against Rome took different forms. Martin Luther emphasized justification by faith, John Calvin the divine decree; but the substance was similar. In either case, the necessity of ecclesiastical mediation was denied and the essence of religion was found in the relation between the individual soul and God.

John Calvin's distinctive contribution to the Reformation was his emphasis on the 'witness of the Spirit'. It was the supreme means of conveying to the believer that the Bible was the Word of God and that it was sufficient for salvation. This doctrine of the 'witness of the Spirit' must be distinguished from that taught by John Wesley, as we have explained elsewhere.[20]

The Reformers' protest was not against the apostolic deposit of 'the faith which was once for all delivered to the saints.' (Jude 3). The protest was against the depository class in Western Europe and the accretions added to the original deposit by the Roman Church. The 'Ten Articles of Religion' (1536) reveal the Anglican position with regard to the relation of Scripture and tradition and the Church's awareness of the undesirable increment which had been added to the original deposit of faith.

It would appear, however, that the earlier Reformers were no less scholastic than the medieval theologians and regarded a dogmatic theology as essential. So, having rejected the Roman hierarchy, they sought a new foundation for their faith, and this they found in the sole authority of the Bible. This doctrinal position was maintained for some three hundred years, until Biblical criticism in the nineteenth century challenged their somewhat literal and fundamentalist approach to the Scriptures.

There was also the question as to who was competent enough to interpret the Bible, in the absence of the Catholic Church. The sole authority of Scripture and the belief that every one could interpret the Bible for himself led to a great diversity of sects, all claiming the right to use the Scriptures as they saw fit, in order to substantiate their particular beliefs, however extravagant and misguided these views may be. Some people went so far as to believe themselves favoured with an individual illumination that left even the Bible far behind!

The Thirty Nine Articles seemed to offer some recognition of both the Catholic view that Scripture and tradition were joint authorities and the Protestant belief in the sole authority of the Bible. The main underlying principle, however, is the priority of Scripture. Article 6 states: 'Holy Scripture containeth all things necessary for salvation. So that whatsoever is not read therein, nor may be proved thereby, is not to be required of any man, that it should be believed as an Article of Faith, or thought requisite necessary to salvation.'

Article 34, however, states that not everything in the Church requires the warrant of Scripture. Custom and tradition may be given approval by Church rule. The Article reads: 'Every particular or national church hath authority to ordain, change and abolish ceremonies or rites of the church ordained only by man's authority.'

In defence of the Church's right to approve customs and traditions, not prohibited by Scripture, Archbishop Thomas Cranmer responded in humorous vein to the Puritans' over-emphasis on biblical direction: 'They say that kneeling is not commanded in the Scriptures and that what is not commanded in the Scriptures is unlawful. Here is the root of the errors of the sects . . . If kneeling is not expressly enjoined in holy Scripture, neither is standing or sitting. Let them lie down on the ground and eat their meals like Turks or tartars.'[21]

Criticism and reason

The emergence of historical criticism in the nineteenth century soon made itself felt in spheres concerned with tradition and Scripture – especially the latter. The wind of change swept through the world of religious thought and belief. It soon became evident that reason was increasingly a force to be reckoned with in secular and Christian circles. German scholars were in the vanguard of theological change and they initiated a revolution in the understanding of the Bible. For some people, not least in Britain, it seemed as though the foundations of their faith were being shaken – indeed there are still 'tremors' at the present time in 'conservative' or 'fundamentalist' circles. Reason has had a mixed reception in the history of religion.

It is perhaps only the few in all ages and in all religious circles who have seen reason as an ally of revelation. The resistance movement has been strong throughout Church history – from the Early Church, through the Middle Ages and the Reformation up to our own day.

British scholars eventually responded to the impact being made by continental theologians as their radical views spread throughout Britain. It was a very disturbing impact and, not surprisingly, it stirred up a storm. David Pailin in his essay on 'Reason in Relation to Scripture and Tradition' entertains his readers by describing how Strauss's views on the 'mythical interpretation' of the Gospels 'can still cause theological thunderstorms after a hundred and fifty years!'[22] We can add that more recently the eruption caused by John Hick's 'The Myth of God Incarnate' is still felt in Christian circles. It would appear that 'Truth' needs to be 'handled with care'. Certainly biblical criticism has stirred up a storm, but it has also shed a lot of light in religious studies and heralded great advances in our knowledge of the Bible and our interpretation of it.

Cardinal J. H. Newman made a significant contribution to the subject of religious belief in his 'Essay on the Development of Christian Doctrine' (1845) – a theme echoed in Maurice Wiles' book on 'The Remaking of Christian Doctrine'. Newman believed that the dogmatic definitions of the church of the fourth and fifth centuries were not only a logical unfolding of what was already there but an addition of something new. Professor Hanson explains that for Newman the only true development was that which took place within the Roman Catholic Church and was tantamount to a new revelation. These theological ideas put forward by Newman were not widely accepted. Hanson adds the significant comment that 'no theologian of a reformed tradition has yet produced a satisfactory or generally acceptable explanation of the development of doctrine.'[23]

The pressure for greater freedom for Roman Catholic scholarship was still in evidence at the time of Vatican II – a time that called for redefinition. Renewed study of the Council of Trent has suggested that the Council had not intended the polarisation of Scripture and tradition. One of the hopeful features of the present situation, says Daniel Jenkins, is that while 'Protestantism is realising how closely Scripture and tradition are intertwined, Catholicism is beginning to realise . . . the full magnitude of the claim of Scripture to authority.' – an authority which needs to be defined in a way that does justice to tradition as 'the living stream of the Church's life.'[24]

John Macquarrie points out that 'what is required is that we should not allow presuppositions or ideas – to dominate our minds to such an extent that we never really face the phenomena, but remain content with some ready interpretation.'[25] One wonders how Macquarrie would relate his admirable reasoning here to the doctrine and practice of infant baptism. He makes his position plain on a later page. 'It may indeed be true,' he writes, 'that there is no clear New Testament sanction for infant baptism . . . Of course from the point of view of this book . . . the almost universal practice of infant baptism in the church throughout its history is an entirely sufficient and satisfactory warrant and authority.'[26]

But there is another side to this situation. One need not assume that the widespread observance of this rite has been satisfactorily answered – answered, that is, because the majority of Christians approve it or, at least, accept it. In examining the validity and meaning of Christian belief and practice, Macquarrie, despite his readiness to support infant baptism solely on traditional grounds, points out that there is room for reason as well as for Scripture and tradition. 'This threefold type of authority,' he says, 'guards against a petrified "fundamentalism" on the one hand and against runaway change on the other.'[27] It is, therefore, still relevant for reason to enquire whether the Early Church had accepted into its traditional practice a religious rite which had insufficient evidence in the New Testament or in the Apostolic community.

A unique revelation?

The background study to the present chapter has drawn our attention to another important feature connected with this enquiry. Looking into the relationship between Scripture and tradition has revealed an impressive unanimity among several writers – belonging to different communions – to the effect that in Christ and his apostles we have a final and unrepeatable revelation – final and unrepeatable because it is *unique*. It is also held that, being unique, it cannot be transmitted in its original, true, or real essence to any other person or at any other time. The revelation in Christ and the apostles' involvement in that revelation are inseparably bound up with the historical situation in which the incarnation and the original deposit of the faith took place.

Prestige has reminded us that the Christian faith was not based on human authority. The facts of the faith were 'given' and the interpretation of those facts was by inspiration. The authority of the apostles was normative and decisive because they were called by God 'at the final and culminating point of God's self-disclosure . . . The tradition received its definite form from the apostles of Jesus Christ.'[28] The apostle was unique partly because he was a witness of the resurrection. (Acts 1,22). He did not receive the Gospel from man (*παρὰ ἀνθρώπου*) but through revelation (*δι'ἀποκαλυψεως*) (Gal. 1, 12). For this reason, the canon of the New Testament was limited to what were believed to be 'apostolic' writings. The apostles were 'unique instruments of the revelation of God in Jesus Christ'.[29]

It is this divine disclosure that makes the New Testament a way of salvation and 'a lamp to our feet'. Commenting on the Tridentine claim to be the interpreter of the Bible, Benjamin Drewery says that 'there is a Scriptural hapax (*ἅπαξ*) – a once-for-all – pertaining to the mighty acts of God in creation and redemption of which subsequent tradition is, in a vital sense, but an unfolding, an elaboration. The precise definition of this priority has exercised the subtlest intelligence of modern scholarship, both privately and (for example) in Vatican II.'[30]

The Bible is clearly a *unique* book – though its nature, its truth, its authority have been clarified partly because biblical criticism has treated it 'just like any other book'. It is a book which tradition can reflect or interpret, but can never transcend. The American John Knox, noting the spotlight which the New Testament focuses on Jesus and his apostles, writes of a 'normative significance which the experience and thought of the church in no later period can have.'[31]

This widely held view – that the Gospel events are unrepeatable, once-for-all – is surely the conclusion the evidence requires. Only the apostles could say of Jesus; 'The life was made manifest and we saw it and testify to it' (1 John 1, 2). It is argued that if the redeeming acts of Christ are unique, then it must follow that the apostles' direct personal witness to these acts must also be unique. And since this redeeming work and witness dominate the New Testament, it is not surprising that the priority of Scripture is indicated in the previous pages of this chapter. In these days of biblical criticism, we may not mean quite the same as our forbears did when we speak of the Bible as the 'Word of God'; but we can turn to no authority comparable to the Scriptures for discerning the mind of Christ and for discovering something of the beliefs and practices of the Apostolic Church – including, of course, the subject of Baptism.

If we see the New Testament canon, observes D. E. W. Harrison, merely as books that happen to have been selected from other literature and pronounced authorative by the Church, then the crucial factor is the judgement of the Church. There is another explanation, however, from which few Christians would dissent, namely that it is the quality of apostolicity inherent in the New Testament writings themselves which explains their canonisation – a *unique* quality, incapable of transmission, and, as is widely believed, a final revelation[32]

Professor F. L. Cross saw tradition as the preserver of Scripture and a means of maintaining the essential link with what is for the Christian 'salvation history'. He holds that the Primitive Church was historical 'in a *unique* sense'. He writes, 'Certain events which took place at a particular time in history were . . . pivotal in God's relations with men . . . The Christian creed was not a system whose truth, if lost, could be recovered by rational argument . . . Her system was rooted in . . . empirical facts in the past; and with these crucial facts contact could be maintained only by an historical continuity of life . . . Tradition, therefore, was integral to the structure of the Church.'[33]

We have undertaken this brief survey of Scripture and tradition for an obvious reason – because we believe it is relevant to our enquiry into the grounds of infant baptism. It would appear that no Christian doctrine or practice has been officially established or authenticated unless it is based either on Scripture or tradition. We have seen how different denominations have inclined either in one direction or the other. There was, on the one hand, the Reformers' emphasis on Scripture alone; and, on the other hand, the prominent place given to tradition by the Council of Trent.

It would appear that even the Roman Catholic Church, when formulating a doctrine on the basis of tradition, has nevertheless felt the need to justify its emergence by claiming that this new belief or practice was at least *implied* in Scripture. Moreover, any doctrine which is seen to be contrary to Scripture would stand little chance of being officially approved on purely traditional grounds. In a letter to Richard Tompson in 1756, John Wesley said that the united testimony of even such authorities as the ancient Fathers and the Reformers would not suffice to establish an unscriptural doctrine.[34]

It is essential, therefore, that in the next chapter we should carefully consider what evidence there may be in the New Testament for the doctrine and practice of infant baptism.

CHAPTER THREE

What Evidence does the New Testament offer?

Most scholars are agreed that there is no direct evidence for the practice of infant baptism in the New Testament. Writers from different schools of thought have tended to converge here. Dr L. S. Thornton refers to the problems which arise from infant baptism 'because the apostolic writings, in their explicit statements, envisage only adult neophytes with a corresponding emphasis upon individual faith and repentance as necessary pre-requisites.'[1] A similar view is expressed by A. T. and R. P. Hanson when they observed that in New Testament times baptism meant adult baptism and that it is 'a much debated question whether there is any evidence for the baptism of infants in the New Testament.'[2] The almost complete silence of the Synoptic Gospels on baptism is explained by W. F. Flemington in terms of its association with the death and resurrection of Christ.[3]

On the question of indirect evidence, however, there are wide differences of view. The relevant material that calls for consideration can hardly be said to be extensive. There are in all eleven occasions in the New Testament when Christian baptism took place. Nine are in the Acts of the Apostles and two in Paul's first letter to the Corinthians. They are as follows:

Acts 2.41	Converts on the Day of Pentecost
Acts 8.12	The Samaritans
Acts 8.38	The Ethiopian
Acts 9.18	St Paul
Acts 10.48	Cornelius
Acts 16.15	Lydia
Acts 16.33	The Philippian jailer
Acts 18.8	Crispus and the Corinthians
Acts 19.5	The 'disciples' at Ephesus
1 Cor.1.14	Crispus and Gaius
1 Cor.1.16	Stephanas

The baptism of households

Supporters of infant baptism lay much emphasis on those Scriptural texts which relate to the baptism of households. They are all in the Book of Acts, with the exception of 1 Cor.1.16. Jeremias gives close attention to these passages. In his book, *Infant Baptism in the First Four Centuries*, he lists the relevant passages as follows: 1 Cor. 1.16 – 'I did baptize also the household of Stephanas'; Acts 16.15 – The half-proselyte Lydia 'was baptized with her household'; Acts 16.33 – The keeper of the prison in Philippi 'was baptized at once with all his family'; Acts 18.8 – Crispus, one of the very few whom Paul said he baptized (1 Cor. 1.14), 'believed in the Lord, together with all his household'.

Jeremias reckons that the 'households' of Crispus and Stephanas were Jewish, whereas the other 'households' were half-proselyte and Gentiles. He draws attention to the meaning of 'household' (*οἶκος*) as indicated by Ignatius when he wrote: 'Greetings to the families of my brothers, along with their wives and children'.[4] Jeremias takes this reference to cover 'father and mother of the household and children of all ages. In addition, relatives living in the house and servants were counted as belonging to the household'.[5]

Jeremias argues that the addition *ὅλος, πᾶς, ἅπαντες* ('the whole', 'all') to *οἶκος* shows that no single member of the household was excluded from baptism. Moreover, 'it is extremely unlikely' that the households of Cornelius, of the jailer, of Crispus and of Stephanas included many slaves to whom reference was made. Therefore, concludes Jeremias, the addition of the words *ὅλος, πᾶς, ἅπαντες* must refer to '*all* the children of the household'.[6]

Support for this interpretation is provided by Stauffer's research into Old Testament sources in which he discovered a constant biblical 'oikos formula' – a term coined by him – a formula of ritual significance which 'not only referred to the children in addition to the adults, but which had quite a special reference to the children and not least to any small children who might be present'.[7] Examples in the Old Testament given by Stauffer include Gen. 17.12f; Exod. 12. 27,30; 1 Sam. 1. 21ff. Parallel examples in the New Testament are 1 Cor. 1.16; Acts 16.15, 33f.

With reference to the New Testament, this does not mean, according to Jeremias, that in every case small children were involved, 'it does mean that Paul and Luke could under no circumstance have applied the oikos formula, if they had wished to say that only adults had been baptized'.[8]

But this makes the big assumption, as Dr Beasley-Murray points out, that 'Luke the Hellenist understood so technical a Hebrew use of the Greek term.'[9] A similar qualifying statement is given by the Revd S.I. Buse when he says that even if the oikos-formula was proven for the Old Testament, 'its relevance for Luke's narratives in Acts would remain doubtful. It is significant that the mention of "households" is in the more Hellenistic stratum of Acts and, as J. Schneider has pertinently remarked [10], we may well doubt whether a Hellenist like Luke when he used the word "house" would have Old Testament ritual language in mind.'[11]

Jeremias reinforces his argument by the following points:

(1) The part that 'corporate personality' and 'family solidarity' played in the ancient world.
(2) It was accepted that the faith of the father should determine the faith of the household.
(3) So, 'if the father of the household became a Christian, the family followed him, not indeed always (1 Cor. 7.12), but usually.'
(4) Baptism in the New Testament was an eschatological sacrament, signifying deliverance from the last judgment. In that situation, an omission of any member of the family, however young, would be thinkable.[12]

It is clear that the 'oikos formula' is a widely held theory quoted in support of the view that infant baptism was practised in New Testament times. Not surprisingly, Jeremias begins his book with an exposition and defence of this theory.

Kurt Aland is unimpressed; and, in his book entitled *Did the Early Church Baptize Infants?*, he puts forward a very different point of view. Aland states that the word occurs 112 times in the New Testament, but in only nine of these instances does it mean a 'family' – that is people in a house. And in three of these nine cases – 2 Tim 1.16; 4.19 and Titus 1.11 – there is no reference to baptism. Aland proceeds to examine the relevant passages.

He deals first with 1 Cor. 1.16, 'the oldest of them', in which Paul says that he has baptized 'the household of Stephanas'. No information is given here about this household, but in 1 Cor. 16.15 f – where *οἰκίαν* may mean the same as *οἶκον* – it is stated that the 'household' of Stephanas 'were the first converts of Achaia and they have devoted themselves to the service of the saints'. Paul says: 'I urge you to be subject to such men . . .' Aland adds: 'That *οἰκια* (*οἶκος*) in this passage relates only to adults needs no argument.

With the best will in the world, children cannot be included in this ministry of leading the church – to say nothing of infants!'[13]

Commenting on 1 Cor. 1.16, Whiteley says: 'A household would naturally include small children, but the argument is not conclusive, since St Paul does not say that he baptized every single member of the household of Stephanas, if indeed it included children at all, which it probably would have done; it is possible that only those "suitable" for baptism would receive it and that childen would be excluded.'[14] Whiteley is not alone in declining to be dogmatic on the subject!

We move now into another uncertain area as we consider the baptism of Crispus. Let us look at the biblical evidence. In 1 Cor. 1.14 Paul writes: 'I baptized none of you except Crispus and Gaius.' Whereas in 1.16, the apostle says that he baptized the 'household of Stephanas'; there is no reference here to his baptizing the household of Crispus. In Acts 18.8., however, we read: 'Crispus, the ruler of the synagogue' (presumably the same person) 'believed in the Lord, together with all his household (*σὺν ὅλῳ τῷ οἴκῳ αὐτοῦ*) and many of the Corinthians, hearing Paul, believed and were baptized.'

It might be assumed from this text that the household of Crispus were baptized – by Paul or somebody else (cf. Acts 10.48) – but it should be noted that this is not explicitly stated. One possibility suggested is that on this ocasion the baptism of the head of the house was deemed to be representative of the rest of the family. Be that as it may, it is clear to Aland that in this 'context there is little hand-hold for a proof of infant baptism'.[15] Jeremias, of course, does not draw that conclusion and sees no necessity to reconcile these passages. He ventures the view that Paul may not have baptized the household of Crispus because they were all female. Well might Jeremias conclude: 'But here we have reached guesswork!'[16]

The Cornelius problem

The word *οἶκος* does not appear in close connection with the baptism of Cornelius; but, in opening up the story in Acts 10, Luke says that Cornelius was 'a devout man who feared God with all his house' (*σὺν παντὶ τῷ οἴκῳ αὐτοῦ*). The term *οἶκος* is used retrospectively by Peter in the report he gave to the 'circumcision party' in Jerusalem. He explained how Cornelius had seen an angel standing in his house and saying: 'Send to Joppa and bring Simon called Peter; he will declare to you a message by which you will be saved, you and all your household.' (Acts 11.13f).

The Lucan narrative in Acts 10 describes the assembled company who awaited Peter's arrival from Joppa. It says: 'Cornelius was expecting them and had called together his kinsmen and close friends' (10.24). It was to these 'kinsmen and close friends' that Peter spoke. As he did so 'the Holy Spirit fell on all who heard the word . . . Then Peter declared, "Can any one forbid water for baptizing these people who have received the Holy Spirit just as we have?" And he commanded them to be baptized in the name of Jesus Christ' (10.44 ff).

Kurt Aland assesses and interprets this baptismal evidence as follows: 'We are not dealing here with an assembly of the *οἶκος* with parents, children and domestic servants, but with a meeting of like-minded adults coming from different families. Of children, or the very young, or infants there is not even a hint here; nor have we to presuppose the presence of slaves in this circle. Women will undoubtedly have been there, including the wife of Cornelius, if he had one, but more than this cannot be concluded from the text.[17]

Once again Jeremias crosses exegetical swords with Aland, saying 'There is room here for debate'! He begins by quoting the angelic message to Cornelius: 'You will be saved, you and all your household' (*σωθήσῃ σὺ καὶ πᾶς ὁ οἶκός σου*) Acts 11.14, and then Jeremias asks: 'Whom does this *οἶκος* comprise?' He rules out Aland's suggestion that Cornelius might have been a bachelor, by drawing attention to Acts 10.2 which states, as we have seen, that Cornelius was 'religious and feared God with all his household'. Jeremias holds that in this passage, where the religious position of the 'house' is described, *πᾶς ὁ οἶκος* can denote only 'the whole family'. He speaks for us all when he adds: 'Unfortunately we are not told of whom the family was comprised.'[18]

Dr Beasley-Murray's comments on Jeremias's interpretation of the Cornelius episode are significant, if not amusing. He says 'the insistence of Jeremias that statements concerning "all" the household must necessarily relate to all members without exception would appear to be reasonable. But has he noticed to what the statements in Acts about the "whole" households refer?' Beasley-Murray quotes Acts 10.44 ff, then adds: 'On Jeremias's principle no doubt is to be entertained concerning the meaning of the passage – *all* the house of Cornelius heard the word, *all* received the Spirit, *all* spoke with tongues, *all* were baptized; the infants present also heard the word, received the Spirit, spoke with tongues and so were baptized. To this *no* exception is possible.'[19]

Dr Beasley-Murray's statement may appear unanswerable – assuming that Cornelius's household included children – but some readers may feel that it is so severely logical as to strain the truth! After commenting in similar terms on the episodes of the Jailer and of Crispus, Beasley-Murray defends his exaggerated style in Pauline language: 'you compelled me to it!' He then reiterates his view that 'Luke, in writing these narratives, . . . has in mind ordinary believers and used language applicable to them.'[20]

It may seem something of an anti-climax, but before we leave this event in Caesarea, we should note that doubt has been expressed as to whether in fact Cornelius was baptized at all. The account says that Peter 'commanded them to be baptized' (Acts 10.48), but it does not record the fact that the command was carried out. Peter's later description of the incident might be taken to imply that for Cornelius water-baptism was superfluous, since he had already been baptized with the Holy Spirit' (11.16). Is this a fulfilment of words spoken by John the Baptist: 'I baptize you with water . . . but He will baptize you with the Holy Spirit' (Luke 3.16)?

In suppport of this view C. S. C. Williams points out that the editors of *The Beginnings of Christianity* 'argue that water-baptism was not in fact used on this occasion, but interpolated by a redactor of Acts'[21]. If Acts 10.47f was a later redaction, designed to regularise the story, and Cornelius did not receive water-baptism, this would presumably apply to his household and to any children in his family. The episode would then support the view that water-baptism was not essential to salvation.

This idea that water-baptism may not be essential brings to mind a remarkable observation by W. F. Flemington – a recognized authority on baptism and not noted for being 'way out' theologically. It is therefore all the more surprising when he writes: 'If Jesus himself had not come from Nazareth of Galilee to be baptized by John in the Jordan, it may be questioned whether baptism would ever have become a Christian sacrament.'[22]

If Cornelius did receive baptism in water, then we have an early instance where the Holy Spirit was bestowed before, rather than accompanying, or following, baptism. So whether or not Cornelius was baptized, it is an unusual episode. We shall consider further these seemingly anomalous elements on later pages, not least with reference to the Syrian Church.

The Lydia household

The most direct reference to the baptism of a household (*οἶκος*) is in connection with Lydia (Acts 16.14f). Aland states, with what seems to us unwarranted emphasis, that Lydia was an unmarried woman or a widow, and therefore 'in this *οἶκος* there were either no children at all, or at least there were no little children or infants.'[23] We are surprised that Aland does not entertain the possibility of her being a *young* widow and therefore perhaps having a young family.

'It is said of Lydia,' writes Jeremias, that 'she was baptized and all her household.' The word 'all' (*πᾶς*) does not appear in the original Greek text of the New Testament – *ἐβαπτίσθη καὶ ὁ οἶκος αὐτῆς*. It is found later, however, in the Western text which 'characteristically expands the narrative by adding *πᾶς* before *ὁ οἶκος*.'[24] One wonders if this addition was due to theological considerations or to the influence of comparable Greek phrases which included the word 'all' in the 'oikos-formula.'

Jeremias sees Lydia's offer of hospitality to the apostles as an indication that she was probably an elderly widow and that 'her house consisted of married children and their children.'[25] But were they all baptized along with Lydia? That is the question!

The Philippian jailer

The 'oikos-formula' is also involved in the narrative concerning the Philippian jailer in Acts 16. 27–34. Let us look closely at the text and especially at the Greek words that are most relevant to this aspect of our enquiry. The keeper of the prison said to Paul and Silas 'What must I do to be saved?' And they said 'Believe (singular) on the Lord Jesus and you (singular) will be saved, you and your household (*σὺ καὶ ὁ οἶκός σου*). And they spoke to him the word of the Lord and to all who were in his house' (*σὺν πᾶσιν τοῖς ἐν τῇ οἰκίᾳ αὐτοῦ*). – Compare the use of *οἰκία* in 1 Cor. 16.15 – 'And he was baptized he and all his immediately (*ἐβαπτίσθη αὐτὸς καὶ οἱ αὐτοῦ πάντες παραχρῆμα*) . . . and he rejoiced with all his household that he had believed.' (*καὶ ἠγαλλιάσατο πανοικεὶ πεπιστευκὼς*). One ancient manuscript (D gig) has *σὺν τῷ οἴκῳ αὐτοῦ* ('with his household') instead of the adverb *πανοικεὶ* ('with one's entire household').

Despite the fact that there are three references to people associated with the keeper (16. 32–34), Aland is reluctant to commit himself as to who they may be. Yet he ventures the following: 'That slaves were included in the group seems . . . to be certain; that the keeper of the prison was married is equally likely, but whether he had children, or whether little childen or infants were in the house, obviously cannot be determined. The report in 16.32 that the jailer received baptismal instruction "with all (σὺν πᾶσιν) who were in his house" does not exactly demand the assumption that infants were included in these πᾶσιν (all).'[26]

Jeremias sees a similar situation obtaining in the case of Lydia and her household (Acts 16.14f). He concludes that 'the way in which the solidarity of the family was taken for granted explains why no reason was found for emphasising or justifying especially the baptism of children.'[27] With reference to the five cases of baptism associated with Crispus, Stephanas, Lydia, the Philippian jailer and Cornelius, Jeremias observes that 'the linguistic evidence forbids us to restrict the concept of the 'house' to the adult members of the family. On the contrary it shows plainly that it is the complete family including all its members which received baptism'.[28]

Aland is unimpressed by these arguments. 'The elevation of this oikos-formula', he says, 'to a theological status seems to me to be utterly unsatisfactory.' He maintains that nowhere in connection with the oikos-passages in the New Testament is a child or an infant expressly named, let alone its baptism[29]

Flemington sees things differently. He holds that the solidarity of the family meant that the baptism of households included children. He reckons that confirmation of this is provided by two passages in Paul's letters in which the apostle addresses children in a way which assumes that they are church members. In Col. 3.20 and Eph. 6.1, he exhorts children to obey their parents 'in the Lord' (ἐν κυρίῳ). The use of this phrase, according to Flemington, implied that these children were members of the church, in which case 'it would seem a justifiable inference that they had been baptized.'[30] One must recognise that Flemington's deduction from these texts is of a conjectural nature.

Children at Pentecost

Were children baptized on the Day of Pentecost? The Biblical account says, 'Now when they heard this they were cut to the heart and said to Peter and the rest of the apostles, "Brethren, what shall we do?" And Peter said to them, "Repent and be baptized every one of you in the name of Jesus Christ for the forgiveness of your sins; and you shall receive the gift of the Holy Spirit. For the promise is to you and to your children and to all that are afar off, every one whom the Lord our God calls to him . . ." So those who received his word were baptized, and there were added that day about three thousand souls.' (Acts 2.37–41)

Who are the children referred to in this passage? Jeremias is in no doubt as to the answer. He rules out the idea that the words 'and to your children' (*καὶ τοῖς τέκνοις ὑμῶν*) refer to the descendants of the hearers. He does this by pointing out that, in view of the apocalyptic expectation of the End, the church would not be thinking in terms of future generations. He allows, however, that at the time Luke wrote – the latter part of the first century – the phrase 'your children' might denote the hearers' descendants.

Jeremias links this passage with the promise of Joel, quoted by Peter in Acts 2.17–21, and reckons that the promise of the Spirit is for the children as for 'your young men' and 'your old men'. 'Thus', he says, 'the children are not coming generations, but the sons and daughters of the hearers. Since the gift of the Spirit (2.38) is linked to baptism, 2.39 contains the challenge to have the children baptized also. Thus in Acts 2.38f. we have before us a witness for the practice of infant baptism in Apostolic times, at any rate in the time of the composition of Luke's twofold work: that is to say, for the baptism of children of Jewish parents on their admission into the Christian Church.'[31]

On the question of the age of these children said to be baptized, Windisch is quoted as saying that we must contemplate children who are old enough to repent (2.38) and to prophesy (2.17).[32] On the question of the maturity of recipients of baptism, Windisch could have cited some words that follow in the same passage: 'And he testified with many words and exhorted them . . . So those who received the word were baptized' (2.40f). Jeremias, however, does not accept this age qualification and holds that the salvation from the final judgment mediated by baptism (2.40; cf. 2.21) 'excludes any limitation of age.'[33]

As we might expect by now, Aland questions this exegesis! He observes that ascribing this passage to the 'Jewish-Christian sphere' is dependent on the degree of historicity we attach to the speeches of Peter in the Acts of the Apostles. On a later page of his first book, Jeremias notes that in Acts 2.39, the Codex Bezae (D) manuscript changes the pronouns from the second person to the first person – that is: 'you (*ὑμῖν*)' and 'your (*ὑμῶν*)' are replaced by 'us (*ἡμιν*)' and 'our (*ἡμων*).'

Thus the western recension of this text reads: 'For the promise is to *us* and to *our* children'. Jeremias adds that 'the statement is now made to refer to Christian children . . . The most natural explanation of the variant is that the formulation: "Be baptized every one of you . . . for the promise is to us and to our children" came naturally to the redactor's pen, because the baptism of Christian children was a custom taken for granted.'[34]

The value of this evidence for infant baptism before AD 150, based on a variant reading, is questioned by Aland. Moreover, he draws attention to the way in which this Codex D manuscript treats the plural personal pronouns 'you (ὑμιν)' and 'your (ὑμῶν)' in other parts of Peter's speech. In Acts 2.17 'your (ὑμῶν)' appears four times. Codex Bezae replaces it twice by 'their (αὐτων)' with 'sons' and 'daughters'. Twice 'D' omits 'your' – with 'young men' and 'old men'. It also leaves out 'your' in connection with the phrase: 'for the forgiveness of sins'.

These scribal changes clearly cast doubt on the reliability of this manuscript. Not surprisingly Aland concludes: 'When we see how D here and in various other passages endeavours to make the text relevant by directly relating it to the reader . . . we shall not be inclined to regard the change of text in 2.39 as reflecting a practice of infant or child baptism in that time.'[35] Jeremias is not prepared to leave it there. He reacts to Aland's interpretation of Codex Bezae's textual changes by saying that he is turning things upside down. 'The opposite is correct; it is just when it is seen that D makes the text relevant elsewhere that the same must be assumed for 2.39.'[36]

This variant reading prompts an interesting and important question – linked with the previous chapter – as to the relationship between the authenticity of a text and the inspiration and authority of Scripture. It is not, however, relevant to pursue the question here.

At the risk of labouring the point, Aland feels bound to sum up his position in a final paragraph. He says that in Acts 2.38f there is not a word about the baptism of children, but only of adult hearers, who are exhorted to repent and get baptized. Aland concludes: 'Contrary to Jeremias, the children here surely denote descendants, as the clause that follows emphasizes, i.e. it is to be understood in a temporal and not a local sense: *πᾶσιν τοῖς εἰς μακρὰν* (to all who are far off) refers to coming generations'[37]. Support for Aland's argument is found in the frequent use of the phrase in the Old Testament with regard to descendants. Moreover, in Acts 13.32f, Paul declares: 'We bring you the good news that what God promised the fathers, this he has fulfilled to us their children.'

If Aland thought that Jeremias would leave it there, he was of course mistaken! Jeremias came back strongly in his second book, which in some places is not exactly tepid, as for example on page 25. Our candid comment here does not diminish our obvious indebtedness to these two distinguished German scholars or our appreciation of their careful, detailed and painstaking researches in the Biblical and historical evidence connected with infant baptism.

But – to come back to Acts 2.38f – Jeremias notes Aland's threefold classification: (a) the adult listeners (*ὑμῖν* – to you); (b) their descendants (*τοῖς τέκνοις ὑμῶν* – to your children); and (c) the coming generations (*πᾶσιν τοῖς εἰς μακρὰν* – to all that are far off). Jeremias makes what seems to us a very relevant and obvious point when he says of Aland's triad: 'Thus there would be no mention in Acts 2.39 of children in the proper sense of the word, but only of descendants, and the passage would have nothing to do with our subject.'[38]

Jeremias deals first with the third group: 'To all that are far off'. He says that the word 'far' (*μακρὰν*) in 2.39 signifies distance not in time – as Aland suggested – but in space, and this phrase does not refer to 'coming generations' – as Aland held – 'but to all those whom God summons from distant lands, i.e., according to the Lucan point of view, the Gentiles (cf. Acts 22.21 – 'far away to the Gentiles' – *εἰς ἔθνη μακρὰν*).'[39]

With regard to the first two phrases: 'To you' and 'to your children', Jeremias states that they must be taken together because they express completeness. 'You and your children' reproduces the list in 2.17 'your sons and your daughters, your young men and your old men', which is likewise a paraphrase for the family in its completeness. Jeremias admits, however, that 'baptism is not expressly mentioned in verse 39' but claims that 'it is implied inasmuch as the fulfilment of the promise of the Spirit is linked in verse 38 with baptism'.[40]

Beasley-Murray, a distinguished Baptist scholar, seldom agrees with Jeremias against Aland, but he does so with regard to the interpretation of the phrase 'to your children' in Acts 2.39. It is, however, a qualified agreement as the latter part of his observation shows. He writes: 'I am inclined to agree with Jeremias that the most natural interpretation of Peter's statement "The promise is to you and to your children" is that it denotes that the promise belongs to the hearers and their children, even as the citation from Joel at the beginning of Peter's speech declares "your sons and your daughters shall prophesy"'. Then Beasley-Murray adds: 'If your children' in verse 39 are the same as 'your sons and your daughters' who shall prophesy in verse 17, the indication is that they are such as can repent and be baptized for the remission of sins and the reception of the Holy Ghost, according to verse 38.'[41]

What does 1 Cor. 7.14 mean?

We turn now to 1 Cor. 7.14 – a difficult passage which has been variously interpreted. It reads: 'For the unbelieving husband is consecrated through his wife, and the unbelieving wife is consecrated through the husband. Otherwise, your children would be unclean, but as it is they are holy.'

Let us look first at Jeremias's exposition. The Christian partner of the marriage sanctifies the non-Christian partner, as the holiness of the children proves. 'One believing member sanctifies the whole household.' Since the children and the heathen husband or wife are not baptized, it follows that the holiness of the children rests not on baptism, but on their descent from a Christian father or a Christian mother. On what premise is Paul able to state, 'But now are your children holy'? It was generally accepted that this was true of all children born in the church, that is to say, children whose father or mother was a Christian.

Commenting on this verse, Henry Cook says that Paul is discussing holiness, not baptism, and his point simply is that the influence of even one Christian parent goes a great deal farther than we sometimes imagine.'[42]

Judaism distinguishes between children born 'not in holiness' – that is *before* conversation to Judaism – and children born 'in holiness' – that is *after* conversation to Judaism. The former were baptized when the parents changed their religion, the latter were not baptized. Jeremias says that 'this terminology of the law concerning proselytes is adopted in 1 Cor. 7.14c, where Paul states that the children of Christian parents are not "unclean" but "holy".'[43]

The inference has therefore been drawn that children born *before* their parents were converted to Christianity would be baptized, but not those born 'in holiness' – that is, born *after* their parents' entry into the church. Aland, however, questions Jeremias's contention that 1. Cor. 7.14 belongs to the realm of Jewish ritual language. He holds that this text, with its mixed marriage ideas, cannot be interpreted in terms of Judaism, which forbids Jewish/Gentile marriage. Nor would the Jewish ethic countenance the idea of holiness being applied to a Gentile partner or his children, while remaining in a non-Jewish faith.[44]

In the German edition of his book, 'Infant Baptism in the First Four Centuries', Jeremias argued that children born of Christian parents in New Testament times were not baptized. Later, however, in the English edition, he changed this view – a view which overlooked the fact that in Judaism all boys, whether born 'in holiness' or not were circumcised on the eighth day. And since, according to Jeremias, baptism replaces circumcision in the Christian Church, (a belief we shall examine in Chapter Seven), the fact that children are 'holy' from birth (1 Cor. 7.14c) does not preclude the possibility of baptism. This leads Jeremias to sum up the situation thus: 'We must accordingly be content with the conclusion that 1 Cor. 7.14c bears no reference to baptism. There is every possibility that the statement "for your children are holy" no more excluded the baptism of children on the eighth day, in place of circumcision, than the saying "your unbelieving husband is holy" excluded the later baptism of the husband. But here we cannot get beyond conjecture.'[45]

Jesus and the children

An incident in the Gospels which has often been associated with infant baptism is the blessing of the children by Jesus.[46] This association goes back to the Early Church. We do well, first of all, to attempt an outline of Jeremias' approach to this episode. He begins, surprisingly enough, by emphasizing that the narrative itself 'has nothing to do with baptism, but is pre-sacramental.'[47] It probably happened on the Day of Atonement when parents brought their children to the elders for a blessing[48]. Jesus 'was indignant' (*ἠγανάκτησεν* – a word found only in Mark) when the disciples tried to keep the children away and he said: 'Let the children come to me, do not hinder (*κωλύετε*) them; for of such is the kingdom of God'.

Jeremias also attaches much importance to the word *κωλύειν* (to hinder) which appears in this story. He says that the term was often linked with baptism – a view supported by Oscar Cullmann, who claims that in a series of baptismal texts – e.g. Acts 8.36 (*κωλύει*); 10.47 (*κωλῦσαί*); 11.17 (*κωλῦσαι*) and Matthew 3.14 (*διεκώλυεν*) – the word *κωλύειν* (to hinder) appears so regularly as to suggest a formula. Cullmann concludes: 'As early as the first century, whenever someone who had come to faith was brought for baptism, enquiry was made whether any hindrance existed, that is, whether the candidate had really fulfilled the conditions demanded.'[49]

Such evidence as we have considered led Cullmann to conclude that during the time in which the Gospel tradition took shape the question of infant baptism was a live one and that the passage about the blessing of the children was quoted in order to dispel doubts about receiving this sacrament – 'Forbid them not' (*μὴ κωλύετε αὐτά*) – there is no hindrance to it.[50]

The belief that there are 'traces of an ancient baptismal formula in the New Testament' leads Cullmann to the conclusion that since the word 'hinder' (*κωλύειν*) in the baptismal stories (e.g. Acts 8.36; 10.47; 11.17; Mt. 3.13) is the same as in Christ's reception of the children (Mk. 10.13–16 and parallels), the 'sole difference' of the 'blessing by the laying on of hands takes the place of baptism'[51]. This would, of course, be a 'waterless-baptism'!

Henry Cook regards this as 'a strange kind of reasoning.' He says that 'there is no suggestion in the story of the blessing of the children that Jesus regarded his action as a baptism, nor is there any evidence that the blessing of the children was so regarded by the New Testament Church.' Dr Cook adds that, 'apart from the verb "forbid" or "hinder", there is no real parallel between the baptismal references . . . and the blessing of the children'.[52]

There are, however, other instances in the New Testament in which the word *κωλύειν* (to hinder) appears – such as Mark 9.39; Luke 11.52 and 1 Thess. 2.16. In each of these instances the term *κωλύειν* (hinder) could not possibly have any baptismal associations. In view of the varied use of the word, one must be careful not to attach to *κωλύειν* in Mark 10.14 (and parallels) a reference to baptism which the context does not warrant. As C. T. Craig wrote: 'It may be correct that the Greek word here translated "hinder" had acquired a technical use in the early church in relation to baptism. Yet it is not very conclusive evidence that Jesus meant as the opposite of "hindering" children the "baptizing" of them.'[53]

Further support for the relevance of Christ blessing the children to infant baptism is sought in Luke's choice of a different word for 'children'. Whereas Mark and Matthew use *παιδία* ('children'), Luke uses *τὰ βρέφη* (the infants). The same word (*βρέφος*) also appears in Acts 7.19. The importance of this different choice of word by Luke may lie in the fact that *βρέφος* would generally be used to signify a younger child – an infant or baby – rather than *παιδίον*. Jeremias draws attention to this difference and says: 'This change was not motivated by the narrative itself and should be explained as arising from the Sitz im Leben of the passage. The early church already practised child baptism as infant baptism, and with this in mind Luke inserted the expression *τὰ βρέφη*.'[54]

Howard Marshall, in his scholarly commentary on the Greek Text of Luke's Gospel, explains that 'the use of the article (*τά*) may emphasise the idea of the class; the children are representatives of the class and the point that Jesus is concerned even about infants is much stressed, although . . . Luke's interest in the pericope is more with children as an example to adults.'[55]

One might well ask whether too much emphasis has been placed on Luke's use of *βρέφη* (infants) in preference to *παιδία* ('children'). Did he distinguish between these two words or treat them as synonymous? It is noticeable that he switches to *παιδία* in the latter part of the narrative: 'Now they were bringing even infants (*βρέφη*) to him . . . Let the children (*παιδία*) come to me.' This verbal distinction seems too slender a foundation on which to base a theological conclusion regarding infant baptism.

What would seem to be of more significance than Luke's use of *βρέφη* instead of *παιδία* is his omission of Mark 10.16 which records how Jesus not only blessed the children but laid his hands upon them. Further Synoptic differences relate to the phrase 'as a child' (*ὡς παιδίον*) in Mark 10.15 (= Luke 18.17) and 'become like children' (*γένησθη ὡς τα παιδία*) in Matt.18.3. Beasley-Murray comments that 'whereas Matt. 18.3 shows that it originally meant "becoming as a child", in Mark and Luke it can mean "he that does not receive the Kingdom of God as a child (i.e. in childhood) will not enter it", so suiting better the application to infant baptism.'[56]

In a summary statement, Jeremias reckons that this story 'in several places contains indirect references to baptism' and that the Early Church 'took it as authority for the practice of infant baptism. We may conclude from this', he says, 'that in Rome at the time when the Gospel of Mark was written (about AD 65) that the children of Christian parents were baptized.' He adds that, in so doing, appeal would be made to the example of Jesus who had forbidden that children should be turned from him and had explicitly promised them a share in the coming kingdom of God.[57]

In this connection, reference might be made to Calvin's interpretation of St Matthew's account of this episode (19.13 ff). He says that by embracing the children, Jesus 'testified that they were reckoned . . . among his flock; and if they were partakers of the spiritual gifts, which are represented by baptism, it is unreasonable that they should be deprived of the outward sign'.[58]

Leaving this almost exclusive confrontation between Jeremias and Aland – if only for a while! – we turn to other New Testament texts to which an appeal is made in support of the practice of infant baptism. The Church of Scotland's 'Special Commission on Baptism' (May 1955) interprets references in 1 John concerning 'children' (*παιδία*) 2.18 and 'little children' (*τεκνία*) 2.1 in terms of baptizing infants. The Report states that their being 'anointed by the Holy One' (2.20) and being 'born of him' (2.29) relates to the reception of the Holy Spirit in baptism. Most scholarly exegetes appear to understand the use of these references to 'children' in this epistle as metaphorical, used fittingly of adult Christians as from a 'Father in God.' A similar use of the term 'children' (*τεκνία*) as applied to adults appears in Paul's letter to the Galatians (4.19) – a letter in which he also refers to the same readers as 'brethren' (*ἀδελφοί*) in 4.28.[59]

This Report also sees a reference to infant baptism in 1 Cor. 10.1f which says that 'our fathers were all under the cloud and all passed through the sea, and all were baptized into Moses in the cloud and in the sea.' If we ask where in this scripture there is an allusion to infant baptism, we are told that it is in the word 'all'. The 'all' must have included children and therefore Paul's allegorical application of the passage to baptism must include the baptism of children.

We admit to some difficulty in taking seriously this exposition in the Report. Those who believe that Scripture provides evidence of the practice of infant baptism in New Testament times do not strengthen their claim by an exegesis which, as it seems to us, is invalidated by the generally accepted criterion of biblical and historical criticism.

Did Jesus validate baptism?

We recall that our study of Christ's blessing of the children included the suggestion that he thought of his laying hands on them in baptismal terms. This gives rise to the prior and larger question as to whether Jesus in fact approved and initiated the practice of Christian baptism. If, as has been suggested, Jesus did not favour baptismal ritual, then obviously, he would not have approved of infant baptism. Apart from the great commission in Matt. 28.19 and Mark 16.16, which raise questions of authenticity or textual soundness, there is little evidence in the Gospels to support the Dominical foundation of Christian baptism. As for Matt. 28.19, one wonders why, in the New Testament, the apostles baptized only in the name of Jesus, if their risen Lord had commanded them to baptize in the name of the Trinity. As for the words 'He who believes and is baptized' (Mark 16.16), attributed to Jesus after his resurrection, these words are not, of course, part of Mark's original Gospel, as manuscript evidence proves. The authenticity of Matt. 28.19 is not accepted by H. H. Rowley.[60] or by Kirsopp Lake[61], though it is supported by P. W. Evans.[62] A. J. Maclean makes the interesting observation that 'it is quite possible that no formula of baptism is given in the New Testament and even that at first there were no fixed words'.[63] It needs to be added that, even if Matt. 28.19 and Mark 16.16 were not spoken by the risen Christ, these texts presumably reflect the belief and practice of the Church at the time of writing.

Dr W. K. L. Clarke says that St Paul's words in 1 Cor. 1.17 'Christ sent me not to baptize, but to preach the Gospel' have been thought to exclude the possibility that he knew a command of our Lord as given in Matt. 28.19[64]. We should also note the shortened form of Matt. 28.19 given by Eusebius in his pre-Nicene writings: 'Go make all peoples my disciples in my name.' (*πορευθέντες μαθητεύσατε πάντα τὰ ἔθνη ἐν τῳ ὀνοματί μου*).[65] How significant is it that the command to baptize and the Trinitarian formula are omitted?

It may be argued that Christ's emphasis on the inwardness of religion and the absence of any reference in the Synoptic Gospels to any baptismal activities by Jesus or his disciples cast doubt on Christ's approval of this rite. Moreover, there is no reference to the disciples being baptized either before or after Pentecost. By whom would they have been given Christian baptism? Was the apostles' Spirit-baptism deemed to have made water-baptism in their case superfluous?

According to the Anglican *The Alternative Service Book 1980*, baptism 'is the sacrament instituted by Christ for those who wish to become members of his church.' Certainly Jesus highly commended his forerunner, John the Baptist, and was himself baptized in the Jordan. Dr J. G. Davies says that 'the origin of baptism lay partly in the imitation of Jesus in his submission to the baptism of John and partly in Jewish proselyte baptism whereby converts to Judaism were purified from their previous contamination as Gentiles'[66].

There is also a contradictory and doubtful reference in St John's

Gospel (4.1f) to Jesus baptizing and/or to his disciples doing so. It is unlikely, however, that the Primitive Church would so readily have baptized converts at Pentecost had they not believed that Christian baptism was in accordance with the mind of Christ. As to the slender evidence in the Gospels to baptism, it is sometimes maintained that the silence on the subject is because the writers were so pre-occupied with other aspects of the life and teaching of Jesus that they took baptism for granted. Perhaps one should be wary of using this kind of apologetic. Some use it to explain the absence of any direct evidence in the New Testament to infant baptism. Such conjecture has its place so long as we do not confuse it with proof.

Dr N. P. Williams argues retrospectively – from effect to cause. He holds that the universal prevalence of Christian baptism presupposes 'some command or expression of purpose given by the Lord himself.' By his own baptism 'in which the interior influx of the Spirit was superadded to the exterior affusion of water, our Lord . . . transformed the water-baptism of John into Spirit-baptism.' Williams adds that John 4.1f is sufficient evidence of an 'expression of purpose' that his followers should practise baptism.[67]

Latourette briefly and clearly surveys this debatable question when he writes: 'Just how and why baptism came to be the method of admission to the Christian community we do not know. We have no record of Jesus himself administering the rite. Our earliest accounts of the Christian groups which succeeded the death and resurrection of Jesus seem to show that baptism was accepted as the invariable method of introduction to membership and to Christian discipleship. Some, however, believe that these accounts reflect the practice of the generation which gave them their present form and not that of the years immediately after Jesus.'[68]

We believe that we have dealt with the main New Testament evidence usually presented in support of infant baptism – except one important subject, namely the widely held view that infant baptism arose in the primitive church as a counterpart of circumcision. We shall devote a later chapter to this suggested relationship.

One way of considering the Scriptural evidence, which we have brought together in this chapter, would be to try to imagine that infant baptism did not exist at the present time but only the baptism of adults. Looking at the Biblical data as dispassionately as possible, would we conclude that we should replace adult baptism by a rite for the baptism of infants? We are not alone in thinking that there seems sometimes to be a distinct difference between the views expressed by those who write with a sense of loyalty to traditional church doctrine and by those biblical scholars who appear to be more ready in their exegesis to follow wherever the Scripture leads.

W. F. Flemington, a supporter of the infant rite, nevertheless concedes that 'the most characteristic New Testament baptismal teaching, originally formulated with special reference to the baptism of adults, must undergo some measure of restatement before it can be applied to a situation in which the typical subject of baptism is an infant.'[69] This scholarly writer ends an article on baptism in 'The Interpreter's Dictionary of the Bible' by saying: 'The direct evidence of the New Testament is insufficient to settle the question either for or against infant baptism; the case must be argued on other grounds.'[70] There are not a few writers who have come to the same conclusion.

We are not told what 'other grounds' Flemington has in mind; but we shall look at 'other grounds' in later chapters. We shall then see what further light our examination of these may throw on the question whether or not infants were, or should have been, baptized in New Testament times.

CHAPTER FOUR

Can the Rite be Traced in the First Two Centuries?

Our aim in this chapter is to consider what evidence there may be for the practice of Infant baptism before AD 200. The mainly contrasting views of Jeremias and Aland in their interpretation of the relevant sources cannot well be ignored in any serious attempt to assess the evidence for and against the baptism of infants in the early church. Here, as in the previous chapter, we are indebted to their scholarly contribution.

The Eastern Church: Origen

Turning to the Eastern Church, where 'the evidence is more scanty' than in the West, Jeremias sees Origen as 'of the greatest importance', and holds that although his evidence was written down between the years 233 and 251, yet it 'takes us back to a considerably earlier period.' Origen (c 185 – c 254) refers to infant baptism as 'a tradition handed down from the apostles' because he knew that 'his father and probably his grandfather had been baptized as *παιδία* (children)', which would date back to the first half of the second century.[1] Origen's travels enabled him to speak of infant baptism as 'the custom of the church' (ecclesiae observantia), that is the Eastern Church, and refutes the idea that infants do not need to be baptized.

It is argued, however, by Argyle that Origen shows no acquaintance with the practice of infant baptism in the time he spent writing at Alexandria and he cites Bigg[2], Harnack[3] and N. P. Williams[4] in support of the view that Origen became acquainted with infant baptism only in the latter part of his life when he lived in Caesaria[5].

According to Aland, if the baptism of infants was based on an apostolic tradition and was universally practised, then Origen's defence of the rite would be unnecessary. It follows, therefore, that there must have been circles holding a different opinion and abstaining from infant baptism. This would prompt Origen to appeal to the 'tradition of the church received from the apostles.' (traditio ecclesiae ab apostolis). Is Jeremias's conclusion correct in claiming that Origen's 'witness holds good for practically the whole Eastern Church of his day'?[6]

With regard to Origen's father, Leonides, he was a Christian and died a martyr under Septimius Severus in AD 202. But there is no evidence that he was a Christian from his youth and not a word about his grandfather. Nor is it established that they were baptized as infants. Young children may have been baptized between 230–250 in Palestine, during Origen's stay there, 'according to the custom of the church', but this custom need not go far back in time.

In connection with another part of the Eastern Church, Jeremias says that the first direct evidence for the practice of infant baptism in Syria is given by Asterius the Sophist (early fourth century) and the Apostolic Constitutions (370–380). As for East Syria, he says that there is no trace of evidence that here infant baptism was practised in the first century.[7]

The Western Church: Aristides

Turning to the Western Church, Jeremias finds in the 'Apology' of Aristides indirect proof for infant baptism at the beginning of the second century. The 'Apology' has been preserved in the Syriac translation – discovered by Rendel Harris in 1889 in the monastery on Mount Sinai. Only fragments of the Greek original remain. Jeremias sees in the 'Apology' a reference to baptism: 'And when a child (*τέκνον*) is born to them, they thank God; and if he die in infancy (*νήπιος*), they thank him exceedingly, because it departed this life sinless.'[8]

Another statement in the 'Apology' (17.4) is regarded as having a similar meaning. 'And if it happens that one of them (the pagans) is converted, he is ashamed before the Christians of the things he has done and thanks God saying: "In ignorance have I done this." And he purifies his heart and his sins are forgiven him.' Jeremias comments that in this passage the focal expression 'to thank God' is a reference to baptism.[9] For Aland, the words 'Thank God' in this context have no such connotation. He reckons that baptism is presupposed much more in the statement that 'he cleanses his heart and his sins are forgiven him'.

A passage in the 'Apology' (15.6), overlooked by Jeremias, is significant because, while it refers to 'children's baptism', it does not refer to infants. The reference is presumably to the children of Christian parents. This passage reads: 'Now they instruct the servants and maids or the children, when any of them have such, that they become Christians, on account of the love which they have for them. When they have become Christians they call them brothers without distinction.'

This Syriac text does not seem to mean children of the servants or of the maidservants. Moreover, the word 'Christian' appears to refer to all of them. In the fragmented Greek text[10] the words 'if they have any' (ἐὰν ἔχωσιν) can be taken to refer to the 'servants and maidservants' rather than to the 'children' – that is, the servants are not the parents of the children.

It also seems clear that the 'children' (τέκνα) are not 'infants' (βρέφη), but are of an age to understand the meaning of baptism and to receive the Eucharist. They are regarded as full Christians. It appears, therefore, that Aristides' Apology 15.6, not only excludes infant baptism, but postpones the baptism even of the children of Christian parents until they are old enough to receive instruction in the faith.

Irenaeus

Irenaeus, Bishop of Lyons in the latter part of the second century, has been regarded as a witness to infant baptism. With reference to Christ, he wrote: 'For he came to save all through means of himself – all, I say, who through him are born again to God (renascuntur in Deum) – infants and children and boys and youth and old men.'[11] Taking this quotation in isolation, Jeremias comments that 'Since Irenaeus, following the fully established and quite unvarying terminology of the church, describes baptism as "regeneration unto God" (regenatio in Deum), he bears witness in our passage to infant baptism and presupposes it as "an unquestioned practice of the church".'[12]

It is pointed out that the words 'born again' in the above quotation can be found in other passages where Irenaeus uses this phrase to mean baptismal regeneration.[13] This evidence has led to the conclusion that infant baptism was practised in the latter part of the second century. This conclusion, however, has been countered by pointing out that Irenaeus in other places writes about regeneration with no baptismal connotation. Moreover, much that Irenaeus has to say on baptism presupposes adult Christians, as Argyle shows[14]. Baptism is offered to one who has faith.[15]; who accepts the 'Rule of Truth'[16]; and who confesses the threefold name, the incarnation, the passion and the resurrection of Christ.[17]

If the above quotation from Irenaeus is seen in its larger setting, then its relevance to infant baptism is doubtful. Irenaeus had said that Jesus, after his baptism, came to Jerusalem as a teacher 'not despising or evading any condition of humanity . . . but sanctifying every age by that period corresponding to it which belonged to himself.' Irenaeus goes on to say: 'He therefore passed through every age, becoming an infant for infants, thus sanctifying infants, a child for children, thus sanctifying those who are of this age, being at the same time made to them an example of piety, righteousness and submission; a youth for youths, becoming an example to youths and thus sanctifying them for the Lord.'

In the light of these observations by Irenaeus, Kurt Aland concludes that the Bishop of Lyons does not appear to have baptism in view here, much less infant baptism. 'He is concerned solely with the fact that Jesus sanctified all humanity in that he . . . lived through all stages of life and was an example to all.'[18]

Clement of Alexandria (c.155-c.220), despite being dismissed by Jeremias as having nothing of importance to say about baptism, does in fact seem to make some significant contribution to the subject. Clement, however, does not appear to make any reference to the infant rite even in places where one might expect him to do so. This situation suggests one of two things: either that Clement had no interest in infant baptism or that it did not exist in his day, at least in his part of the world.

In Clement's 'Paedagogos' 1.5, which has the meaningful heading: 'All who concern themselves with truth are children of God', passages about children are expounded, including the story of Jesus blessing the children.[19] But he interprets 'children' as adult Christians – compare 1 John 2 – even when he quotes Matt. 21.16 which quotes Psalm 8.2 'Out of the mouth of babes and sucklings thou has brought perfect praise.' Although in Paedagogos 1.5 a page is given to the word 'infant' (*νήπιος*), there is no reference to real children or to baptism.

Baptism is considered by Clement in Paedagogos 26. 1–3; 30. 1–32.1, but again there is no mention of the baptism of infants. In sections 39–42, there is a meditation on birth and nourishment of children, but it is illustrative of adult Christians with no implication of infant baptism. As 'Stromateis' Book IV, chapter 2 indicates, baptism is for forgiveness of past sins and relates to 'the repentance of a one-time unbeliever.' (*ἡ τοῦ ποτὲ ἀπίστου μετάνοια*). It is a rite which presupposes that 'the foundation of redemption is the faith that proceeds from a man's volition' and is therefore not applicable to young children.

Hippolytus: Apostolic Tradition

Much importance has been attached to the 'Church Order' of Hippolytus (died c.236) which is said to have had the same outstanding significance for the West as Origen had for the East. Dom Gregory Dix says that 'the Apostolic Tradition of St Hippolytus is the most illuminating single source of evidence on the inner life and religious polity of the early Christian church.'[20] Only a few fragments of the original Greek manuscript have survived, so one has to make do with various translations – translations which go back to a common textual tradition dating long after the death of Hippolytus.

Most of what it says about baptism, shortly after AD 200, is designed for adults and normally required a probationary period of three years. It shows how carefully candidates for baptism were chosen and that they were instructed in the Christian faith even before they became catechumens. They were treated as church members, but not admitted to the Eucharist and the kiss of peace.[21]

A regulation in the 'Church Order', thought to reflect the situation early in the third century, reads as follows: 'First, the little ones should be baptized. All who can speak for themselves should speak. For those, however, who cannot, their parents or another who belongs to the family should speak.'[22]

The Latin tradition of the original Greek text goes back to the end of the fourth century – the earliest manuscript is said to date from around AD 500 – but the existing fragments do not include the chapter on baptism. Since the texts immediately before, and after, the chapter on the baptism of children and infants treat in some detail only with adult catechumens, it appears possible that the chapter on infant baptism could be a later interpolation after the time of Hippolytus. If so, this evidence does not relate to the early years of the third century.

While the theory that this chapter was a later insertion, prompted by doctrinal considerations, would offer some support for Aland's case against infant baptism in the early church, he nevertheless chooses to reject it. He does so according to the principle of 'lectio difficilior', that is, a scribe is unlikely to insert a more difficult reading in a text unless there was a good reason for doing so. Moreover, since the baptism of infants was already being practised in the early third century in Africa (Cyprian) and in Palestine (Origen), there seemed to be no good reason why the infant rite was not being practised also in Rome in the time of Hippolytus (AD c.220).

There is another reason for our discussing this issue here. According to Jeremias, what Hippolytus writes relates not only to his own day, but to earlier times. It is true, he says, that the Apostolic Tradition, as far as its composition goes, must be dated about 215, but its material is older, and it would be a mistake if we were to reckon the work merely as evidence for the beginning of the third century. 'For Hippolytus, who probably incorporated the Church Order into his book *Περὶ Χαρισμάτων ἀποστολικὴ παραδοσις* as its second part, had no intention of introducing new rules for church action, but, as the title of his work indicates, of setting down the older (apostolic) tradition. And this is true of infant baptism.'

Elements in this statement are questioned on the ground that a Church Order had the intention of establishing the status quo of its own time by means of the usual appeal to the Apostolic Age. Church Orders are said to look forwards not backwards. Aland says 'assuming that the section on the baptism of children and infants really does stem from Hippolytus, his Church Order takes us no further back than Origen does, namely to the end of the second century'.[23]

Tertullian

We now turn to Tertullian (c.160–c.215), Bishop of Carthage – moralist, apologist and theologian – whose writings take us to the end of the second century and into the third.[24]. The evidence he provides has possible implications for earlier times with regard to the question whether infant baptism was established in the first two centuries. A. R. Whitham points out that 'Tertullian's treatise on baptism is noteworthy as the first Christian monograph on this subject.'[25] Whereas Hippolytus was the last Western theologian to write in Greek, Tertullian was the first Christian to write in Latin, though he had equal facility in Greek, as some of his publications show.[26]

It is in his writings that the 'Fierce Tertullian' is known, as few details of his life are certain. Perhaps we may be permitted to wander a little from the path set by this book by briefly noting the interestng biographical sketch which David Wright ventures to draw[27]. He says that Tertullian was reared in the cultural paganism of Carthage and had a literary, rhetorical and perhaps a legal training. The fortitude of the martyrs probably led him to become a Christian. The effect on the Early Church of this bishop's conversion to Montanism must have been dramatic and startling. Ronald Knox (1888–1957), a Roman Catholic scholar and son of an Anglican bishop of Manchester, sums up Tertullian's conversion by saying: 'It was as if Cardinal Newman had joined the Salvation Army'![28]

Retracing our wandering steps, back to the question of infant baptism in the second century, we note that in 'De Paenitentia' (6.3–24), Tertullian opposes the tendency to postpone joining the church, because of the belief that, in view of the forgiveness expected in Baptism, one could continue in sin as long as one remained unbaptized! This leads Jeremias to express astonishment that in his book 'De Baptismo' (ch.18) – written about the same time (AD 200–206) – Tertullian urges the postponement of baptism in special cases, such as children and unmarried people.[29]

It is held that 'De Baptismo' was written to meet a special situation – the baptism of converts. Hence Tertullian's doubts about the legitimacy of infant baptism relate to the children of pagans joining the church. Jeremias adds that the reservations expressed in De Baptismo 18 were not intended by Tertullian to cover the baptism of the children of Christian parents.[30]

Tertullian's question: 'Why does the age of innocence hasten to the remission of sins?' seems to reflect a tendency in Carthage to baptize children. With Matt. 19.14 in mind: 'Let the children come to me, and do not hinder them' for to such belongs the kingdom of heaven', Tertullian writes: 'Let them "come", therefore, when they grow older; let them "come" when they are able to learn, when they can be instructed whether they should "come"; Let them become Christians when they can know Christ.'[31]

This can be taken to mean: baptize children only when they are old enough to understand the Christian Faith and can confess Christ. Tertullian's main theme seems to be: The postponement of baptism is preferable[32]. This advice is also offered to spinsters and widows, because he sees them as being particularly susceptible to temptation[33]. Some of the grounds that he gives for delaying baptism are not very convincing, such as: (1) the sponsor's untimely death and (2) the unpredictable character of the infant baptised.

Flemington points out that nowhere did Tertullian produce what would have been a conclusive argument against the practice, namely that infant baptism was not a usage of apostolic days, nor did he anywhere so much as suggest such a possibility.[34] Flemington is using the argument from silence and that, as we observed earlier, is not the equivalent of proof.

James Bulloch is somewhat in sympathy with Flemington's point of view when he writes: 'No reliable evidence for infant baptism is available until the end of the second century, but no conclusion can be drawn from this, not so much because new members were predominantly converts as because of the extreme scarcity of information . . . Tertullian made it plain that infant baptism was common and that he did not care for it. Had it been an innovation he would gladly have said so.'[35]

If Bulloch is right in suggesting that infant baptism was common at this time, why was Tertullian so pre-occupied with baptismal activities appropriate only to adults when he wrote: 'Those who are on the point of entering upon baptism ought to pray, with frequent prayers, fastings, bendings of the knee, and all-night vigils, along with the confession of all their sins.'[36]

The influence of so important a person as Tertullian may have slowed the development of infant baptism at the beginning of the third century; but, as we shall see in the next chapter, the tide was too strong for anybody to hold back. In his first and latest writings, Tertullian does not deal with the baptism of the infants. 'De Spectaculis' (4.1) is concerned with baptismal confession (renouncing the devil) and is made 'with our mouth' (ore nostro) – a ritual practice which would seem to exclude infants. In 'De Corona', he describes a baptismal rite, in which after immersion three times a mixture of milk and honey is received. So far the involvement of children need not be ruled out, but Tertullian would seem to exclude babies when he says that 'from that day we refrain from the daily bath for a week.'![37]

Tertullian says that sinfulness begins at 'the puberty of the soul', that is 'at about the fourteenth year of life' and he comments that 'it drives man out of the paradise of innocence.'[38] This rules out belief in 'original sin' and therefore the need of cleansing from the 'inherited taint' often associated with infant baptism. We shall consider the relationship between 'original sin' and baptism in a later chapter.

In 'De paenitentia', Tertullian emphasises the pre-requisite of repentance before baptism – again a requirement which babies cannot be expected to meet. It would appear that, in 'De Baptismo', we have evidence of the very beginnings of infant baptism in

Carthage and Africa. Tertullian's resistance was unsuccessful; the new powers were too strong and infant baptism spread ever more widely until fifty years later we find it as the norm. Moreover, the bishop's conversion to Montanism in 207 would considerably weaken his influence as he sought to resist the development of the baptism of infants.[39]

Michel Meslin draws attention to the fact that a number of patristic texts reveal how the practice of baptism developed along lines designed for adults and not easily adaptable for infants. He says that 'the baptismal ritual was quickly enriched through such additions as interrogations . . . a triple renunciation of the devil . . . a triple immersion . . . the anointing of the neophite with the holy chrism and the laying on of hands by the bishop or priest.'[40]

James Bulloch also sees the early development of baptism as being shaped with adults in mind. 'The church very early insisted on a lengthy period of preparation . . . Those desiring baptism were to pray, fast, keep vigil and show evident signs of repentance in a change of life, while they received exorcism and instruction.'[41]

The Didache

The Didache ('The Teaching of the Twelve Apostles') is said to be the oldest text on the subject of baptism outside the New Testament. Its date is doubtful – perhaps early second century – but it is thought to reflect primitive Christianity and might well have been included in the Canon. While there are a number of references to baptism in the second century, the only sources that describe the rite are the 'Didache' (7) and Justin's 'First Apology' (61 and 65).[42]. The first six chapters simply give a summary of what was taught in a form to be recited prior to baptism. Chapter seven is a special treatment of the subject. This preparation, however, is clearly not designed for infants.[43] Baptism was preceded by fasting (possibly derived from Judaism) and was performed in the name of the Trinity[44] or 'into the name of the Lord'[45], as in the New Testament.

Baptism, as described in the Didache, was followed by the Eucharist – a ritual which generally presupposes adult involvement. Affusion is here an acceptable alternative to immersion, although the latter appears to have been the more common in the first four centuries and was usually performed out of doors 'in running water'.[46] The hesitation shown towards visitors, in the Didache, implies a time of probation before a convert can be admitted to the rite of baptism – a situation which indicates adult participation.

The subject of baptism also appears in the letter of Barnabas, written early in the second century and using the Old Testament allegorically. It refers to the candidates descending into the waters of baptism 'full of sins and defilement of the flesh' – a description that can hardly be applied to infants. The Shepherd of Hermas alludes to a preparatory interval of proving and testing before baptism.[47] It implies probation and states that baptism cleanses previous sins. Again the preparation and the ritual appear to have no reference to infants. The baptismal water is seen as conveying the seal of the Holy Spirit and having a regenerative effect whereby the candidates 'go down into the dead and come up alive'.[48]

R. M. Grant points out that the evidence from the early second century has to do chiefly with the meaning of baptism and the eucharist; the actual rites, except in the Didache, are taken for granted. 'It is . . . after 150 that we have evidence to give a somewhat clearer picture of what actually went on in the Christian assemblies.'[49]

Justin Martyr

We turn now to Justin Martyr (c100–165) – a Christian philosopher, martyred in the reign of Marcus Aurelius. The sixty-first chapter of his 'First Apology' provides detailed information about baptism – a description which appears to rule out infants, as the account which follows seems to indicate. The rite is offered only to 'all who are persuaded and believe that the things taught and declared by us are true and who promise that they can live accordingly'. They must seek forgiveness with prayer and fasting.[50] This is followed by baptism in the threefold name, followed by prayer, the kiss of brotherhood and finally the Eucharist in bread, wine and water.[51]

Flemington regarded Justin's 'First Apology' as providing evidence for the practice of infant baptism as early as the first century. He quotes Justin's statement that living in his own day were 'many men and women of sixty and seventy years of age, who became disciples of Christ from their childhood.' (*οἱ ἐκ παίδων ἐμαθητεύθησαν τῷ χριστῷ*)[52]. Flemington says that 'the verb *μαθητευῶ*, used here by Justin in the passive, is the same verb that is used . . . at the end of Matthew's Gospel – "Make disciples of all the nations, baptizing them . . ."' (*μαθητεύσατε πάντα τὰ ἔθνη,βαπτίζοντες . . .*)[53]

Flemington attaches what seems to us undue importance to the finer point that *ἐμαθητευθησαν*, in the aorist tense in Greek, would represent a definite or complete action, whereas an imperfect tense could indicate a continuous or repeated action. On this slender verbal distinction he draws the weighty conclusion that the baptism of these 'men and women of sixty and seventy years of age', referred to by Justin, was not preceded by continuous instruction in the faith, but indicates a particular moment at which these people in their childhood 'became disciples'. 'Thus', says Flemington, 'the most natural interpretation of the passage seems to involve the baptism of these people as infants. Sixty or seventy years from the date of the First Apology takes us back to about AD 80 or 90'.[54]

After a somewhat lengthy and detailed exposition – into which we need not go – Jeremias maintains that *ἐκ παιδων ἐμαθητευσαν τῳ χριστῳ*[55] means 'They became disciples of Christ as children (through baptism)' and places these infant baptisms towards the end of the first century. He concludes rather tamely by saying: Admittedly it is only an indirect piece of evidence, because baptism is not mentioned expressis verbis – a conclusion that hardly strengthens his previous argument.

Argyle holds that Justin clearly understood Christian baptism to be administered in the threefold name to believers only. The recipients of baptism were they who 'are persuaded and believe' the Christian teaching, who exercise conscious faith, who have fasted and prayed. 'This washing is called illumination (*φωτισμός*), because they who learn these things are illuminated in their understandings.'[56]

Illumination, says Anthony Hanson, was a figure often used for baptism in the early church.[57] The same point is made by Maurice Wiles when he wrote: 'Illumination in the writings of the Fathers simply means baptism. The "illuminands" are the baptized' – illumination comes when the light of saving knowledge is imparted. To appreciate and experience this clearly requires the maturity of an adult mind.[58]

We have already observed that there is direct evidence for the practice of infant baptism in the third century and have considered and questioned the claim that some writings in the early part of that century indicate that the infant rite was not a recent innovation but had been practised long before AD 200.

With characteristic emphasis, Jeremias says that neither Tertullian nor Origen nor Cyprian give us the slightest support for the hypothesis that infant baptism was an innovation in their time or was felt to be such. On the contrary, they are unanimous in showing that it was then the natural and traditional practice of the church. 'We have already seen . . . that this holds good for Hippolytus and Irenaeus as well.'[59] That, at any rate, is the judgement of Jeremias. Most scholars, however, would agree that there is no direct evidence for infant baptism in the first two centuries.

In this connection, we recall how in the previous chapter the absence of direct evidence of infant baptism in the New Testament was explained by arguing that the biblical writers omitted to mention this practice because they took it for granted. A similar line of argument has been followed with regard to the absence of any direct reference to the baptism of infants in the first two centuries. It is suggested that the theological writers of that time did not attempt to present a full picture of church activities and therefore it is not surprising that the practice of infant baptism was not mentioned. This suggestion calls for careful consideration.

Burkhard Neunheuser, in a balanced statement, says that the baptism of adults is presupposed throughout the New Testament and the early Christian period. As yet we find no reference to the baptism of young children. 'But this is no proof, of course, that the practice was unknown . . . No special rite of infant baptism was ever devised. In the early days the baptism of children was . . . a sort of appendage to the baptism of adults . . . The catechumenate did not include children.'[60]

The main issue, however, centres on the question of indirect evidence. As we saw earlier, Jeremias and Aland, both of whom have carefully examined the sources in the first two centuries, take up different positions. We noticed how Jeremias claimed to find in certain writers implications that point to infant baptism at an earlier date, as, for example, the suggested baptism of Origen's father and grandfather when they were children. 'They are of an indirect nature, but they confirm each other. The oldest of them takes us back to Apostolic times, probably to the times when the Gospels of Matthew and Luke were written.'[61] For Aland, this is speculation rather than historical fact.

Polycarp's testimony

One such instance of indirect evidence for infant baptism is seen in the account of Polycarp's martyrdom.[62] A probable date of Polycarp's death is AD 167.[63] When, in the Arena in Ephesus, Polycarp was challenged by the Roman Proconsul to revile Christ, he uttered the well-known words: 'For eighty-six years I have served him and he never did me any wrong. How can I now blaspheme my king who saved me?'

Deducting eighty six years from the time of his martyrdom, Jeremias concludes that Polycarp must have been baptized as a child in about AD 81. Maclean reckons that Polycarp died around AD 155 and that he was not much older than eighty six at his death. From this calculation, Maclean concludes that Polycarp was baptized as an infant about AD 70[64]. Gregory Dix agrees with Maclean's calculation. He says: 'The inference from Mart. Polycarpi IX is that Polycarp had been baptized in infancy about AD 70.' He adds that infant baptism, accompanied always by infant confirmation[65], goes back to the second century, probably to the first.[66]

Irenaeus supports the view that Polycarp's youth was set in the first century and says that Polycarp was made a Christian and consecrated bishop of Smyrna by the apostles.[67] Jeremias rejects the suggestion that Polycarp was about fourteen years old when he was baptized, and points out that this would make the bishop impossibly old at the time of his martyrdom. The reasoning here assumes that the beginning of Polycarp's 'service' for Christ coincided with his baptism. Jeremias concludes: 'Thus we have in Mart. Polyc. 9.3 an indirect confirmation given us of the practice of infant baptism in the years round about AD 80'.[68]

The firm conclusion expressed here by Jeremias prompts us to say that we have noticed in the writings of this distinguished scholar a tendency sometimes to use emphatic statements – such as 'we may conclude with certainty', 'the undoubted fact', 'it is certain'[69] – assertions that concern matters about which there does not seem to be any such absolute assurance. It was this dogmatic tendency which appeared partly to fuel Aland's criticism of Jeremias. On the other hand, we must add that, in our study of this subject, we have also come across some excessive claims made by the opponents of infant baptism – claims which do not seem to be warranted by the available evidence. It is clear that in the sphere of early church history, as elsewhere, truth is an elusive commodity.

With these observations in mind, we turn to the situation in Bithynia, as revealed in the correspondence between Trajan, the Roman Emperor, and Pliny, his proconsul, about AD 112. In a rather sweeping statement, Jeremias says that 'we may conclude with certainty that among the very young there were numerous children of parents who had been converts from heathenism; and since Pliny considers the possibility that the very young (teneri) should be brought to trial and punished in the manner of adults, we must take it that they had become through baptism full members of the church.'[70] This statement seems to us to be a non-sequitur – the conclusion does not necessarily follow from the premise. Moreover, Hans Lietzmann says that 'in Bithinia about AD 100 and in Rome even about AD 200, it was usual to proscribe night-time between Saturday and Sunday for the baptismal ceremony . . . the night in which the Lord rose again.'[71]

The baptismal significance which has been attached to Polycarp's 'eighty six years' in Christ's service is applied also to a statement by Polycrates, Bishop of Ephesus in 190/91. 'Brethren I have lived in the Lord sixty-five years'.[72] Polycrates, like Polycarp, does not mention baptism, but it seems to Jeremias that the reference to sixty-five years indicates more than his age. 'This passage, taking us back to the year 125/6 as the year of Polycrates' birth, also favours the conjecture that baptism took place soon after birth, rather than there was an age-limit for baptism.'[73]

Not surprisingly, Aland disagrees with this conclusion and argues that to interpret Polycrates' word to mean that 'he was baptized as a child about AD 125' is to make the mistake of reading into the text what is not necessarily there. 'For to belong to the Christian Church for sixty-five years gives no information as to the time of baptism and does not need to include infant baptism.'[74]

We now consider the relevance of the First Letter of Clement – a letter which goes back to an earlier date than any evidence produced by Jeremias – back in fact to the first century. While Clement has little, if anything, to say directly about baptism, there is, however, an illusion to the Spirit of grace, which might mean the Holy Spirit given at baptism[75]. There are two further possible allusions in the description of the deluge, which Noah proclaimed, as 'regeneration'[76] and the phrase 'through him our foolish and darkened mind springs up into the light.'[77]

The First Epistle of Clement was sent in about AD 96 from the Church in Rome to the Church in Corinth by messengers who are named in this letter[78] and who 'have walked among us from youth to old age unblameably.'[79] These elderly messengers, reckoning backwards from AD 96 were presumably born about AD 30. It appears, therefore, that they were born 'pagan', as the Church of Rome does not appear to have been established before AD 40. It should be noted that the word 'baptism' is not used; but if and when they were baptized it seems clear, in view of the above reckoning, that they would not be infants at the time of baptism. Hence 'from youth' (*ἀπο νεόυητος*) in 63.3 clearly does not refer to infancy.

Christian inscriptions

Our aim in this chapter has been to see what evidence there may be for the practice of infant baptism in the second century. It may therefore be thought irrelevant for us to consider here Jeremias' claim to find traces of the baptism of infants in Christian inscriptions, since none of these is dated prior to AD 200. Our reason for looking briefly at this evidence is because these inscriptions have been taken to imply that the infant rite was so well established in the third century – in Africa, Italy and perhaps Palestine – as to presuppose the existence in earlier times. This is a line of argument which we have already met on previous pages.

Only in a single case do the inscriptions refer to an infant – a child living only for a few hours. Jeremias comments: 'From the words "in pace" ("in peace") we may infer that the little child, who died nine hours after his birth, was baptized.'[80] But does 'in pace' indicate that baptism had taken place? – especially in view of the holiness of children held at that time, a subject we discussed in the previous chapter in connection with 1 Cor. 7.14. If the child was baptized, it was presumably 'emergency baptism', which even Tertullian recognized, but this particular instance can hardly signify that infant baptism was a general practice.

In cases where baptism is not mentioned, they would seem to offer no evidence in support of the infant rite. Indeed, some of the these inscriptions might provide evidence against the view advanced by Jeremias. In certain instances, where baptism is mentioned, the reference appears to indicate emergency baptism – one case being that of Marcianus, who was in fact a boy of twelve! This evidence draws the following comment from Aland: 'The inscription actually shatters the thesis that infant baptism was administered to Christian childen and at the same time it tears a very large hole in the idea that infant baptism was obligatory in the third century.'[81]

Looking back over his review of material from the early centuries offered in support of infant baptism, Aland sums up by saying that the first unambiguous testimonies for infant baptism emerge about the middle of the first half of the third century. 'Despite the thesis maintained by Jeremias', says Aland, 'the inscriptions, which are the sole testimonies we possess besides the patristic writings, do not permit us to assume that the usage attested in the "Church Order" of Hippolytus and by Cyprian was compulsory for all Italy and all Africa.' Perhaps the situation envisaged in the 'Church Order' did not apply even for the whole of Rome, since the Marcianus inscription comes from that city. It is argued that the inscriptions, far from supporting the position of Jeremias, decisively weaken it. Moreover, the 'Church Order' reveals the practice of baptizing children of maturer years as well as the baptism of infants.

Jeremias sums up his argument by saying: 'The statements of Origen, Hippolytus and Tertullian, which carry us back into the second century . . . constitute the scaffolding which supports the rest of the evidence . . . Everywhere, with the exception of Eastern Syria, we find in the second century infant baptism as an old and established usage of the Great Church, which both East and West agree in tracing back to the apostles.[82]

Suffice it to say that our enquiry in this chapter has not found clear and compelling evidence in support of this definite and unequivocal judgment. With regard to the question whether the first two centuries reveal instances of infant baptism being administered, Hans Conzelmann succinctly concludes: 'The sources say nothing about the baptism of children or even infants.'[83]

Donald Lake is of the opinion that 'until about the end of the fifth century adult believer's baptism was the normal practice of the church. This fact is demonstrated by the emphasis in the Early Fathers on careful preparation for baptism and the necessity to live a sinless life after baptism.'[84] Beasley-Murray says that the earliest explicit reference to the baptism of a very young child falls just before AD 300. R. Huna (died AD 297) counselled that a child whose father had died and whose mother wished him to become a proselyte should receive the bath 'according to the judgment of the court': 'What is our justification for this? Because it is for his advantage, and an advantage can be applied to a man without his knowledge of it.' Such a statement assumes that the child was too young to answer for himself.[85]

Williston Walker goes back over a hundred years earlier in search of the first reference to the baptism of an infant. He says that 'the strong probability is that, till past the middle of the second century, they were those only of years of discretion. The first mention of infant baptism, and an obscure one, was about 185 by Irenaeus.'[86]

We conclude this brief survey set in the second century by quoting E. C. Whitaker, to whose work in the sphere of baptismal liturgy we are much indebted. He writes: 'The Gospel was first preached to adults . . . to whom the appeal was first made that they should repent and be baptized. Whether infants were baptized from the first is a matter for debate . . . There is no clear and solid historical evidence to support either side.' Whitaker goes on to point out that the rite developed with adult baptism as its purpose and that no particular accommodation was made for infants in the service.[87]

CHAPTER FIVE

The Origin and Development of Infant Baptism

As we move into the third century, there is clear and increasing evidence of the existence of infant baptism in the Early Church. The chief witnesses are (1) the 'Church Order' of Hippolytus; (2) the Synodal letter of Cyprian; and some sayings of Origen. Whatever doubts there may be regarding the practice of baptizing infants in the New Testament and in the first two centuries, there is firm evidence for infant baptism from the beginning of the third century. Admittedly, in recent years, such eminent scholars as Cullmann and Jeremias have held that in the New Testament, even in the Gospels, there is evidence for the existence of the infant rite; but, as we have seen, writers of the calibre of Aland and Beasley-Murray have dissented strongly.

Professor Alan Richardson summed up the history of infant baptism by saying that it 'has been practised by the church in an unbroken tradition from the third century until the Reformation, when the Anabaptists and later the Baptists renounced the practice and proclaimed the necessity of "believers' baptism".' Richardson adds that 'the churches of the Catholic Tradition and many Protestant confessions (including Lutheran and Presbyterian) have retained the practice of infant baptism.'[1]

In this chapter, we shall first seek an answer to the question as to the origin of the baptizing of infants and then attempt a brief account of the development of this rite in subsequent centuries. This historical survey, carried over into the next chapter, will include some grim and tragic features. It will show the cost in human suffering as a consequence of opposing the baptizing of infants. History makes clear that the establishment or perpetuation of infant baptism has not been an unmixed blessing. The result in personal terms and in Denominational devisiveness is all too apparent. The practical and theological problems relating to the rite of confirmation, to which infant baptism gave rise, and the question of restoring the wholeness of Christian initiation will be discussed later in this book.

Of course, it can be argued – with some cogency – that truth must be followed whatever it involves or wherever it leads. But – to ask the ancient question – 'What is truth?' in this context. It would generally be agreed that, if infant baptism is biblically and theologically authenticated, then it must be practised whatever the cost. The conditional premise in this last sentence is one which was partly dealt with in chapter three when we considered the claim that infant baptism is traceable in the New Testament. The theological aspects will be studied on later pages.

How did the infant rite begin?

Before we embark on this brief historical survey, let us ask how it was that infant baptism seemed suddenly to emerge in the third century. It is not surprising that scholars are not agreed on the answer to the question. Maurice Wiles reminds us that 'the origins of the practice of infant baptism are a matter of fierce debate at the present time . . . What led to its adoption? We have virtually no evidence', he says, 'from which to judge – indeed the lack of any sign of debate about the issue (in the Primitive Church) is one of the arguments used by those who believe that the practice must have gone back to the very beginning of Christian history.'[2]

H. G. Wood points out, however, that 'even in the third century infant baptism cannot be described as a church custom' and that 'it is probable that the custom arose from the pressure of parents and not through the direct advocacy of the church. If this is so, the reason for the adoption of the custom may perhaps be sought outside the idea of the remission of sins.' Wood goes on to say, quoting Höfling, that John 3.5 'played an all-important part in developing . . . infant baptism'. It would appear that the mere statement that one must be born of water to see the kingdom of God would disturb Christians whose children had died unbaptized. Wood adds that to such doubt and fear the practice of infant baptism owes its origin.[3]

The reason for the emergence of infant baptism is considered by Abraham Booth in his book 'Paedobaptism Explained'. He says that there is no evidence for the infant rite before the end of the second century and that it began then because some parents believed that their children's salvation could be assured or effected by the instrument of baptism.[4] It is said that the idea 'extra ecclesiam nulla salus' (outside the Church there is no salvation) made people anxious to have their children baptized.

In support of this view that parents played a part in establishing infant baptism, Robert Grant writes: 'From the second century onwards, many of those who became Christians were born of Christian parents, and apparently for this reason infant baptism came to be widespread early in the third century.'[5] On a later page, Grant refers to 'the novel practice of infant baptism' as a 'most important liturgical innovation.' 'This custom', he says, 'explicitly recommended by Hippolytus and in Origen's later writings called "apostolic", cannot be found in Christian literature before Tertullian, though it may have arisen in some localities toward the end of the second century.' Grant adds that this 'reflected the extent to which the church was beginning to consist of families hereditarily Christian, and was accompanied by a new emphasis on the doctrine of original sin.'[6]

Jeremias takes Aland to task over his suggestion that in Origen's view infant baptism was 'a consequence of the idea that even new-born babes are sinful'.[7] Jeremias says that this is to stand the argument on its head, since Origen reasons the other way round, deducing the fact of original sin from the practice of infant baptism. This line-up of cause and effect is accepted by N. P. Williams who writes: 'The Church actually does baptize infants as soon as possible after birth . . . therefore infants must be infected from the womb with a hereditary taint.'

Williams goes on to say that there is no clearer instance of the control exercised by liturgical or devotional practice over the growth of doctrine than that provided by the study of relations between the custom of infant baptism and the doctrine of original sin.[8] In the opinion of Argyle, 'the doctrine of original sin, while it does not appear to have been a cause of the introduction of infant baptism, nevertheless helped to establish it.[9] Origen's fertile and original mind led him to base the necessity of baptism on the pollution acquired at birth[10] and the need to remove by this rite the sins committed in a previous life.[11]

Whatever may be the merits of these divergent views, there is no doubt that many thinkers – including no less a theological heavyweight than Augustine – have regarded the belief in original sin as a cause, perhaps the main cause, of the emergence and perpetuation of infant baptism. This, however, is not the place to develop this discussion further, as we shall be considering in a later chapter the suggested relationship between original sin and the baptizing of infants.

Beasley-Murray was clearly much impressed by a letter he received from a missionary, the Revd Leslie Wenger, about his experience in India. His letter illustrated the difficulty facing a Christian community in a non-Christian environment. He said that attempts had been made in India 'to introduce legislation which would take away the children of converts from their parents and place them under the guardianship of the nearest Hindu relative' He goes on to say that 'one can see the great desire for converts to ask to have their children 'marked for Christ', so as to ensure that they too would be recognized as Christians.' Leslie Wenger wondered if in this Indian situation we have a clue as to the beginnings of infant baptism, since the sense of separation from the world was strong in the early church. Beasley-Murray adds that 'it has long been felt that the growth of infant baptism was a popular movement springing from below rather than one promoted by authority in the churches.'[12]

Non-Christian influences

In another of his books, Beasley-Murray discusses in a rather strident manner what he considered to be the origin of the infant rite. His views on this question – and the way in which he expresses them – must surely have raised many theological eye-brows. He admits that a definitive answer is not possible, but 'broad hints' suggest to him that 'infant baptism originated in a capitulation to pressures exerted upon the church both from without and from within.'[13]

In support of this point, an article by Hans Windisch is quoted – an article in which this German scholar writes: 'Although the sacramental element already exists in primitive Christianity, the infant baptism of the Catholic Church signifies a "falling away" from primitive Christianity.[14] Oepke, a supporter of infant baptism, is also cited as saying: 'The sacrament in Christianity is from the beginning a hybrid phenomenon, half-spiritual symbolism and half-primitive magic.'[15]

Beasley-Murray says that the implication of Oepke's remarkable statement is that it was this 'half-primitive magic' in early Christianity which made the rise of infant baptism possible. In support of this conclusion, he observes with reference to 1 Cor. 15.29 that 'the attitude that could adapt the baptism of believers to baptism for dead people, that they may gain the benefits believed to attach to the rite, would find it a short step to baptize infants, that they too might receive its blessings.'[16]

Attention is also drawn to a Swedish writer, H. J. Evander, another exponent of infant baptism, who says metaphorically that 'in Paul's baptistry there was as yet no font for small children.' But, he adds, the field was made ready for infant baptism (1) partly by the sacramental-magical character which baptism gradually took under the influence of the mystery cults: (2) partly through the analogy with circumcision on the eighth day; (3) partly through the teaching on original sin; and (4) finally to the conception of the church as the exclusive institution of salvation, into which one came through baptism and from which it was desired not to exclude the infants.[17]

Lampe observes that the years between the apostles and Tertullian were 'the century of the common man' – a time in the Christian community when there was 'no single character of outstanding spiritual and intellectual power . . . to face the critical period of consolidation, and the development of its doctrinal system.'[18] Following Lampe's luminous description of the church's social setting, Beasley-Murray depicts the little Christian congregations as being ill-equipped to withstand the impact of 'the guilds and other hero cults and . . . the numerous mysteries', possibly tinged with Judaistic ideas.[19]

Jeremias also has something to say about the possibility of pagan influence on the sacrament of baptism in the Early Church. With reference to what he calls the crisis in the fourth century in regard to the postponement of infant baptism, he writes: 'The acute crisis, therefore, lies in the decades following the recognition of Christianity as the religion of the State, i.e. in that period during which countless numbers of pagans were flocking into the church. It is no surprise to find that the superstitious conception of baptism which many of these pagans brought with them also had an influence upon Christian circles.'[20]

Lampe says that Christians brought into their assemblies ideas current in their non-Christian environment. 'It was in this age of confusion . . . that the liturgical tradition took shape'. On a later page, he says that the failure of the post-apostolic writers to develop Paul's teaching on justification dims the New Testament doctrine of baptism. 'In particular the seal of the Spirit, received in baptism, begins to be conceived in quasi-magical terms as a mark impressed upon the soul by the . . . baptismal ceremonial,[21] a stamp whose purpose is to safeguard the recipient from the hostile powers of the Devil and preserve him . . . for the enjoyment of immortality.'[22]

Questions have been raised concerning certain elements in Gregory Dix's claim that the apostolic *παράδοσις* (tradition) of practice, like the apostolic *παράδοσις* of doctrine, antedates by two or three decades the writing of the New Testament – a theory which we discussed in chapters two and three. 'Dix, like many others,' writes Beasley-Murray, 'has glossed over the indubitable fact that in this tradition the simple structure of the New Testament baptism has become a complex system of initiation rites and in these rites a most unexpected and extraordinary emphasis is laid on exorcism.'[23]

Beasley-Murray goes on to list other features of the developing ritual of baptism as revealed in such liturgical documents as the 'Apostolic constitutions' and the Sarum ritual. He then adds that 'a ritual of this order . . . is not a hair's breadth removed from incantation. It is an adulteration of the religion of Christ by pure animism . . . It is difficult to resist the conclusion that the doctrine of baptism in the liturgical tradition has become suffused with the exorcistic idea.'[24]

This Baptist scholar takes the matter further: 'It is sometimes asked, Where is the voice of protest against the introduction of infant baptism, if it were a post-apostolic innovation? I am constrained to ask, Where is the voice of protest against this blatant accommodation of the apostolic doctrine of baptism to pagan infiltration into the Church? I know of none. On the contrary, the great thinkers of the church seem to have been blind to the process going on in their midst.'[25]

A writer of a very different churchmanship from Beasley-Murray has a relevant word here. The Roman Catholic theologian, E. J. Yarnold, S. J., refers to the secretive ways in which the early church observed the sacraments of baptism and the eucharist – a practice known as 'Disciplina Arcani'. He says that in the early church it is possible that 'there was the wish to imitate the secrecy of the Greek and Roman mystery-religions.' Yarnold goes on to say that baptismal sermons at that time included an emphasis on awe (an emotion typical of mystery-religions) which the Christian mystery of baptism would arouse. He also points out that Constantine provided Christian mystery-sites at Jerusalem 'where the Christian God (like Persephone at Eleusis) died and rose again. Jerusalem indeed was the source from which several liturgical innovations seem to have spread.'

As Yarnold observes, the 'Disciplina Arcani' could not take place at a time when infant baptism was normally practised. Otherwise, with children around, the secret would soon be out! 'Consequently from the middle of the fifth century, as infant baptism became normal, the practice of mystagogic catechesis and disciplina arcani became redundant and lapsed.'[26]

It is suggested that the sub-apostolic church opened its doors to 'contemporary paganism' owing to the fact that converts to Christianity were unable to rise to the heights of apostolic teaching. Beasley-Murray sums up his position as follows: 'The New Testament gives no evidence that infant baptism was practised in the primitive church; its theology of baptism is lofty, with no taint of magical conceptions, and it does not allow of the application to the baptism of infants.' This summary statement should be weighed in the light of the evidence we considered in chapter three.[27]

'In the succeeding century', continues Beasley-Murray, 'the doctrine of baptism was considerably modified in the direction of a lowered and externalized sacramentalism. This theology is capable of being applied to the baptism of infants, since the emphasis falls on the efficacy of the rites and on the materials used.[28] By the close of the period infant baptism appears to be established . . . The modified views made possible the application of the rite to infants, and . . . the process of externalizing the mode of its operation became accelerated.'[29]

Perhaps by reason of sensing the impact of his extreme views – or his way of expressing them – Beasley-Murray qualifies the above statements, and disarms the reader!, by saying: 'Nevertheless, I am ready to admit that the principle, that the origins of an institution do not necessarily serve as a criterion for its developed condition, may be applied here also. The undesirable practices and conceptions of the early centuries, following the death of the apostles, could conceivably be regarded as regrettable, but inevitable, concomitants of developments that were to issue in something entirely good.'[30]

We have discussed Beasley-Murray's views at some length, not only because his scholarship in the sphere of baptism is widely recognized and respected, but because he represents, in general, the views of certain other writers on this debatable subject.

John Ebdon's radio broadcasts, the result of his rummaging through the BBC sound archives, were always introduced by the announcer as likely to lead to 'no definite conclusions'! The same could be said of any enquiry into the origin of infant baptism. Williston Walker would agree. He writes: 'Why infant baptism arose there is no certain evidence.' The practice did not 'become universal till the sixth century, largely through the feeling already noted in Tertullian that so cleansing a sacrament should not be lightly used.'[31]

Some scholars, however, would question Walker's time-scale and would maintain that, within thirty years of the publication of Tertullian's De Baptismo, Hippolytus of the Western Church and Origen of the Eastern Church held that infant baptism was the usual form of initiation and that it was traceable to apostolic authority. In this connection, we recall how Cyprian (c.200–258), Bishop of Carthage, in the middle of the third century, wrote a letter to Bishop Fidus, conveying the unanimous decision of the North African bishops, that infants should be baptized on the second or third day after birth and not, as Fidus had suggested, on the eighth day in order to correspond with circumcision.[32] This appears to be the first clear evidence for the baptism of new-born babies.

The development of Infant Baptism

There appear to have been at least three important ways in which the rite of baptism had developed since New Testament times. One was the introduction of catechetical instruction, sometimes very lengthy; a second was the elaboration of the ritual; and a third was a development in the interpretation of the sacrament. It is difficult to dissent from the view that 'the shape of the liturgy' was designed for adults rather than for infants.

Some degree of the extent of this development is indicated by Cyril of Jerusalem (c.315–386), in his catechetical lectures in the fourth century. He says: 'We are handing on to you a mystery, a hope of the age to come. Guard the mystery from those who would waste this prize.'[33] With reference to these changes, Donald Bridge says that 'it is easy to see how quickly thereafter the church came to hold the erroneous views of the rite particularly associated with the Middle Ages.'[34]

As we have seen, the postponement of baptism in the fourth century shows that, although infant baptism was established, it was not universally practised, not required of necessity. Cyril's Catechetical Lectures deal with a baptismal liturgy that is clearly designed for adults. The directions to the candidates, both in terms of their mental and physical involvement, presupposes a person mature enough intelligently to respond. Cyril's 'Mystagogical Catecheses' (Lectures 19–23) deal with a highly developed and complicated liturgy that no child, let alone infant, would be able to participate in or appreciate in any meaningful way.

It is doubtless for this reason that Gregory of Nazianzus (c.325–390) recommends that baptism be deferred until a child is old enough to understand and respond to baptismal questions – the only exception he allows is in the case of a child who is not likely to live. But Gregory qualifies this recommendation by saying that baptism should be withheld until the children are 'three years old (or a little more or a little less) when it is possible for them to hear and answer something about the sacrament. For then, even if they do not completely understand, yet they will receive the outlines.'[35] We can only say that the children known to Gregory must have matured very much earlier than is generally the case nowadays! Gregory distinguishes between the baptism of infants and adults by pointing out that for infants it is no more than a 'seal', whereas for adults it is a 'cure' for sin and also the 'best seal' – a recovery of grace and of the image of God.[36] He sees infant baptism solely as a dedication to God. We shall consider this aspect of initiation in chapter nine.[37]

Chrysostom (c.345–407) looked favourably on the practice of infant baptism, though he himself was not baptized until he was over twenty years of age. This fact and his baptismal teaching show that, in the Eastern Church, the infant rite was not universally practised. He taught that Christian character is the Spirit's seal, which he links with baptism and by which the recipient is recognized by God – it is a form of illumination (*φώτισμος*).[38] While Chrysostom links circumcision with infant baptism, his criticism of the Jewish rite detracts from the value of baptizing infants when he says: 'For what benefit to his soul can an infant derive from it, since he has no knowledge of what is done to him and has no sense.'[39]

Augustine

Augustine of Hippo (354–430) was the first to give to infant baptism a theological foundation. His mother, Monica, prevented his being baptized as a child for fear of post-baptismal sin – a decision which, later in life, did not commend itself to Augustine.[40] He held that infant baptism was necessary because of the original sin and guilt which every child has inherited from Adam, following 'the fall'.

Donald Lake has a relevant word here. He points out that it was not until the fifth century that the Syrian Church made infant baptism obligatory; previously it was the exception rather than the rule. But a theological foundation was found with the emergence of the doctrine of original sin. 'And it was Augustine more than anyone else who lent his theological genius to this issue.'[41]

Not all comments on Augustinian theology express an unqualified approval. The belief that an unbaptized baby, by reason of 'original sin' is without salvation has prompted Henry Cook to say that he wished Augustine 'had heeded the words at his conversion more thoroughly. He did "take" the Book and "read" it, but unfortunately he did not throw away the Manichaean spectacles beforehand; with the result that his reading of the New Testament was sadly discoloured; and, great saint and thinker that he was, Christianity has paid a heavy price for his influence.'[42]

Augustine explained that the removal of original sin at baptism did not eradicate the tendency to sin – concupiscence remained.[43] He held that the Holy Spirit was given at baptism by the laying on of hands – even in the case of infants.[44] The grace of Christ thus bestowed upon the child remained inviolate unless and until in later years he became steeped in deliberate sinfulness. This view that baptismal grace may be lost through grievous sin was echoed by the Council of Trent (1545–1565).[45]

Augustine developed the doctrine of the baptismal character (*σφραγίς*) which was said to distinguish the baptized person from the unbaptized – a doctrine anticipated in the Shepherd of Hermas, the Acts of Thomas and Cyril of Jerusalem. Although Augustine taught that the absence of baptism could imperil one's eternal salvation, he nevertheless recognized the Martyr's 'baptism of blood' and the 'baptism of desire' (Desiderium Sacramenti). Much of Augustine's teaching spanned the centuries and was developed by the schoolmen, particularly by Thomas Aquinas. The 'Sacrament of desire' came to be interpreted as an anticipation of sacramental grace – a doctrine accepted by the Council of Trent.[46]

It has been said that Augustine's doctrine of 'original sin' and 'original guilt' carried such weight and influence that infant baptism was established firmly and universally for a thousand years – a situation which involved the inevitable eclipse of adult baptism. The end of the adult rite also meant, of course, the end of the 'catechumenate' – though the term was sometimes applied to infants. Instruction in the Christian faith gradually became post-baptismal, except in those times of distressing indifference or negligence when no instruction was given either before or after baptism.

While Pelagius rejected Augustine's doctrine of original sin and guilt, he supported the rite of infant baptism. He held that this sacrament was a mystery through which, ex opere operato, even infants could receive regeneration and salvation. The Pelagians, whose assessment of human nature was more optimistic than Augustine's, held that infants, being innocent, do not need baptism for the remission of sins, rather as the gateway into the kingdom. But what happened to infants who died unbaptized? The Pelagians, like many people since, could give no satisfactory answer, except to suggest that they would obtain eternal life, but not the kingdom. Augustine was not the only one who has questioned this distinction.[47]

Survey of early centuries

Looking back over these early centuries, Yarnold refers to the regular baptism of children as attested by Tertullian, Origen, the Apostolic Tradition and Cyprian in the third century and by Asterius the Sophist in the fourth century. The evidence, however, does not show whether this practice was universal or whether Christian parents could without censure postpone the baptism of their children to maturer years. It would appear that, around the middle of the fourth century, the baptism of children became exceptional, but towards the end of this century the practice of child baptism was revived. Gregory of Nazianzus supported child, but not infant, baptism and Augustine, early fifth century, offered a theological justification for the baptism of children too young to have faith.[48]

Yarnold points out Augustine's questionable motive in urging the postponement of infant baptism: 'Let him alone, let him do as he pleases; he is not baptized.'![49] Saints not baptized in infancy, despite having Christian parents, included: Ambrose, Augustine, Chrysostom, Gregory of Nazianzus (a bishop's son), Jerome and Paulinus of Nola (353–431). Yarnold shows that this postponement of infant baptism meant the upgrading of the catechumenate, which was now 'regarded less as a first preparation for baptism than as admission to a second-class membership of the church.' The ceremony sometimes seems to have included: (1) the sign of the cross; (2) salt on the tongue; (3) laying on of hands; and (4) exorcism.[50]

Our interest here in the Paulicians concerns, of course, their attitude to baptism. J. G. Norman says that they were an evangelical sect whose 'characteristic doctrines include: adoptionist Christology; rejection of Mariolatry, images and hagiolatry; the authority of scripture; believers' baptism.'[51] They questioned the soundness of infant baptism and the view that an infant had original or actual sin. F. C. Conybeare says that the Paulician Catechism states that Jesus first required 'faith, repentance and then He gave the command of holy baptism.'[52] It will be recalled that we considered the Dominical institution of baptism in chapter three.

The Paulicians held a service of blessing for infants when eight years old – a service in the home with minister and church members present, who prayed for divine blessing on the child's preparation for baptism in the future. We shall discuss the desirability and relevance of 'the blessing of children' in a later chapter.

The Middle Ages

Between the sixth and eighth century, the candidates for baptism were assumed to be infants and were involved in a ritual that was much more suited to adults. The creed and Lord's Prayer were recited to the infants, in theory for them to learn! The ritual included the Effeta, when the noses and ears of the candidates were touched with saliva, the anointing of the breast and back with exorcised oil, together with the renunciation of Satan; and finally the reciting of the Creed on behalf of the infants who had in theory now learnt it!

The actual baptism included a threefold question and answer, the command of Matthew 28.19 being carried out, though without repeating the traditional Trinitarian formula – a formula that was not included in the baptismal ritual of the Roman Church until the eighth century. After baptism, the infant was anointed on the head and the priest said: 'Almighty God . . . anoints thee with the chrism of salvation in Christ Jesus unto eternal life.' Then the Bishop prays: 'Almighty God . . . who has regenerated thy servants by water and the Holy Spirit and hast given to them forgiveness of all their sins, send, Lord, upon them thy Holy Spirit.'[53]

J. D. C. Fisher says that by the end of the fifth century infant candidates for baptism so far exceeded any others that, in John the Deacon's account of Roman practice, no trace survives of the long-term preparation for initiation. Fisher also points out that there is conclusive evidence showing that the subjects of initiation in the seventh century were infants, but this conclusion is somewhat modified by the fact that the word 'infantes' in the Gelasian rubrics could be used of any person, whatever his age, who had been spiritually reborn in baptism, as shown in the writings of Zeno of Verona, Augustine and Caesarius of Arles.[54]

W. J. Grisbrooke has shown that from the late eighth or early ninth century, we have the oldest surviving liturgical documents of the Byzantine rite. They are in a Greek manuscript called the 'Barberini Euchologion', which consists of two sets of texts dealing with the liturgy of initiation. They include many of the usual elements that have made up a baptismal liturgy in the past and are here used for either infant or adult initiation. A comparison of the second set of these texts (including two prayers for infancy) with the modern Byzantine baptismal rite shows that there has been remarkably little change for over a thousand years.[55]

The Waldenses deplored the indiscriminate baptism of infants that sometimes followed a national leader's acceptance of the Catholic faith. The situation has been summed up as follows: 'Salvation by believing response to the preached Word and salvation by sacramental manipulation lay in mortal combat with each other all through medieval times.'[56] Reginald Kissack, in an erudite article, says of the Waldenses that 'the vestigial community of the Cottian Alps provided the early Protestants, in their mainly theological or ecclesiological debates, with a splendid reposte to the question: "Where was your church before Luther?"'[57]

A powerful protest against infant baptism was headed by Peter of Bruys in the twelfth century. He maintained that a person is baptized 'after he is ready to recognize his God and to believe in him. We do not, as you charge us, rebaptize him, because the man who has not been washed with the baptism by which sins are washed away ought never to be called baptized.'[58]

Thomas Aquinas

Thomas Aquinas (1224–1274), the greatest theologian and philosopher of the Medieval Church, deals at some length with the subject of baptism, particularly in part three of his 'Summa Theologiae'. He sees this sacrament as a channel of divine grace – grace being regarded as an impersonal force. While he believes baptism to be essential to salvation, he puts forward the interesting Augustinian doctrine that if a person, intending to be baptized, is prevented by sudden death, his salvation is assured by means of the 'baptism of desire'.[59]

According to Aquinas, the baptism of a child was necessary to effect regeneration and to eradicate original sin. While recognizing that an infant could not exercise the faith required by this rite, he held that the faith of the parents and the church could serve as a substitute and ensure for the child a dying and rising with Christ. Aquinas traced the seven sacraments to Jesus and held that baptism, confirmation and ordination left a permanent stamp on the soul, which means that these three sacraments could not be repeated. The baptismal efficacy associated with ex opere operato also featured in his teaching.

By the thirteenth century, in the Western Church, sprinkling rather than immersion was used in the baptism of babies; whereas, in the Eastern Church, immersion continued to be the usual practice. The gradual displacing of adult baptism by the infant rite and the consequent disappearance of the catechumenate meant, as we have seen, that instruction in the faith followed rather than preceded baptism. In many cases, the instruction was never given. Where it did take place, it was usually linked to confirmation several years after the child was baptized.

As we move into the fourteenth century, Dr J. R. H Moorman offers a brief and clear description regarding the practice of infant baptism. 'Every Church', he writes, 'was provided with a font in which infants were normally baptized on the day of their birth. The service was in two parts, the first taking place outside the door of the church, the second at the font. The service was long and elaborate and full of symbolism, such as the exorcism of the evil spirit, the "effeta" or unction with spittle,[60] the anointing with oil, and the putting on of the white chrisom cloth, which the mother of the child returned when she came to be "churched".'[61]

In the Middle Ages there developed a significant intertwining of Church and State – a relationship in which entry into the church by infant baptism was seen as involving entry into the citizenship of one's country. A somewhat similar situation had existed in the deepening relationship of Christianity and the Roman Empire under Constantine; and, going farther back in history, in the religious and racial significance of circumcision for the Jews.

Chapter Six

Infant Baptism during and after the Reformation

Anthony Hanson reflects on the fact that 'serious objections can be raised against the baptism of infants. Ever since the Reformation there has been a substantial body of Christians who refused to practise paedobaptism, deferring baptism to an age of discretion.'[1] The subject not only caused bitter disagreement between Protestant and Catholic, but also deeply divided the various reforming groups.

Colin Buchanan points out that the service used for the baptism of infants, which the Reformers inherited from the Medieval Church, is traceable, despite its accretions, to the rite used in Rome by the Early Church and perhaps also to the baptismal ritual used, towards the end of the sixth century, by Augustine of Canterbury. 'While great gaps in the historical evidence exist, yet a real continuity with the baptismal uses described in Justin Martyr (c.150) and Hippolytus (c. 215) can be seen.' No special rite for infant baptism was ever devised. 'The adult rite of the Primitive West . . . became the infant rite of Medieval England. It was this rite which the Anglican Reformers inherited.'[2]

By the sixteenth century, the general rule was for babies to be baptized before they were a week old; thus baptism became associated with the giving of the name – a christening. Sarum rites required godparents to teach the children their prayers and to ensure that they were confirmed. Some elements in the catechumenate such as the 'scrutinies'; the 'handing over' of the Creed; and the Lord's Prayer were omitted as being beyond the comprehension of infants. Other features, including the reception at the church door, the giving of salt and the exorcisms were retained. The baptism, performed by a presbyter, was by immersion in the name of the Trinity. Confirmation was conferred by the bishop when the child was at least seven, the rite being associated with the gift of the Spirit. The significance of Confirmation and its relationship to Baptism will be considered in chapter eleven.

Fisher indicates very clearly the Reformers' five objections to the Medieval Latin rite of baptism:
(1) Since the Scriptures show that the essence of baptism is the use of water in the name of the Trinity, it follows that the other elements are not essential – such as the blessing of the font, the use of oil, candles, salt and spittle. (2) These additions have given rise to superstition. (3) Private baptism without a church congregation is to be deprecated. (4) Not enough thought was given to the choice of suitable godparents. (5) The service lacked meaning because it was in Latin.[3].

Despite the Reformers' emphasis on personal faith, most of them were in favour of infant baptism. Since their faith was founded on Scripture, they felt bound to seek support for the baptism of infants in the New Testament. They put forward the following arguments:

(1) The divine covenant promised to Abraham and his descendants was extended through the New Covenant to Christian parents, whose children were therefore qualified to receive baptism as an entry into the family of God.
(2) The Jewish initiatory rite of circumcision was taken to certify that Christians should have their children baptized as a sacrament of initiation into the church.
(3) Christ's welcome of little children was interpreted to mean that the church should receive infants into the church by baptism.
(4) If, as in 1 Cor. 7.14, the children of one believing parent were 'holy', then it follows that children of two believing parents must be 'holy', and therefore qualify for baptism.
(5) Households baptized in the New Testament must have involved children.[4]

Martin Luther

It has to be said, however, that doubts concerning the validity of infant baptism were widespread during the Reformation. Luther was not immune. In 1522, he wrote: 'I have always expected that the devil would touch this sore point . . . We ourselves are in great conflict concerning it.'[5] As one would expect, Luther rejected the Catholic view of ex opere operato in relation to infant baptism.[6] Yet he saw the infant rite as well illustrating how helpless humanity can be saved by the grace of God – for faith, without grace, is not enough.

The difficulty mainly lay in Luther's well-known emphasis on personal faith – a faith which he saw as an essential prerequisite for receiving the sacrament. The Eucharist presented no problem, but how could he relate his doctrine of faith to his acceptance of infant baptism? There were two possibilities – neither satisfactory – one was to attribute implicit faith to the unwitting child, the other was to regard the faith of the sponsor as being vicariously conveyed to the infant.

Bernard Reardon points out that Luther found it possible to support infant baptism, despite his emphasis on faith, by denying that infants lack faith and by avoiding what he considered to be the errors of the Roman opus operatum and of Anabaptism. Luther held that faith is unconsciously present in the child. The baptized infant is set in a new relationship to God, involving forgiveness and salvation, while the meaning of baptism is apprehended as he grows up. 'The stress', says Reardon, 'falls characteristically on the objectivity and prevenience of the divine promise and grace.'[7]

Fisher shows that Luther, in his 'Greater Catechism', defended infant baptism by saying that 'it is not of the utmost importance whether he who is baptized has faith or not, for this will not make the baptism wrong: everything depends on God's Word and command. . . . For my faith does not make the baptism, but receives baptism.'[8] Fisher adds the significant comment that Luther's argument 'is not wholly convincing, and seems to attribute to the baptism of an infant an objective efficaciousness inconsistent with what he said elsewhere about the necessity of personal faith.'[9]

At one time Luther said: 'We hopefully assume the child to be a believer and thus regenerate. The baptism then strengthens the seed of faith'.[10] Melanchthon, a supporter of Luther, advised caution, pointing out that confusion and disruption would ensue if some people were baptized as infants and others as adults. He estimated that as a result 'an openly pagan way of life would come about'.

Not all the contemporaries of Luther supported his baptismal reforms. Some preferred to retain the medieval rite and called for a handbook that would explain and interpret the ancient ceremonies. John Gropper (1503–1559), a member of the Cologne chapter and an opponent of Lutheranism, met this demand by producing the 'Enchiridion Christianae Institutionis'. This was translated from the Latin into English and published in Cologne in 1538. It emphasised that the two essential features in baptism were the Trinitarian formula and the element of water – water being regarded as the sacramental means by which the person baptized is spiritually cleansed and regenerated.[11]

Zwingli

Ulrich Zwingli (1484–1531) shared Luther's doubts regarding the validity of infant baptism. He was at one time priest at the Great Minster in Zurich and joined the Reformers in 1523. 'Nothing grieves me more', he said, 'than that at present I must baptize children, for I know it ought not to be done.'[12] Zwingli's dependence upon the support of the civic authorities at Zurich influenced, if not determined, his actions regarding infant baptism, about which he did not appear to have a compelling conviction. His dilemma and his compromise are apparent when he wrote: 'If we were to baptize as Christ instituted it,[13] then we would not baptize any person until he reached the years of discretion, for I find infant baptism nowhere written or practised' in the New Testament. 'But we must practise it now so as not to offend our fellow men.'[14]

The Order of Infant Baptism issued by Zwingli in 1523 retained many ceremonies of the old Latin rite for which biblical warrant was doubtful. The limited extent of this revision was probably due to political considerations. In a second revision in 1525, he rejected the doctrine that sacraments convey the grace which they signify and indicated that 'nobody is saved except by faith.'[15] This revised rite states that 'all the additions which have no foundation in the Word of God have been removed.' At least in theory Zwingli seemed to favour believers' baptism, but he cannot persuade himself to give up the infant rite. In 1525, he wrote: 'This error misled me also some years ago, so that I thought it much better to baptize children after they have come to a riper age.'[16]

Zwingli's vacillation regarding infant baptism seems to stem from his theology of the sacrament. He apparently did not regard baptism in itself as a means of grace, nor as a necessity, but as essentially a symbol of initiation, 'representing', as Bernard Reardon says, 'but not effecting an inward change in those who receive it.' In this respect, Zwingli deemed the Anabaptists to be mistaken in their belief that a spiritual change is necessarily linked with the baptismal ritual. Zwingli ruled out the connection between 'original sin' and the need for baptism, but he put forward the argument – with his hand on his heart? – that infant baptism went back historically to the Apostles and that it was the Christian entry into the New

Covenant corresponding to circumcision[17] – the Jewish entry into the Old Covenant.[18]

Following in the wake of Luther and Zwingli, there were 'reformers' who, having imbibed the principles of the Reformation, concluded that the Scriptures required penitence and faith as the prerequisites for the sacrament of baptism and therefore only believers' baptism was biblical.[19] Infant baptism, therefore, was deemed invalid and contrary to Scripture. Foremost in holding and practising these convictions were the 'Anabaptists' who, as the name implies, re-baptized believers who had been baptized as infants. It was a significant and important movement with an intense and tortuous history, but it had the distinction of being 'the spiritual soil out of which all Nonconformist sects have sprung.'

The Anabaptists

The 'evangelical Anabaptists' laid emphasis on the literal exposition of the Scriptures as interpreted by the Holy Spirit. They admitted to their Christian Community only those who had received believers' baptism. Some Anabaptists, known as 'spiritualists', stressed the revelation conveyed to the individual by the Holy Spirit. This direct and personal communication of God's message tended to take precedence over the Bible, the Church and the sacraments. This individualism and subjectivism sometimes led to misguided and undesirable excesses in religious experience. It is, however, the 'evangelicals' who are the more relevant to our study in this chapter.

These Anabaptists spread rapidly and attracted many people to their ranks. The authorities felt threatened and overwhelmed by this popular movement, with the result that the Diet of Speier (1529) decreed the death sentence for all Anabaptists. For many of them the penalty for practising believers' baptism was indeed a heavy one. They were vulnerable and had little influence because they were not well organised, nor did they have powerful leaders or political supporters, due partly to the persecution they had to endure.

In the second quarter of the sixteenth century, many Anabaptists were executed. But, as in ancient history, the oppressed Hebrews produced 'a godly remnant', so it was with the Anabaptists. And as persecution of the Apostolic Church made the early Christians move out of Palestine with their missionary message, so it was with the Anabaptists – persecution served to spread the movement.

Ardent in their recognition of the superior authority of the Bible, the Anabaptists did not sufficiently take account of the Spirit's leading since New Testament times, nor make enough allowance for the sociological differences since the first century. An appreciation of both these factors would have given them a truer interpretation of the Bible, enabling them to distinguish in Scripture between essential doctrine and contemporary custom. We looked at the principles involved here when we considered the claims of 'Scripture and Tradition' in chapter two.

W. M. S. West writes: 'As Luther's teaching centred upon "sola fide" and Zwingli's and Calvin's upon the sovereignty of God, so the Anabaptists' thought centred upon the New Testament "ecclesia" – separated, of course, from State control.'[20] For the Anabaptists, the Church – as the word 'ecclesia' (ἐκκλησία) suggests – consisted of Christians who by believers' baptism had been 'called out' from the world into a fellowship of 'covenant people'. Such convictions they felt to be inconsistent with infant baptism.

The chief reason for the rejection of believers' baptism by Luther and Zwingli appears to be their acceptance of the Medieval social order, in which Church and State belonged together in a unified whole. Infant baptism was seen as the means of initiation both into the Church and into society. To reject the infant rite was regarded as rejection of the church and rejection of the State – hence the charge of anarchy against the Anabaptists and the cruel persecution that followed. Leonard Levy makes the horrific statement that Queen Elizabeth 'burned five or six Arians and Anabaptists whose crimes included the beliefs that Christ was not God and that infant baptism was unnecessary.'[21]

It is not surprising, therefore, that the Anabaptists produced 'a theology of martyrdom'. History does not seem to have done them justice. In modern times there is much evidence that many of them turned their cruel treatment into 'a refining fire' and answered their persecutors with lives of virtue.

One of the most distinguished and influential of the Anabaptists was a Dutch priest, Menno Simons (1496–1561), who lived in the first half of the sixteenth century. His growing concern about infant baptism was intensified when he heard that Sicke Freeks, a tailor, had been executed simply because he had received believers' baptism, after having been baptized as an infant. Cornelius Dych says that Simons's 'spiritual pilgrimage was a gradual transition . . . from a routine reliance on tradition to a deep personal faith in Christ and a reliance on the Scriptures as the final authority in matters of faith.'[22] Despite the dangers that faced him, he agreed to be leader of an Anabaptist group which later became known as the Mennonite Church. Simons believed that the Catholic Church had fallen from its apostolic purity in both its doctrine and life. As a person and as the author of a book on baptism, he has wielded a powerful influence especially in Baptist circles.

Whereas Zwingli judged it prudent not to act upon his questioning of infant baptism, there were others whose deep convictions compelled them to put into practice their disapproval of the infant rite. They paid the price for their courage and suffered severely. They were cruelly persecuted for their opposition to the baptism of infants and their practice of rebaptizing adults.

It is sad to see Zwingli siding with the civil authorities and attacking in print those who would not have their babies baptized. It is hard to understand, in this religious conflict, how Christians could inflict such suffering on fellow Christians with whom, in some cases, they had previously worshipped and pondered the Bible. Can the defence of any doctrine or ritual ever justify such cruelty between Christians? It is disillusioning and depressing to observe how often tolerance has been conspicuous by its absence in the history of the Church.

John Calvin

The support of infant baptism given by John Calvin (1509–1564) is seen in his relationship both with the Catholic Church and the Anabaptist movement. Moreover, the Order of Baptism drawn up by Calvin in 1542 – included in the 'Form of Prayers' – is different from both the Lutheran and Anglican baptismal rites. Turning aside from much that Luther taught on baptism, Calvin made the priority of grace central in the exposition of his doctrine. Reardon says that 'while Calvin is certain of the objectivity of the subject, he is at pains to avoid any suggestion of an ex opere operato efficacy, which Luther at times seemed to teach.'[23]

Calvin emphasised the priority of grace as the essence of the sacrament rather than the personal experience of the individual being baptized. He held that the divine initiative justifies, and is illustrated by, infant baptism. He makes clear that baptism is conditional upon the Divine decree. This election ante-dates our birth for 'God adopts our babies before they are born.'[24] Calvin gave close attention to the teaching of the Anabaptists and attacked their practice of baptizing believers and not children – a policy which he regarded as having a divisive influence in the church.

Unlike the Anabaptists, Calvin stressed the relevance of the Old and New Covenants. He saw them as having much in common – distinguished mainly in that initiation into the Old Covenant is by circumcision, whereas entry into the new is by baptism. Moreover, since circumcision was normally an infant rite, so baptism should be administered to infants. This parallel, of course, can be drawn only with regard to boys.

In dealing with the spiritual state of the baptized infants, Calvin, as we would expect, emphasised the operation of grace. He said that he 'would not rashly affirm that they are endued with the same faith which we experience in ourselves, or have any knowledge at all resembling faith.'[25] He held that for infants repentance and faith lay in the future, whereas for adults repentance and faith must precede their baptism.[26] Calvin looks at the advantages of infant baptism both from the point of view of the parents and the children. The parents see 'with the bodily eye the covenant of the Lord engraven on the bodies of their children.' The children will look back in later life and claim the promises of God made on their behalf by their sponsors.[27]

To this end, Calvin's 'Form of Prayers . . .' requires the minister to say to the sponsors that they must promise when the child 'comes to the age of discretion to instruct him in the doctrine . . . summarized in the confession of faith . . . and generally in all that is contained in holy scripture . . .' In this baptismal rite, Calvin also refers to 'many other ceremonies . . . very ancient but . . . invented at will . . . have not been founded upon the Word of God and . . . so many superstitions have arisen out of them, we have no hesitation in abolishing them . . . It is certain that the chrism, candle and other such pomps are not of God's ordinance, but have been added by men.' Calvin went on to say that 'we have such a form of baptism as Jesus Christ has ordered, as the apostles have preserved and followed, as the primitive church has used.'[28]

Such was the impact of Calvin's teaching and influence that many of the Anabaptists and Waldensians were drawn into the Calvinist fold, even in some cases to the extent of having their children baptized! Looking back in 1564, Calvin wrote: 'I was constrained also to compile the form of baptism while I was at Strasburg, and they brought to me the children of the Anabaptists from five to ten leagues away.'[29]

Donald Bridge, to whom I am indebted in this chapter, offers a useful summary statement: 'Within a century Calvinism had replaced Anabaptism as the most influential expression of Christianity in the Low Countries, and had become the persecuted but defiant Protestantism of France and Scotland, and the Christian orthodoxy of England and her colonies. The whole content of the baptismal controversy had altered. In the Middle Ages, paedobaptism stood for Catholicism, and adult baptism for evangelical "heresy". During the Lutheran Reformation, paedobaptism symbolized state Christianity, and adult baptism symbolized voluntary Christianity. Through Calvin's reforms, paedobaptism came to represent a predestinarian view of the Gospel, while adult baptism accompanied a strong emphasis on human free-will.'[30]

John Knox

A brief reference should be made to John Knox (c. 1514–1572). While we are more concerned here with his teaching than his life story, we would at least recall how this colourful and courageous character, threatened by Mary Tudor (a Roman Catholic), fled to Frankfurt and then to Geneva. While at Geneva, Knox used a baptismal rite based on the form of service drawn up by Calvin. He shared with Calvin the view that infants may obtain salvation without baptism, since baptism does not effect but only seals the salvation already gained. Knox also agreed with Calvin that women should not baptize infants, even in a case of emergency.

This last point recalls the widely-held belief, going back to the early church, that baptism is valid provided that water is used and the Trinitarian formula pronounced, irrespective of the worthiness, or otherwise, of the officiant. Whenever the correctness or character of the minister has affected the validity of the sacrament, confusion and division have tended to arise, as seen in the bitter conflict between Stephen, Bishop of Rome, and Cyprian, Bishop of Carthage, in the third century, over the re-entry of the lapsed into the church.

To return to Knox – with the accession of the Protestant Queen Elizabeth, he made his way back to Scotland. Knox was strongly opposed to the Latin rite; and in his 'Disputation with Friar Arbuchill (1547)' concerning baptism, he wrote: 'God has not ordained . . . spittle, salt, candle, cuide, hards, oil and the rest of the Papistical inventions.'[31] Knox did not leave the matter there. In 1556, he wrote that 'baptism now used in Papistry is not the true baptism . . . but an adulteration . . . to be avoided by all God's children.' Yet anybody who undergoes this baptismal 'profanation' is not to be baptized again 'for the Spirit of regeneration . . . hath purged us from that poison which we drank in the days of our blindness.'[32]

During the first half of the sixteenth century in England, the baptismal rite that was most used was in the 'Sarum Manual', containing all the ceremonies which Luther abolished in 1526. In the latter part of 1537, the 'Bishops' Book'[33] was produced, dealing among other things with the seven sacraments. The following quotation is drawn from the section on baptism which appears in C. Lloyd's book, 'Formularies of Faith': 'That the promise of grace and everlasting life . . . pertaineth not only unto such as have the use of reason, but also to infants . . . that they . . . must needs be baptized and that by the sacrament of baptism they do also obtain remission of their sins . . . and be made thereby the . . . children of God. Inasmuch as children dying in their infancy shall undoubtedly be saved thereby, and else not.'

It is significant that these last three words, implying that unbaptized infants will not be saved, were omitted six years later in the 'King's Book' (a revision of the 'Bishops' Book') which simply states that baptism 'is offered unto infants . . . that if they die in the state of their infancy they shall undoubtedly be saved.' The state of the unbaptized child will be raised again later in this chapter.[34]

In Puritan times in the seventeenth century, the Church of England generally speaking could be said to be Catholic in its organisation and Protestant in doctrine. The Church and the State somewhat coalesced in a religiously restrictive sense. Everybody was required to be baptized in infancy; to be confirmed when reaching years of discretion; and to attend the worship of the church. The Dissenters turned away from the State Church and saw in the New Testament the true body of Christ, consisting only of people who were spiritually regenerate. They were a sort of 'gathered church', who in later times became the Congregationalists and Independents. Their insistence on regeneration as an essential qualification for entry into this Christian community led to a belief in, and practice of, believers' baptism and the rebaptism of those seeking membership who had been baptized as infants. It was tantamount to a re-emergence of Anabaptism.[35]

David Edwards gives an interesting account of the Puritan's attitude to the conventional features of the baptismal liturgy. He writes: 'They were uneasy when the priest used the sign of the cross on the infant's forehead; it reminded them of the tricks of a pagan magician. They also disliked the custom by which the godparents were chosen more for social than for theological reasons, while the natural parents were not featured.' Can this be said of the present day? Edwards goes on to say that the 'Puritans wanted the emphasis to be more on the parents' faith as justifying the practice of infant baptism. They also objected to midwives and other women baptizing privately infants thought to be in danger of death.' Calvin and Knox would have agreed, as we saw earlier in this chapter. Edwards points out that such objections to the Prayer Book's arrangements for baptism implied the whole 'reforming of the Reformation'. For the Puritans, 'religion should be based . . . not on social conventions but on personal faith, not on superstitious custom but on the Holy Bible.'[36]

Commonwealth irregularities

We should bear in mind that during the Commonwealth (1649–1660) ministers of various denominations were appointed to take charge of the churches. It was an unprecedented and irregular arrangement. Infant baptism was practised by some and not by others. The result was that, as time passed, there were many young people who had not been baptized, including Baptists, Anglicans and Presbyterians. The Society of Friends (the Quakers), of course, observed neither the infant nor the adult rite of baptism – since sacraments were considered irrelevant to the realm of the Spirit. This situation, with so many adults unbaptized, led to the inclusion for the first time in the Book of Common Prayer (1662) of a rite of baptism for those who are 'of riper years'.

In Bedford, in the seventeenth century, a 'Gospel Church' was formed, with John Gifford as its leader – a church independent of the State and keen to communicate the Christian message. They laid stress on a personal faith in Christ and on quality of life. They favoured the baptism of believers by immersion, but they were accommodating not to exclude those who had received infant baptism. Moreover, they did not try to prevent any of their members from having their babies baptized at the Anglican Church, if they so wished. It has to be said that such readiness to respect the various sentiments of fellow Christians contrasted strikingly with the bitterness and intolerance that generally existed in those days between the denominations.

John Bunyan (1628–1688), after a chequered career, joined Gifford's 'Gospel Church' and in due course succeeded him as pastor. Bunyan, who was not a sacramentarian, did not lay any essential emphasis on baptism. In deference to his wife's wishes, he agreed to his infant son being baptized at the parish church. Bunyan's openness about baptism aroused much opposition and personal abuse. The former Bedford tinker, the author of 'Pilgrim's Progress', surely the finest Christian allegory in the English language, responded by an appeal to love and tolerance. With reference to baptism and holy communion, he said: 'I count them not as fundaments of our Christianity'.[37]

Baptism for John Bunyan was not in itself an essential means of entry into the church, but an outward sign of the new life in Christ. Christian experience was a prerequisite of the rite and was not dependent upon the sacrament or effected by it. This is a far cry from ex opere operato – the view that the efficacy of grace in the sacrament of baptism could operate irrespective of the recipient's participation or awareness, as in the baptism of infants. We shall consider the relationship of grace to baptism in chapter nine.

The fate of the unbaptized child has exercised the minds of many Christians down the ages. Earlier in this chapter, we saw how the issue was treated in the 'Bishops' Book' and the 'King's Book' in the sixteenth century. The subject was raised by the General Baptists in their 'Confession of Faith' in 1660. Needless to say, the 'Confession' rejects infant baptism, describing it as 'Scriptureless'. It states that infants who die too young to commit sin are subject only to the 'first death, which comes upon them from the sin of the first Adam; and not that anyone of them . . . shall suffer for Adam's sin eternal punishment in hell.'[38]

The Orthodox Creed of the General Baptists (1678) rejects the 'Popish doctrine' which teaches that 'infants that die without baptism . . . cannot be saved.' This Creed also says 'Neither do we believe that infants dying in infancy without baptism go to purgatory or limbus infantum'. The 'Confession' claims that children who die too young to sin are saved by God's grace, by Christ's merit and by the operation of the Holy Spirit. These views in the seventeenth century gave rise to much controversy. What particularly aggravated the situation was the fact that the rejection of infant baptism was said to lead to serious political disturbance and national instability. That is why Anabaptism was rejected as 'the canker of religion and the gangrene of the State.'[39]

Richard Baxter was in two minds with regard to the validity of baptizing infants. He says that he soon discovered the error of this doctrine when he found in Scripture that repentance and faith were prerequisites 'and that signs cannot, by moral operations, be the instruments of a real change in infants, but only of a relative; and that to dream of a physical instrumentality was worse than popish.'

Later, however, Baxter modified his stance and regarded infant baptism as 'a sign to enter them church members and solemnize their dedication to Christ . . . and to confer on them remission of sins . . .'[40] But neither the Scriptures nor the contemporary theological defence of infant baptism offered him sufficient reassurance as to the validity of the infant rite. For this reason he could not bring himself to undertake ministerial service and turned instead to academic circles.

The Thirty-Nine Articles and Catechism

Number twenty seven of the 'Thirty Nine Articles' of the Church of England states that 'Baptism is not only a sign of profession and mark of difference whereby Christian men are discerned from others that are not christened, but is also a sign of regeneration or new birth, whereby, as by an instrument, they that receive baptism rightly are grafted into the Church; the promises of the forgiveness of sin and of an adoption to be the sons of God by the Holy Ghost are visibly signed and sealed; faith is confirmed; and grace increased by virtue of prayer to God. The baptism of young children is in any wise to be retained in the church, as most agreeable with the institution of Christ.'

The shorter catechism of the Anglican Church says it more succinctly and states the conditions: 'Baptism is not to be administered to any that are out of the visible church, till they profess their faith in Christ and obedience to Him; but the infants of such as are members of the visible church are to be baptized.'

Since the principal purpose of this chapter and the previous one is to offer a brief survey of the beliefs and practices of infant baptism over the centuries, this is clearly not the place to consider the Scriptural and theological implications of these Anglican and other statements. We shall consider these implications on later pages and recall the relevant features of our study of the New Testament evidence in chapter three.

The above directive in the shorter catechism that 'infants of such as are members of the visible church are to be baptized' would commend itself to the Puritans. In the words of William Perkins: 'The faith of the parents maketh those their children to be accounted in the covenant, which by reason of their age do not actually believe.'[41] In chapter three, we considered Paul's statement in 1 Cor. 7.14 that children born of a Christian parent were 'holy'. In agreement with this view is a claim made by the 'Directory of Publique Worship of God' (1644) that children of believing parents are 'foederally holy' prior to baptism. From this premise, the 'Directory' concludes 'that outward baptism is not so necessary that through the want thereof the infant is in danger of damnation.'[42]

'The History of Infant Baptism', written by William Wall in 1705, was deemed for many years to be of great importance. It is pointed out, however, that the evidence which he produces from the early Fathers is regarded as questionable. Wall concedes that the patristic writers are referring to the baptism of adults, but argues that this was the time when pagans were being received into the church. Yet one is inclined to observe that some of these heathen converts must have had children and to inquire whether or not infants were baptized.

As for unbaptized infants, William Wall seems to believe that they can be safely left to the mercy of God, despite the widespread doctrine that original sin, without baptism, can imperil the soul's salvation. He also claims that, since national churches require infants to be baptized, it follows that those who oppose infant baptism are schismatics and are in error. Those who opposed paedobaptism at this time were presumably in the minority and being 'the few' were regarded as necessarily wrong – an assumption that recurs often in the history of the Church, both ancient and modern.

John Gale, in his learned book 'Reflections', reckons that Wall, in his defence of infant baptism, has been biased in his selection of the historical evidence and in his interpretation of it. Gale argues that neither Jesus nor his apostles approved or practised the baptism of young children – a question we considered in chapter three. Gale maintains that there is no evidence of infant baptism prior to the middle of the third century – a view that calls for some qualification in the light of our study on earlier pages. It needs to be added that the views of William Wall and John Gale wielded an influence, not only upon their contemporaries in the eighteenth century, but in the nineteenth as well.

The Evangelical Revival

In a comprehensive article on baptism, Donald Lake dismisses the eighteenth century by merely saying that rationalism 'set aside not only sacramentalism but also ecclesiastical institutionalism which included baptism.'[43] One wonders how he came to overlook the relevance of the Evangelical Revival. Admittedly, it was the Revival itself which dominated the religious scene rather than any controversy over baptism – a controversy which ebbed with the passing of the Puritan Age and did not surface again in any strength until the twentieth century.

It is not relevant here to deal with this Revival movement as such – a subject we have dealt with elsewhere[44] – except to observe that it made a considerable impact on the religious and social life of Britain and across the seas. One historian, W. E. H. Lecky, considered that it saved England from a French Revolution.[45] Yet the message and purpose of the Methodist Revival could not ignore the doctrine and practice of infant baptism, as it was stated or implied in the 'Book of Common Prayer'.

The main aim of the Revival was to convert people, turning them from a life of sin and indifference to a spiritually regenerate life, made possible by repentance and faith in the redeeming work of Christ. But how was this to be related to the Anglican baptismal ritual, which declared to be 'regenerate' all those who had been baptized in infancy? – which presumably included most of the people of Britain. Was it not irrelevant and superfluous – almost heretical – to proclaim the need for a spiritual 'rebirth' to those who had already been 'reborn' in baptism?

It is not surprising, therefore, that the preaching of such revivalists as John Wesley and George Whitefield, and the hymns of Charles Wesley, caused much consternation and stern opposition. The Revival message was based on the assumption that being 'born of water' in infancy was no guarantee that the child in later life would not need the conversion experience of being 'born of the Spirit'. There was, however, some difference in the interpretation of the infant rite between the Calvinistic Whitefield and the Arminian Wesley.

Prior to his 'assurance of salvation'[46] on 24th May 1738, at Aldersgate Street in London, John Wesley, a priest in the Church of England, apparently believed in 'baptismal regeneration'. After he felt his 'heart strangely warmed'[47], he developed a doctrine relating infant baptism to adult conversion in terms that were more in line with the transformed lives of his converts than with the orthodox teaching of the Anglican Church.

Wesley taught that at baptism a child is born again by the Holy Spirit and delivered from 'original sin'. But the innate disposition to sin was not eradicated and led to personal sin as the child grows up, thus making a spiritual conversion necessary – that is another 'regeneration' in which he is actively and consciously involved. Not surprisingly, Wesley's baptismal doctrine did not commend itself to all of his followers – some of whom came to adopt a rather flexible and imprecise attitude to the sacrament, ruling out any commitment to 'baptismal regeneration'.

The practice of baptizing adults led many of Wesley's converts to join the Baptist Church – a situation which prompted him to write his 'Treatise on Baptism', which was designed to vindicate both the infant and the adult rites. It is significant that Wesley did not baptize those adult converts who had received infant baptism in the Church of England; but he did see fit to baptize converts who had been baptized as infants by the Dissenters.

The Oxford Movement

We turn our attention now to the Oxford Movement whose emphasis on the sacraments made a great impact in the middle of the nineteenth century – an impact that is still widely and deeply felt. Their baptismal doctrine was stated in John Keble's preaching and was published in 1869 with the title 'Village Sermons on the Baptismal Service'. Keble interpreted baptism as a coronation whereby the lowliest infant becomes a priest and king in his relationship with God. He likened the sacrament to a spiritual marriage with Christ in which the individual became in baptism completely united with his Lord. Keble made clear that the validity of infant baptism depended chiefly and essentially on two things: (1) The material used, namely water. To make baptism effective, however, the water must be consecrated. (2) The form of words: 'In the name of the Father, and of the Son, and of the Holy Spirit.'

John Keble also held that a child, once baptized, is permanently saved, because of the inherent grace of God in the rite – unless in later years he deliberately sins. We shall consider the vital and debatable question as to the essence and effectiveness of grace in chapter nine. Keble believed that, while 'original sin' is banished by baptism, the corrupted nature remains, but 'the Holy Spirit entering in at baptism mends our nature and opens the door both to the Church and Kingdom.'

An assessment

In a scholarly book, to which I am indebted in this study, D. M. Himbury looks back over the centuries of doctrinal disputation and offers an assessment in summary form: 'The history of baptismal controversy in Britain has not always been a happy one. It has been the cause of much bitterness and has led to extravagant denunciation on both sides. Numerous non-theological factors have influenced the course of the discussion in every period. Yet it has also produced works of great learning and has provoked all sections of the Christian community to define, with theological exactness, their own view of the church and sacraments.'[48]

CHAPTER SEVEN

The Relevance of Circumcision and the Covenant

Before we discuss the relationship between circumcision and infant baptism, let us look briefly at the origin and significance of this Jewish rite.

It is thought likely that in early Jewish history the rite was carried out at puberty or at marriage. Genesis 17.25 says that Ishmael was circumcised when he was thirteen years old. It was usual for the rite to be practised at childhood or puberty rather than infancy in non-Hebrew races. There is no clear indication as to when the Jews transferred circumcision to infancy, but the switch had certainly taken place by the fifth century BC when Genesis 17.12 and Leviticus 12.3 were written. In the first century AD the performing of the rite on the eighth day was accompanied by the naming of the child, as shown in one of the infancy narratives with reference to John the Baptist (Luke 1.59) and Jesus (Luke 2.21).[1]

Circumcision in Hebrew religion was a sign of the Covenant between Yahweh and Israel (Gen. 17. 10-14). The rite was carried out, not only on Hebrew children, but also on slaves and on any resident alien who wished to observe the Passover. Circumcision seems to have been widely observed before the Babylonian Exile (sixth century), though it does not appear to have commended itself to some prophetic circles, nor to the Deuteronomic school. Nowhere does Deuteronomy urge physical circumcision. Instead, the writer spiritualizes the rite by talking in terms of circumcision of the heart. (Deut. 10.16; 30.6). Jeremiah makes the perceptive judgment that some people are physically circumcised, but not circumcised in heart. (Jer. 9.25f).

After the Exile, this distinctive Jewish rite became increasingly important and was considered to be a mark of Jewish faithfulness. In the second century BC, the Book of Jubilees declared that a child who is uncircumcised 'belongs not to the children of the covenant which the Lord made with Abraham, but to the children of destruction'.[2] We feel ourselves under no obligation to accept the view that 'the higher angels and many of the early patriarchs were born circumcised'![3] While converts to Judaism were generally required to be both circumcised and baptized, certain Jewish leaders of the Tannaitic era held that baptism alone was enough.

In New Testament times, circumcision presented a problem to the early Christian Church, as its missionary enterprise took the Gospel of Christ into the Gentile world. The argument between Jewish and Gentile Christians needed the Council of Jerusalem (Acts 15) to find a formula acceptable to both parties, but even then the conflict rumbled on to disturb St. Paul's missionary activities, as revealed in the Acts of the Apostles and the Pauline letters.

Despite the fact that Paul himself had been circumcised (Phil. 3.5) and that he in turn had circumcised Titus (Gal. 2.3), he was emphatic in denying the need for physical circumcision and led the way in the spiritual interpretation of the rite. For the apostle what really mattered was neither circumcision nor uncircumcision, but 'faith working through love' (Gal. 5.6); 'a new creation' (Gal. 6.15); 'keeping the commandments of God' (1 Cor. 7.19). Paul maintained that 'circumcision is a matter of the heart, spiritual and not literal' (Rom. 2.29) and that the Christian can be 'circumcised with a circumcision not made with hands by putting off the body of flesh in the circumcision of Christ'. (Col. 2.11).

The purpose of Circumcision

As for the purpose of circumcision, three of the many reasons advanced are:

(1) To cure disease and to promote fertility;
(2) as a form of sacrifice;
(3) as an act of initiation.

A combination of these views probably explains the original purpose of circumcision. The rite was chiefly an initiation into the covenant community. As Genesis 17.11 says, 'You shall be circumcised . . . and it shall be a sign of covenant between me and you' (cf. Rom. 4.11). The common name in modern Judaism for the circumcision ritual was 'covenant'. The rite was regarded as of divine origin and an occasion of joy. Three figurative representations of circumcision are found in the Bible:

(1) Circumcision of the heart – a heart open to God's command. See Deut. 10.16; 30.6; Jer. 4.4; Lev. 26.41; Rom. 2.28f; (cf. Col. 2.11).
(2) Moses was 'of uncircumcised lips'. (Exod. 6.12.30).
(3) Jeremiah refers to uncircumcised ears. (Jer. 6.10) – the RSV says 'their ears are closed'.

David Pawson draws attention to two further factors in the history of circumcision. The first was the mosaic covenant at Sinai. After this, the descendants of Abraham were bound to the law. Circumcision then became a 'seal' of righteousness by works. Only when this change is realised will Paul's closely argued case against circumcision be understood. See Galatians 5.3. The rite's involvement with law detracts from it being a symbol of grace. According to Karl Barth, 'the sign of the election of the holy lineage of Israel, which, with the birth of the Messiah, achieved its goal, so that therewith the sign has lost its meaning, since it has no further significance.'[4]

We follow this brief historical survey with a consideration of the various ways in which the relationship between circumcision and infant baptism has been interpreted. We look first at the Jewish background.

In support of the view that primitive Christian baptism has Hebrew antecedents, Jeremias points out that *βαπτίζειν* (to baptise) and its derivatives originate in the vocabulary of Greek-speaking Jews and that *εἰς το ὄνομα* ('in the name') is Jewish baptismal terminology.[5]

In an article on baptism, Michel Meslin explains how proselytes to Judaism, after answering questions, were circumcised and then, seven days later, were baptized by immersion; though Philo and Josephus were silent on the subject – silent perhaps unintentionally rather than by design. Scholars are generally agreed that proselyte baptism was pre-Christian and that it was also practised in the time of Jesus. It has been suggested that the origin of the rite is traceable to the need for women converted to Judaism to have an appropriate ceremony of initiation, since circumcision was not applicable to them. There is, however, no reference to it in the Scriptures. Nowhere in the Old Testament does it say that a Gentile convert to Judaism should be baptized.[6]

W. F. Flemington sees the analogy of Jewish proselyte baptism as giving some warrant for the practice of infant baptism in New Testament times. We recall that, when Gentiles enter Judaism, they and their children would be circumcised (if male) and later baptized. The Hillelites separated the two rites by seven days and, according to Jeremias, made baptism the decisive act in joining the Jewish community.[7] A child's inability to make promises was regarded as no hindrance. It was agreed that action could be taken on behalf of another, provided it was for his good. But one wonders who decides this issue and how 'good' is defined. Children born after parents had entered the Jewish community were not baptized, only circumcised (if male). Colin Buchanan holds that 'if Christian baptism had its roots in proselyte baptism, then the presupposition would be strong that Christian baptism was given to children with their parents, and they were thus included with them in the covenant people of God.' In a footnote on the same page, Buchanan makes the interesting observation that 'if the non-baptism of those born within Judaism were pressed, it would prove too much! It would set up a situation where children born to believers were so involved tribalistically in their parents' faith, that they needed no baptism at all, neither as infants nor as adults, but were reckoned as initiated from the start.'[8] Jeremias reasons along similar lines: 'If in later Judaism children born "in holiness" (i.e. having a Christian parent) were not baptized, then we must assume that the Christian church also forebore to baptize the children of Christian parents. In this case, children born before their parents joined the church would have been baptized, but not those born "in holiness".'

Circumcision and the seal

To return to Flemington – he held that the Jewish practice of circumcision, the rite of initiation into the old covenant, would have encouraged the early Christians to have their children baptized, since baptism was the way into the Christian Church. He said that 'Paul viewed baptism as a counterpart of circumcision' and quotes Col. 2.11f in support. 'This parallel' argues Flemington, 'may be implied by the use of *σφραγιζομαι* (to seal) in reference to baptism' and he draws attention to the use of the cognate noun, *σφραγις* (seal) in connection with circumcision in Rom. 4.11.

The above reference to a 'seal' (*σφραγις*) turns our attention to some comments by Whiteley: 'The baptism of infants', he says, 'is compatible with the historical evidence, but is not demanded by it. It is made more probable by the fact that, in Rom 4.11, St Paul speaks of circumcision which was undoubtedly administered to infants as a "seal" (*σφραγις*).' We should also observe that the cognate verb, *σφϱαγιζειν* (to seal) may refer to baptism and is used in 2. Cor. 1.22; Eph. 1.13 and 4.30. Whiteley shows that the 'Shepherd of Hermas' certainly applies the term *σφαγις* (a seal) to baptism.[9], [10], [11]

One of the distinctive features of the baptism of John was that it was directed to Jews – Jews who, like John himself and the early apostles, had presumably been circumcised. Here, as in the practice of proselyte baptism, the male recipients were both circumcised and baptized. In both these situations, baptism was added to circumcision rather than displacing it. With regard to the later transcendence of infant baptism as an initiatory rite into the Christian community and its eventual displacement of circumcision in the early church, Dr H. H. Rowley observed: 'It is surely one of the unsolved mysteries of Christian scholarship why the leap should be made from Jewish lustration, proselyte baptism and circumcision to what is a completely different and unrelated rite.'[12]

According to Jürgen Moltmann, the early Christian baptism was connected genetically with the repentance movement of John the Baptist and with the baptism of Jesus in the river Jordan. He holds that baptism in the primitive church had 'no genetic connection at all with Israelite circumcision or the purificatory rites of the mystery religions, although analogies can be discovered.'[13]

In view of the lack of early evidence, Johannes Schneider doubted whether infants of a proselyte to Judaism were baptized with older members of the family.[14] Moreover, we have no evidence that the baptism of John included children. We recall that the earliest clear reference to the baptism of an infant is shortly before AD 300 – an occasion when R. Huna (who died in AD 297) recommended that a widow, who wished her child to be baptized, should have her wish granted, 'according to the judgment of the court' – a court which ruled in favour 'because it is for his advantage.'[15]

One Covenant or two

No writer in the Reformed tradition has propounded the view that the sole basis of infant baptism is the one covenant with more extreme statements than Pierre Marcel in his book, 'The Biblical Doctrine of Infant Baptism' – a sweeping and dogmatic title which, in logical terms, begs the question. Beasley-Murray goes so far as to say that no book on this subject has seemed to him so unworthy. This Baptist scholar adds: 'The exegesis and deductions drawn from it frequently have seemed to me unworthy of the seriousness of the discussion'.[16] When due allowance is made for the fact that this assessment comes from a writer with Baptist convictions, one has to acknowledge that other scholars in different communions are mainly in agreement with his criticism of the book.

Let us consider Beasley-Murray's critical review in summary form. Marcel claims, on the authority of Scripture, that the only foundation of baptism is the covenant of grace which ensures 'our adoption and reception into the covenant'.[17] Marcel adds that 'with the rejection of the covenant of grace every possible foundation of infant baptism disappears.'[18] Baptism is seen as the sacrament of the covenant. Marcel's argument is based on the following considerations:

(1) There has always been only one covenant of grace, essentially the same in all dispensations, whether termed the old or new covenant.
(2) There has been only one Gospel – the Gospel offered to Abraham (Gal. 3.8). Hence Abraham's rejoicing to see Christ's day (John 8.56).
(3) Faith in God's promises has always been the condition of salvation. Abraham is the model of all believers (Gen. 15.6; Rom. 4.9-25; Gal.3).
(4) The Church stems from the Israel of God and belongs to the same covenant of grace. (Rom. 11. 16ff)
(5) The sacraments of the two dispensations mean the same – 'since the sacraments were seals . . . by which the promises of God were sealed, and since no promise of God has been made to man except in and through Jesus Christ (2 Cor. 1.20).'

Marcel, by reference to such texts as Deut. 10.16; Jer. 4.4; and Rom. 4.11f, attempts to establish the identity of baptism and circumcision. Circumcision was in the Old Testament all that baptism is in the New. This unusual exposition sees circumcision as the sign and seal of forgiveness, justification, conversion, sanctification and eternal life. He links the two rites together by concluding: 'Their usage and efficacy are identical, as are also the conditions of admission.'[19]

It is, therefore, argued that infants should be baptized into the new covenant as infant sons were circumcised into the old covenant. The chief error in this interpretation is considered to be the overemphasis on the unity between the old and new covenants and the failure to appreciate the distinctive elements in the two dispensations. The 'promise' and the 'fulfilment' represent the notable distinction between the old covenant and the new. Failure to differentiate between these two covenants causes one to confuse what is transient with what is permanently real.

To appreciate the significance of circumcision in the Old Covenant we need to strip it of any later theological interpretations that tend to obscure its original nature and purpose. The Deuteronomic and prophetic use of the imagery of circumcision to convey moral and spiritual ideas transcends the basic meaning of the rite. This is illustrated in Jer. 4.4 and in Deut. 30.6: 'The Lord your God will circumcise your heart and the heart of your offspring, so that you will love the Lord your God with all your heart and with all your soul, that you may live.'

The New Testament

Moving into the New Testament, we recall the various ways in which Col. 2.11 has been interpreted, particularly the phrase: 'the circumcision of Christ' (ἡ περιτομή τοῦ χριστοῦ). Many have taken it to mean 'Christian circumcision' and have identified it with baptism. In the particular context and the pagan environment in which 'Colossians' was written, and mindful of the Christian Gospel of salvation, Paul in this letter would appear to be using this debatable phrase to signify the crucifixion of Christ. Colossians 2.11 has been intrepreted to mean that the Christian has already been circumcised in Christ's death and has entered effectively into it through his baptism. Therefore he needs no circumcision administered by human hands. In other words, circumcision of the heart is equivalent to redemption through Christ.

Lampe maintains that in Col. 2.11f baptism is contrasted rather than compared with circumcision. He writes: 'The real correspondence to which St Paul points is between the Christian possession of the Spirit as the result of his faith-response to the grace of God in Christ, and the inward "circumcision of the heart" to which the great prophets had looked forward.'[20] According to Jeremias, Paul in Col. 2.11 calls baptism 'Christian circumcision' and describes it as the Christian sacrament which corresponds to Jewish circumcision. Jeremias concludes that 'the description of baptism as "Christian circumcision" makes it very probable that the procedure in baptism was the same, that is, that children of every age were baptized along with their parents when . . . converted to Christianity.'[21]

Erich Dinkler was of the opinion that parallelism between baptism and circumcision cannot be assumed. 'In Col. 2.11' he wrote, 'the word circumcision is used as a metaphor for baptism, but this single verse cannot be used as a basis for generalisation. The religious distinction of the father of the family is not taken up by the earliest Christianity, which emphasised instead the individual person before God'.[22]

In his interpretation of Col. 2.11, Whiteley says that Christians are 'not circumcised physically, but divested of their lower nature' and adds that Paul in the next verse associates this metaphor with sharing Christ's burial in baptism. 'St Paul's doctrine of baptism,' he writes, 'is wholly realistic; but, precisely because it transcends comprehension, he can point to this mysterious reality only by means of such metaphors as circumcision, adoption, burial and incorporation . . . a reality which transcends the powers of literal language and therefore compels the apostle to have recourse to the language of symbols.'[23]

Paul's doctrine of the covenant in Galatians, chapter 3, shows that the real 'sons of Abraham' are those who share Abraham's faith. He assures his Christian readers (whoever they were) that 'in Christ Jesus you are all sons of God through faith . . . and if you are Christ's, then you are Abraham's offspring, heirs according to promise.' In these words are reflected the extent to which the two dispensations are continuous or discontinuous. The qualification for entry into the new covenant is made plain by Paul – it is by faith in Christ, with whom the covenant with Abraham has been superseded and fulfilled. Gal. 3 lends little support for that form of the covenant theology which speaks exclusively of 'the one covenant of grace.'[24]

The Church of Scotland Interim Report of the Special Commission on baptism states that 'the New Testament appears to take it for granted that infants are to be initiated in the new covenant as they were into the old,' and quotes, in support of this viewpoint, Acts 2.39: 'The promise is to you and *to your children*'.[25] On this premise, the 'Report' draws the inference that 'here we have an unequivocal insistence that children come within the covenant and that the promise of the Spirit in baptism is for them too.'[26] Not all scholars are persuaded that the dogmatic conclusions contained in the Scot Report necessarily, or indeed rightly, follow from the evidence adduced.

On the question whether the children of Christian parents were immediately baptized, it is suggested that the practice was different in Jewish Christian circles from what it was in the Gentile churches, in view of the differences regarding the rite of circumcision. The Jewish Christians, especially in Jerusalem, circumcised their children but did they also baptize them? It seems clear from Gal. 5.2ff. that Paul's Gentile converts did not circumcise their infants and it might appear from Acts 21.21 and from the Galatian letter that converted Jews in Gentile country were discouraged from practising the rite of circumcision. Aland, however, quotes Haenchen's comment on Acts 21.21: 'According to Luke's representation, the elders plainly did not believe the charge'.[27]

There does not appear to be any firm historical ground for drawing 'a straight line from the circumcision of infants to the baptism of infants' for the following reasons:

(1) There is no proof that the Jerusalem Church administered both circumcision and baptism at the same time.
(2) The decreasing influence of the Jerusalem church over other churches in the first century.
(3) In the Gentile world, Jewish law and circumcision did not remain in force.

Jeremias dogmatically asserts, however, that Col. 2.11 proves that baptism took the place of circumcision and that infants were baptized in the Jerusalem and Pauline churches – a conclusion which Aland for one does not accept.[28] It is, nevertheless, interesting to observe that for the adult pagan entering the Christian Church, as distinct from his entering Judaism, it could be said that baptism had taken the place of circumcision. Add to this situation, the fact that many converted Jews, who had already been circumcised, were then baptized as Christians.

Whiteley draws attention to Paul's awareness of the important distinction between the outward and inward aspects of circumcision. In Rom 2.25 the apostle says: 'Circumcision has value, provided you keep the law; but, if you break the law, then your circumcision is as if it had never been.' It is clearly the inwardness of religion that matters most to Paul, as the next verse shows: 'If an uncircumcised man keeps the precepts of the law, will he not count as circumcised?'

How does this apply to the relationship between baptism and circumcision? The New Testament does not appear to offer a clear answer. The primitive church were not of one mind regarding the connection of the two rites, either in belief or practice. It would appear that the Jewish Christian church circumcised their male children and that they also baptized converts to Judaism. It has been pointed out that in a sphere where circumcision was well established, there was little likelihood of baptism being seen as the fulfilment of the Jewish rite; nor would the two rites be given the same meaning.

The Early Church

Having stressed that all the early forms of baptism in the primitive church were designed for adults, Dr James Bullock goes on to say that the early church lacked the extreme individualism of modern life. She thought in terms of the covenant and the household of God, and had warrant for infant baptism in the Old Testament precedent of circumcision, meaningless for the Christian of today but entirely authoritative for the first three centuries.[29]

With reference to the treatment of baptism in the Epistle of Barnabas,[30] Robert Grant observes: 'The rite is comparable to circumcision, but unlike circumcision it is unique; furthermore circumcision has now been abolished. Baptism is the "seal" of the new covenant, and it relates the newborn Christian to the eschatological hope of the community. All the explicitly baptismal passages in Barnabas make this clear.'[31]

It is pointed out that, in the early part of the second century, Justin Martyr (c.100–165), in his Dialogue with the Jew Trypho, describes baptism as a 'spiritual circumcision' in contrast to the 'circumcision according to the flesh', which was characteristic of the old covenant – 'a spiritual circumcision' involving God's forgiveness and the 'seal of the Spirit'.[32]

Chrysostom (c. 350–407), the erudite Bishop of Constantinople, held that, while the Jews had circumcision, the Christian Church had the earnest (*ἀρραβών*) of the Spirit, which is conveyed in baptism.[33] A. W. Argyle maintains that Chrysostom, in treating baptism as the counterpart of circumcision, unwittingly exposes the weakness of infant baptism. This fourth century Father describes baptism as the painless circumcision made without hands (Col. 2.11), which, unlike the Jewish circumcision, has no fixed season and can be applied to infants and adults. Chrysostom here appears to have overlooked the circumcision of adult converts to Judaism. Chrysostom questions the efficacy of both infant baptism and circumcision when he says of the latter: 'For what benefit to his soul can an infant derive from it, since he has no knowledge of what is done to him and has no sense.'[34]

Augustine of Hippo (354–430) saw baptism as a parallel rite to circumcision. He held that circumcision prefigured Christ's resurrection by which we were regenerated. Circumcision in the Old covenant corresponded to baptism in the New. As circumcision was essential for entry into Hebrew religion, so baptism was a necessary initiation into the Christian Church.[35] Flemington traces a reference to circumcision in Augustine's confrontation with the Donatists. Augustine argues that even if the apostolic authority behind the universal practice of infant baptism was not supported by any church council, yet the meaning of the rite might be gained from the analogy of circumcision.[36]

The Middle Ages

West refers to the fact that, in the Middle Ages, Christianity and humanity seemed to become merged into a spiritual world empire. He adds that as in the old dispensation circumcision had been the initiation rite into society, so infant baptism, viewed as we should say today sociologically, whatever may have been its theological meaning, was reckoned to bring the child into the membership of the community.

The relationship between circumcision and infant baptism figures in a confrontation which Zwingli had in 1525 with certain people who held Anabaptist convictions. These people refused on conscientious grounds to have their children baptized. Bernard Reardon sums up this situation, with its sad consequences: 'Zwingli (1484–1531), who disliked sectarianism, opposed them in person, urging that baptism, as the Christian counterpart of Old Testament circumcision, ought to be retained. The Council (of Zurich) was persuaded by this reasoning and formerly enacted that no break of the rule of child baptism be permitted. Among those who preached defiance of the new law was Feliz Manz, who for his obduracy suffered the penalty of death by drowning.'[37]

On a later page, Reardon adds: The universal practice of infant baptism could be defended not only on historical grounds – Zwingli thought it probable that it went back to the apostles themselves – but on theological grounds as well, as admitting, like circumcision under the Old Covenant, to membership of the Israel of God.[38]

Further mention should be made of some evidence to which we

referred in the last chapter. We recall how, in line with the Medieval rite of baptism, an explanatory handbook, the Encheridion Christianae Institutionis, based on the canons of the Council of Cologne, was produced by John Gropper (1503–1559) in 1538. The relevant part for our purpose in this chapter, taken from an English translation of the original Latin, is as follows:

'Even from this very passage (John 3.5) the impious Anabaptists are refuted, who impiously reject and refuse the baptism of infants. For in the old law God ordered infants to be circumcised, so that they might join the synagogue . . .So too through baptism, which has superseded circumcision, children are to be brought into the church, lest they should be excluded from the kingdom of God, which Christ clearly declared to belong to them . . . And just as the covenant of circumcision did not less apply to infants for the reason that they did not understand what was done, so neither does baptism avail less in the case of infants for this reason that they do not yet understand the covenant of divine grace.'[39]

The problems presented by infant baptism to Protestant circles with their emphasis on the prerequisite of faith were partly dealt with by drawing attention to the parallel rite of circumcision. Calvin recognized that baptism requires repentance, but indicated that this applied also to circumcision (Jer. 4.4). Herbert Wood writes: 'The rule that baptism should follow faith is not invariable, for circumcision comes after faith in Abraham and before intelligence in Isaac'. Is this statement based on Patriarchal 'history' or on the theology of much later times? Wood goes on to say that 'the parallel with circumcision was the chief ground for defending infant baptism as agreeable to the scriptures, while Mark 10.14f. and 1 Cor. 7.14 [40] were the chief reasons for supposing it to be agreeable with the institution of Christ'.[41]

Calvin and the Covenants

The essential features of the theological debate centring on the covenant of grace and circumcision are highlighted in the arguments between Calvin and the Anabaptists. The latter saw the old and new covenants as discontinuous. They also maintained that participation in a sacrament must be preceded by an experience of repentance and faith on the part of the recipient – and therefore infants were not eligible. Calvin disagreed. He held that the covenants – the old and the new – had a similar basis, aim and purpose. The two rites of circumcision and baptism differed only in external form – circumcision for the old covenant, baptism for the new.[42]

From the premise that circumcision has been administered to infants – a rite said to symbolize repentance and faith – it is argued that baptism can also be applied to children. In the case of infant baptism, however, the involvement of repentance and faith may more appropriately and realistically be seen as awaiting future fulfilment when the child is old enough to satisfy the personal requirements – 'with faith as subsequent response rather than essential pre-requisite'.[43]

John Calvin's baptismal service administered at Geneva is found in the 'Form of Prayers', to use the shortened title, issued in 1542 – a form very different from the Lutheran or Anglican rites. The service states that, although the infants of Christian parents are corrupted by Adam's sin, yet God does not refuse to accept them as his children 'for the sake of his covenant'. For this reason, God 'has wished from the beginning that in his church infants should receive the sign of circumcision, by which he represented then, all that is today signified to us by baptism.'[44]

Thomas Cranmer (1489–1556), who seems to have preferred a simple baptismal ritual, made many references to baptism in his writings. In his 'Confutation of Unwritten Verities', he questioned the Sarum rite's sole dependence on tradition. Cranmer supported infant baptism by reference both to ancient custom and the Bible.[45] In his 'Confutation', he maintained that 'the baptism of infants is proved by the plain scriptures. First, by the figure of the old law, which was circumcision. Infants in the old law were circumcised; ergo, in the new law they are to be baptized.' After quoting what he considered to be supportive evidence from the promise to Abraham, from the words of Jesus and from the teaching of St Paul, Cranmer concludes: 'By these and many other plain words of scripture, it is evident that the baptism of infants is grounded in holy scripture.'[46]

We should not overlook the fact that Cranmer's argument here does not take into account the position of female children. If the baptism of infant boys necessarily relates back to circumcision in the old covenant, to what does the baptism of infant girls relate back?

As assessment

On the question of the relationship between circumcision and infant baptism, David Pawson offers the following summary:

(1) There is no evidence that the physical rite of circumcision has been transmuted into the physical rite of baptism.
(2) As a 'seal' of righteousness, it belonged to Abraham.
(3) As a 'sign' of God's promise, it belongs to Christ and reaches its terminus in him.
(4) As a 'type' of putting away the flesh, it is needed as a 'spiritual operation' by all Christians in addition to baptism.
(5) As a custom, it may be adopted for social (or presumably medical) reasons.
(6) But as a physical rite of initiation, it belongs to the old Israel, not the new.[47]

Neville Clark, in a chapter on The Theology of Baptism, says that the implications of baptism are never to be derived from the circumcision of old Israel. 'Rather is it in the light of Christian baptism or, to be more exact, the cross-resurrection governing baptism, that circumcision is weighed, vindicated and condemned'.[48]

In other words, the old covenant is both negated and fulfilled by the cross and resurrection of Jesus – the momentous event in Christian history and thought that determines interpretation, and helps to settle the issue, of continuity or discontinuity with regard to the old covenant and the rite of circumcision.

CHAPTER EIGHT

Original Sin and Infant Baptism

However convinced clergy or ministers may be that God would not send an unbaptized infant to hell, they will usually respond urgently to baptize a child who is not likely to live. In some cases the parents who are anxious for their baby to be 'christened' have no church connections and little knowledge of Christian initiation. Why then should they press for baptism? What is the cause of their concern? It would appear that beneath the surface of their minds there is a lurking fear, probably indefinable and inexpressible, that their child's eternal destiny is somehow threatened or at least may be liable to some serious spiritual disadvantage. This concern is not as deep or as widespread as it was in times past, but it is still real enough in some sacramental theology and liturgical practice to justify our enquiry in this chapter into the relevance and validity of original sin, especially in relation to the necessity of infant baptism.

Scriptural evidence

Beginning with the Bible, we can find comparatively little evidence in Scripture for the doctrine of original sin. Many people turn first to the book of Genesis – especially to the story of Adam and Eve in the Garden of Eden. It is true that some Jewish writers in the pre-Christian era based their doctrine of original sin on the third chapter of this book. But a close study of this passage shows that this story does not say that Adam's sin caused any corruption of human nature, nor any loss of divine gifts, nor any adverse influence on posterity. Adam and Eve were banished from the Garden and no longer given access to the tree of life. The Yahwistic writer says nothing about original sin.

Subsequent sins mentioned in Genesis, such as the murder of Abel by Cain, are not linked to Adam's fall. Moreover, not all of Adam's descendants are represented as bearing the taint of his transgression. Nor is there any exposition of Eden's tragic events in later parts of the Old Testament.

It is true that there are several references to universal sinfulness but there is no indication that this sin is traceable to Adam's disobedience and fall. This universal sinfulness finds expression in such passages as follows: 'The imagination of man's heart is evil from his youth.' (Gen. 8.21). 'There is no man who does not sin.' (1 Kings 8.46). 'If thou, O Lord, shouldst mark iniquities, Lord, who could stand?' (Psalm 130.3). Jewish rabbis as in the Book of Enoch tended to attribute such widespread depravity, not to Adam's sin, but to the fall of 'the sons of God', whose remarkable activities appear in the strange account in Genesis 6. 1-4. It seems to the scriptural writer that as a result of these events the human race became increasingly sinful, as the following verse states: 'The Lord saw that the wickedness of man was great in the earth and that every imagination of the thoughts of his heart was only evil continually' (Gen. 6.5).

Then follows one of the saddest and most disillusioning texts in the Bible: 'And the Lord was sorry that he had made man' (Gen. 6.6). One wonders if the Yahwist, who made this tragic observation, asked himself: 'Did not the Lord know in advance that man would let him down?' It is not a question – interesting and intriguing as it is – that we can pursue here, though we shall touch on it towards the end of this chapter when we briefly consider the origin of evil.

The first teaching we have about the Fall and original sin is found in the inter-testamental literature. Ecclesiasticus 25,24 traces death and sinfulness to Eve. 'From a woman was the beginning of sin; and because of her we all die.' 1 Enoch. 69.4f makes the strange observation that fallen angels tempted Eve and led men into wickedness by teaching them the art of writing. According to 2 Esdras 7.118f, Adam is mainly to blame: 'O thou Adam, what has thou done? for though it was thou that sinned, the evil is not fallen on thee alone, but upon all of us that come of thee.' The Apocalypse of Baruch makes it clear that 'Adam first sinned and brought untimely death upon all' (44.15). The effect of Adam's sin was physical death. Sin was due to the individual's misuse of free-will, so that in theory one could avoid sin. The Rabbinical writings take a similar line. They stress two things: (1) Adam's sin meant death for all men and (2) Death is punishment for individual sin.

Much is said in the Rabbinic literature about the glory of Adam's status before the Fall and of the cosmic results of his transgression. The evil inclination mentioned early in the Old Testament is enlarged upon here; but the bias to evil is not attributed to Adam's sin until the Christian era. The crude legend that Eve was tainted by Satan (or the serpent) and her sinfulness conveyed to posterity appears in several forms.

The data for a doctrine of original sin are in the Book of Wisdom, but they are not formulated into a coherent concept. In 2.23f, we read: 'God created man for immortality and made him the image of his own eternal self. It was the Devil's spite that brought death into the world and the experience of it is reserved for those who take his side.' In Genesis 3, the 'serpent', though presented as a malevolent being, is not regarded as an evil spirit. It is here in the Apocrypha where the 'serpent' of Genesis is first identified with the Devil. Is it in the mind of the writer of Wisdom 2.23 that, if Adam had not sinned, he would never have died physically, but would have lived for ever?

With regard to the meaning of 'sin' and 'guilt', Whiteley says that 'neither in the Bible nor in subsequent theology is there a standard definition universally acceptable . . . Sin is normally reserved for conscious, purposeful violation of known law.' Guilt is a concept derived from law and remains even when one is not conscious of it. In Pauline theology, we are all sinners. Merit has no place in his system.[1]

It was St Paul who was first in the Bible clearly to link original sin with the Fall in Genesis 3. Looking back from Christ to Adam, he saw a parallel between the redeemed Christian living in Christ and the sinner involved in Adam's transgression. 'As in Adam all die, so also in Christ shall all be made alive' (1 Cor. 15.22). Paul's teaching on original sin is summed up in Rom. 5.12, 'Sin came into the world through one man and death through sin and so death spread to all men because all men sinned.' Cyprian and Ambrose held that all humanity shared in Adam's sin, which is passed on by natural generation. The so-called 'Ambrosiaster' found proof of this involvement in Adam's sin by a questionable exegesis of a phrase in the original Greek of Rom. 5.12. He translated ἐφ' ᾧ by the Latin phrase 'in quo' – '*in whom*' (i.e. Adam) all have sinned.' Other church Fathers followed 'Ambrosiaster', including Augustine of Hippo, in this interpretation. But the consensus of scholarly opinion translates ἐφ' ᾧ as 'because'. '. . . death passed to all men *because* all men sinned.'

Romans 5.12-21 appears to be the only passage in Paul's writings – indeed in the New Testament – which links human sinfulness with Adam's sin. But no explanation of the connection is given. He says that sin entered by one man and death through sin. Two questions arise: First, did Paul mean that death came because all sinned personally or because all sinned when Adam sinned? The latter alternative relates better to the apostle's parallel between Adam and Christ. The second question is this: What was the mediating link between Adam's sin and the sin and death of posterity? Is it simply God's appointment or the seminal existence in Adam of his descendants? The nearest Paul gets to an answer is in the parallelism he draws between the pernicious legacy of the 'first Adam' and the redemption transmitted to believers by the 'second Adam'. (cf. 1 Cor. 15.21f.)

'How we can think of man as still responsible,' writes John MacQuarrie, 'can perhaps best be seen if we consider the doctrine of original sin.' This notion 'points to some basic tendency towards sin.' The view is that we do not start from innocence then fall into sin, but that we are already in sin. Such a situation, however, rules out individual responsibility, yet accountability is an essential element in personal sin.[2]

Dr C. R. Smith agrees with Macquarrie in defining 'original sin' or, as he prefers to call it, 'racial degradation' in terms of society. He says that it has been regarded as 'an exploded doctrine, but like some other such doctrines it survives explosions.' He holds that 'not only good things but evil ones come to every child . . . For theological purposes it does not matter whether they come by heredity or environment or both . . . but all agree that there do come both good influences and evil influences to every child . . . merely because he is inevitably societary'.[3]

The Early Church

The Fathers of the early church did not directly adopt the teaching of St Paul, nor borrow from Jewish literature. They started afresh to elaborate a doctrine of original sin. In this sphere, the chief pioneers before Augustine were Irenaeus, Origen and Tertullian. Their doctrine arose from a personal study of texts, philosophical tenets or institutions, though no attempt was made to give a precise formal account of original sin until the time of Augustine. Controversy first centred on the origin of the human soul. The Eastern Fathers favoured 'creationism' – each soul individually created and joined to the body, the residence of original sin. The Western Fathers taught that the soul was derived by natural generation from the parents. Both the Western and Eastern Fathers, however, had a rather optimistic view of man and laid relatively little emphasis on the Fall and on its consequences for mankind. Their main concern seemed to be that the human race had lost its supernatural disposition towards righteousness. They did not lose sight of the fact, however, that a doctrine of original sin was perhaps the most satisfactory theological justification for the baptism of infants. 'Whether this condition of human sinfulness', as Prof. Bruce Vawter says, 'implied personal guilt . . . or merely the sharing of a defectable and deprived human nature was a matter for debate in early patristic theology.'[4]

The Shepherd of Hermas, of uncertain composition and date, suggests that children are not tarnished with original sin. He refers to 'little children who do not know the wickedness that destroys the life of men.'[5] Believers are said to be like 'babes, into whose heart no guile enters, neither have learned what wickedness is'.[6]

Robert Grant, having concluded as we noted on earlier pages, that infant baptism cannot be found in Christian literature before Tertullian, goes on to say that 'it reflects the extent to which the church was beginning to consist of families hereditarily Christian, and it was accompanied by a new emphasis on the doctrine of original sin.'[7]

The unscriptural phrase 'original sin' was first used by Tertullian (c. 160–220). He held that 'children of believers' are by their birth 'marked out for holiness and therewith for salvation.' They are, however, according to John 3.5, made holy only by baptism. Prior to baptism, their soul is in Adam and therefore burdened with original sin.[8] Tertullian taught that mankind was seminally present in Adam, the sin being transmitted by propagation. It has been pointed out that while Irenaeus never, and Origen seldom, refer to universal sinfulness as deriving from Adam's Fall, Tertullian is emphatic in linking man's depravity with Adam's sin. He derives his doctrine, not so much from Scripture, as from the Stoic's traducianist theory of the soul's origin. 'The idea that the soul is a branch of Adam's absorbing its sinfulness, led to a belief in original sin'.[9] During his Montanist days, Tertullian says that 'practically no birth is pure' and that 'every soul is enrolled in Adam until it is enrolled anew in Christ'.[10]

E. G. Hinson shows that Irenaeus distinguished between the 'image' (εἰκών) and the 'likeness' (ὁμοίωσις) in the Genesis creation story, as did the Gnostic Valentinus, and held that the Fall affected only the 'likeness'. The 'image' was unaffected. But the loss of the divine 'likeness' caused a disordered human nature, involving death and enslavement to Satan. Irenaeus saw sin as wrong moral choice by the exercise of free-will. The Fall attenuated free-will, but did not obliterate it. [11]

Dr J. N. D. Kelly points out that whereas Irenaeus, Tertullian and Clement of Alexandria, accepted the Genesis story of the Fall as historical fact, Origen (185–254) saw it as a cosmic myth and raised the origin of sin from an earthly setting to a transcendental level. The scene of the Fall is set,not in Eden, but in a supra-mundane sphere. Origen taught the pre-existence of each soul, endowed with free-will. All these rational pre-existent souls – except the soul of Christ – chose evil and so lost their place in Paradise.

Following this Fall, God made the world and bound these sinful souls to a human body as a penalty. The punishment was residence in flesh. The Fall consisted in the entry of offending souls into this world – a part of purgatory to be used as a training ground for the hereafter.[12] This means that Origen's theory of the Fall is pre-cosmic and offers an explanation of universal sinfulness.

Origen's belief that children are born already sinful finds support in such scriptural passages as Psalm 51.5 and Psalm 58.3. This view is also reinforced by the baptism of infants. He regards Adam's sin and his expulsion from the Garden of Eden as an allegory of pre-cosmic sin – a theory which denies that individual sinfulness was transmitted by Adam's Fall. Rather is it the result of each soul's pre-existent waywardness. As to the cause of sin, Origen held that evil resided entirely in the exercise of man's free-will.[13]

The teaching of Athanasius (296–373) on the Fall has been regarded as a mixture of Platonism and the Biblical account in Genesis. He contrasts man in his natural state and man as a recipient of God's favour. Though a finite being created from nothingness, Adam was enabled to participate in God's Word and to receive the Divine image. This provided him with supernatural knowledge and rationality and placed incorruption and immortality within his reach. In order to maintain his privileged status, God placed him in the Garden of Eden. Here is the source of the concept of 'original righteousness', which has been defined as including freedom from concupiscence, bodily immortality, impassibility and happiness.[14]

The general view in the West stressed more than did the East the supernatural blessedness of man's primitive state and the solidarity of the race with Adam. Taking Ambrose and 'Ambrosiaster' together, following Dr J. N. D. Kelly, we note that Ambrose presents Adam in a most heavenly form. He fell by reason of pride. The sin of his soul corrupted his body and resided there.[15]

Ambrose (340–400) in his more general teaching, indicates that the guilt attaches to Adam himself and not to us. Our personal sins (propria) are to be contrasted with those we inherit (haereditaria). Baptism removes the former, and the latter are removed by the washing of feet.[16] In 'De Sacramentis' (if written by Ambrose), he says that 'the serpent's poison' is removed by feet washing.

In the early church, during the fourth and fifth centuries, the ceremony of feet-washing – reflecting the episode in John 13 – followed the act of baptism. It was generally considered to be an object lesson designed to encourage baptismal candidates in humility. Ambrose, however, claimed that the rite had a sacramental efficacy in protecting the neophyte against inherited sin from Adam.[17] E. C. Whitaker enlarges on this by saying that Ambrose taught that 'just as a man's own sins were washed away in baptism so the washing of the feet washed away the hereditary sins which he derives from Adam, whose feet were tripped by the serpent.' This sacramental interpretation was approved by St Augustine, but rejected in Rome and in Spain.[18]

Elsewhere, Ambrose says that on judgment day we shall be punished, not for hereditary sin, but for our own sins. Baptism is necessary for infants, for it admits them to the kingdom of heaven. He holds that inherited corruption is transmitted by physical generation. Christ escaped this taint by his virginal conception.[19]

The Greek Fathers provide some evidence which appears to rule out their belief in original sin. Gregory of Nazianzen (330–389) and Gregory of Nyssa and Chrysostom teach that newly-born infants are free from sin. Chrysostom (c. 344–407) did not accept the doctrine of inherited transgression nor the view that concupiscence in itself was sin. He understood Romans 5.19 ('by one man's disobedience many were made sinners') to mean that Adam's Fall made posterity liable only to punishment and death – a point of view akin to Pelagianism. Dr Kelly says that 'there is hardly a hint in the Greek Fathers that mankind as a whole shares in Adam's guilt, i.e. his culpability. This partly explains their reluctance to speak of his legacy to us as sin, and of course makes their indulgent attitude to children dying unbaptized understandable.[20]

Gregory of Nyssa (c. 335–395) rejected the idea that an unbaptized infant who dies will suffer the wrath of God, for he is not as yet tainted with sin. In his treatise 'On the untimely Deaths of

Infants', he teaches that the soul of an infant who has died before attaining the age of reason will receive such blessing as it is capable of receiving, and that such child-souls may grow in the knowledge of God till at last they achieve full intellectual and spiritual maturity.[21]

Augustine and Pelagius

Augustine (354–430), in opposition to Pelagius, developed the doctrine of original sin – a doctrine introduced by Cyprian and by Ambrose. He taught that all men were born sinful and guilty and were deserving of eternal damnation. Since Adam's Fall, the body had dominated, instead of being subject to, the human spirit. Originally, nature was 'natura sana', but it has become 'natura vitiata'. He regarded Adam as originally perfect – 'original righteousness'. He was endowed with 'free will' – liberum arbitrium – but, since he used it wrongfully, he was condemned and all men with him, for they had shared in his transgression. Since original sin involved guilt, it followed that the unbaptized, even infants, were deserving of damnation. Augustine held that Adam's transgression had made human nature so depraved that sinful man was not capable of willing what was good. This gave rise to his teaching about divine grace and consequently his doctrine of predestination – beliefs that made a great impact on theological thought in subsequent centuries, not least at the Reformation and particularly in Calvinism.

No theologian has stressed man's share in Adam's transgression more than Augustine. He found support for this view, as did 'Ambrosiaster', in the incorrect Latin translation 'in whom all sinned' (in quo omnes peccaverunt) for the original Greek phrase ἐφ' ᾧ in Romans 5.12. Although the human race is much marred by original sin, he does not regard mankind as utterly depraved. He says that 'the spark . . . of reason in virtue of which he was made in God's likeness has not been completely extinguished'.[22] Turning to that horrific aspect of Augustine's teaching on the eternal damnation awaiting the unbaptized, Dr Kelly says: 'Even helpless children dying without the benefit of baptism must pass to eternal fire with the Devil, although their sufferings will be relatively mild as compared with those of adults who had added sins of their own to their inherited guilt.'[23]

In the early church, it would be difficult to find two theologians more different than Augustine and Pelagius (fl. 383–409). There was, however, at least one surprising similarity – they both supported infant baptism; though for different reasons. In contrast to Augustine, Pelagius rejected the doctrines of original sin and guilt and stressed unconditional free-will and responsibility, though he linked free-will to the constraints of divine law. He denied that there was any hereditary transmission of sin from Adam through the reproductive process. We sin by imitation of Adam's Fall and not because of a corrupted nature. The sin of Adam transmitted to posterity neither depravity nor death. Infants, although innocent, need baptism only as a benedictory rite and in order to enter the kingdom of God. Yet, there is no possibility of a merciful God sending unbaptized babies to hell. Instead, they would go, as Henry Chadwick says, to 'some third place, or limbo, of natural felicity.'[24] To these merciful and worthy sentiments we would add that the mind cannot rest in the thought that a world, created by the God whom Jesus revealed, can allow evil to remain endlessly beyond the control of His loving purposes for all his creatures. Jesus, whose knowledge of God was supreme, assured us that the Divine Shepherd seeks even His most wayward sheep until all the flock are safely home, however far the wandering and however long it takes.

Pelagius, a British monk of much knowledge and sincerity, argued that no one is guilty of sin unless he is aware of willing it. Moreover, he denied that there was any special pressure on man's will to choose the good. A creationist, he believed that the soul was created anew by God and was not produced by progenitors. Sin is in the soul, not the body. Pelagius held therefore that every infant is a fresh creation and begins life in a state of goodness. Tertullian's belief in the purity of the new-born infant is therefore shared by Pelagius, who held that infants are as Adam was before the Fall. He reasoned that if a child inherits original sin, then the child of baptized parents ought to inherit original righteousness. André La Cocque draws attention to Pelagius's claim that man can attain perfection by the exercise of virtues and asceticism. Moreover, man is entirely responsible for his sins because he has freewill. 'If sin is innate, it is not voluntary; if it is voluntary, it is not innate.' Pelagius accepted the latter alternative.[25]

Pelagius is quoted as saying: 'Nothing good and nothing evil, for which we are judged to be worthy either of praise or blame, is born with us. For we are born not fully developed, but with a capacity for either conduct. We are made naturally without either virtue or vice, and before the action of our proper will the only thing in man is what God has formed in him.'[26]

Partly to meet such 'heresy', the Church Council of 418 condemned (1) the theory that Adam was created mortal; (2) the view that infants should not be baptized; (3) the failure to recognize that baptism remits original sin; (4) the idea that the unbaptized can be saved.[27]

Early in the fifth century, Celestius held many similar views to Pelagius. Though in general agreement with the doctrine of infant baptism, he did not regard it as essential to eternal salvation. Nor did his qualified approval of the infant rite imply that he accepted the doctrine of original sin. He held that the source or cause of wrongdoing lies, not in any inherited corruption in the basic nature of man, but in the misuse of his freedom. Moreover, free-will and irresistible grace were for Celestius incompatible. He also opposed the ideas of total depravity and predestination.

He followed another unorthodox line when he claimed that Adam was created as a mortal being and that he would have died even if he had not transgressed. He took a farther step away from contemporary orthodoxy by teaching that infants are now as Adam was before he fell from 'original righteousness'. It is obvious that his approval of infant baptism did not fit logically into his theological system. Not surprisingly, these views were condemned by the church council of AD 418.[28]

Julian

The Christian Church has had some distinguished 'heretics'! Pelagius and Celestius were two of them. Another was Julian, Bishop of Eclanum (380–c.455) – a learned and formidable advocate of Pelagian theology. In AD 418, he challenged the 'Epistola Tractoria', in which Pope Zosimus condemned Pelagius and Celestius, – with the expected result that he was deposed from his See and banished from Italy for a time. Julian was the most systematic exponent of Pelagianism. He defined free-will as 'the possibility of committing sin or of abstaining from it' and rejected the idea that all men shared in the Fall of Adam.[29]

Julian called Augustine's doctrine of infant baptism extremely erronious and blasphemous. His voluminous writings, being heretical, have not survived, except in sizable quotations in Augustine's last treatise, the 'Unfinished Work'. On the subject of original sin, Julian is quoted as saying: 'You ask me why I would not consent to the idea that there is a sin that is part of human nature? I answer, it is improbable, it is untrue, it is unjust and impious. It makes it seem as if the Devil were the maker of men. It violates and destroys the freedom of the will.'

Against Augustine's view that even new-born infants are tainted with original sin, Julian writes so intensely that one almost expects his heated words to burn the paper on which they are written! 'Tiny babies, you say,. . . are burdened with the sin of another. Tell me then, who is this person who inflicts punishment on innocent creatures . . . You answer: God. God! He who commended his love to us . . . He it is, you say, who judges in this way. He is the persecutor of newborn children. He it is who sends tiny (unbaptized) babies to eternal flames . . . You have come so far from religious feeling, from civilized thinking, so far indeed from mere common sense, in that you think that your Lord God is capable of committing a crime against justice such as is hardly conceivable even among the barbarians.'[30]

In the ninth century Eastern Church, the Paulicians appear to have denied the validity of infant baptism and dismissed the view that infants were in any sense sinful. Theologians in the Medieval Church, as they sought to explain the nature and transmission of original sin, generally interpreted it in terms of the absence of original righteousness. At the Fall, man had lost his supernatural endowment, but he had retained his natural faculties unimpaired.

Anselm (1033–1109) contributed new ideas and defined original sin as the 'privation of the righteousness which every man ought to possess' and so, unlike Augustine, he separated it from concupiscence. It is transmitted by procreation, because mankind was present 'seminaliter' in Adam. Abelard (1079–1142) held very different views from those generally taught in Medieval times. He rejected the belief that Adam's transgression conveyed condemnation to posterity; to say that mankind 'sinned in Adam' seemed to him a misuse of the word 'sin'. Abelard was condemned by the Council of Sens in 1140 for not recognizing that original sin involved guilt. The rationalism of Abelard was shared by others who denied the guilt of original sin (*reatus culpae*) but who recognized its punitive results (*reatus poenae*).[31]

Thomas Aquinas

Thomas Aquinas (1224–1274), the greatest theologian and philosopher of the Medieval Church, regarded original sin as a disordered condition, involving the loss of original righteousness or superadded graces. But he believed that natural goodness and freewill had survived Adam's Fall. He declined to identify concupiscence with sin. He held that Adam was created 'pure nature' to which were added supernatural gifts by which a man could control his inferior powers. He does not associate original sin with personal guilt and so it follows that, whereas unbaptized infants do not gain the beatific vision, they are spared punishment and suffering. Yet a child must be baptized in order to be made regenerate and freed from original sin. For posterity, Adam's Fall left a legacy of pride, a weakness of the will and a darkened mind. Only divine grace can cure this moral and spiritual malady. Aquinas thought that original sin transmitted by the first man to the human race can best be understood when set alongside the redemption of the world by Christ. For Paul and for Aquinas, it was a significant and contrasting parallel of tragedy and triumph.[32]

Despite diversities of views, original sin remained a doctrine of traditional Christianity – Catholic and Protestant. J. D. C. Fisher refers to the pressure placed upon parents in the fourteenth, fifteenth and sixteenth centuries to bring their children to baptism within a few days of birth. 'In this connection, it is necessary to bear in mind the tragically high mortality rate among infants in the Middle Ages and until recent times, and to reflect how this would weigh upon the mind of a church convinced . . . that Augustine's doctrine of original guilt was true and unanswerable.'[33]

The Council of Trent

The scholastic doctrine of original sin, especially as Aquinas understood it, became the official doctrine of the Roman Catholic Church at the Council of Trent. Benjamin Drewery outlines the decree of the Fifth Session on original sin as follows:

(1) The sin of Adam lost him 'the holiness and righteousness in which he had been constituted' and so he incurred the wrath of God, death and captivity to the Devil.
(2) 'Bodily penalties' and 'sin which is the death of the soul' have been 'transfused' to the whole human race by Adam, through 'propagation' not 'imitation'.
(3) 'This sin of Adam' is removed solely through the reconciling merit of Jesus Christ, applied through baptism (infant or adult) to humanity. The baptism of infants, guiltless of actual sin, is

valid 'that what they contracted by generation may be washed away by regeneration.'

(4) By Christ the whole essence of original sin is removed, not merely 'alleviated' (radi: literally 'scratched') or no longer 'imputed'. Yet there remains after baptism 'concupiscence' or the 'formes peccati' (literally: the 'tinder' of sin, i.e. the raw material, liability of sinning). This, however, in the regenerate is not properly 'sin' but 'of sin and inclining to sin'.

(5) The blessed Virgin Mary is exempt from this proviso.[34]

Protestantism, in the sixteenth century, interpreted original sin in terms of Augustinianism, which the Schoolmen had rejected. Generally speaking, Lutheranism and Calvinism agree in emphasising the total depravity of human nature and declaring concupiscence to be sin. On the main doctrinal issues, there is much in common with the Roman and Anglican Churches.

Zwingli (1484–1531) accepts the traditional belief that sin started with Adam's Fall, by which he lost his primal innocence – a fall that has affected all posterity. Yet the divine image is not completely lost. He interprets original sin more in terms of a disease (morbus est et condicio) rather than as guilt. Zwingli also took the traditional line in support of infant baptism by suggesting that it went back historically to the apostles. In theological terms, he linked it with circumcision in the Old Covenant. He deserted tradition, however, by rejecting any connection between the infant rite and original sin.[35]

In the 'Consultation' (to use the brief title) of Archbishop Hermann (1477–1552) of Cologne, there is a 'Form of Catechism' directed to 'all them that bring infants to holy baptism'. It begins: 'Beloved in Christ Jesus, we hear daily out of the Word of God . . . that all we from the Fall of Adam are conceived and born in sins, and that we are guilty of the wrath of God, and damned through the sin of Adam, except we be delivered by the death and merits of the Son of God.' The 'Administration of Baptism' in Hermann's 'Consultation' includes this prayer: 'Impute not to these infants the sin of Adam issued into them and engendered by their parents . . . but let the death and merit of Thy Son our Lord Jesus Christ prevail in them.'[36]

In his interpretation of Christ's blessing of the children in Matthew 19.13ff – said to be typical of the Church's approach – Calvin declares that since 'the whole race of Adam is shut up under the sentence of death, all from the least even to the greatest must perish, except those who are rescued by the only Redeemer.'[37] The Order of Baptism, drawn up by Calvin in 1542, included a 'Form of Prayers', in which a plea is made on behalf of an infant being baptized that God will receive him 'remitting to him the original sin of which the whole lineage of Adam is guilty.'[38]

Menno Simons (1496–1561) – a Dutch priest and founder of the Mennonite Sect – was interested to read of St Cyprian's approval of adult baptism, but other statements by the early Fathers sowed doubt in his mind. 'They taught me,' he said, 'that children are by baptism cleansed from original sin. I compared this idea with the Scriptures and found that it did violence to the blood of Christ.'[39] Reardon adds that Menno's objection to infant baptism, 'although reinforced by the argument that the presence of original sin in infants would seem to entail their damnation, is mainly founded on the absence of any explicit reference in the New Testament.'[40]

The Anglican Articles

Article 9 of the Anglican Formularies expressed a more pessimistic view of mankind than did the Council of Trent. Following Augustinian theology, the article says that 'the fault and corruption (depravatio) of the nature of every man, that naturally is engendered of the offspring of Adam, whereby man is very far gone from original righteousness and is of his own nature inclined to evil.' The article rejects the Pelagian view that the Fall made no impact on the human race. In the other extreme, however, it avoids the Calvinist view of total depravity. Logically speaking, of course, if man were totally corrupt, he would be incapable of recognising his corruption.

To quote the Article again: 'Original sin . . . is the fault and corruption of the nature of every man . . . and therefore in every person born into this world it deserveth God's wrath and damnation.' On this authoritative statement, Beasley-Murray comments that 'if forgiveness of sins in infant baptism is to be taken seriously, no less language than that will do, though no Anglican theologian will be found who subscribes to it . . . The logic of infant baptism is too cruel for modern man.'[41] In this matter, the 'Book of Common Prayer' serves only to endorse the Church of England Articles. Anglican approval of the doctrine of original sin, transmitted by generation, is explicitly stated in 'The Administration of Public Baptism of Infants' which begins: 'Forasmuch as all men are conceived and born in sin . . .' Moreover, as E. C. Whitaker points out, the 1662 'Book of Common Prayer' following that of 1549 includes prayers for the blessing of the font beginning: 'O merciful God, grant that the old Adam in these children, etc.'[42]

In the seventeenth century, Jeremy Taylor (1613–1667) argued that Adam's sin neither made us liable to damnation nor made us vicious. He rejected the view that unbaptized infants were damned as inconsistent with God's goodness. He denied that the loss of Adam's graces was a punishment of the human race, because it diminishes divine justice. He also did not believe that the Fall led to total depravity. Original sin is not an inherent evil, not sin in the strict sense. It is stain rather than sin. It involves the loss of supernatural endowments and encourages concupiscence.

E. B. Pusey (1800–1882), the leader of the Oxford Movement in the nineteenth century, wrote about original sin in his 'Village Sermons on the Baptismal Service', published in 1869. He says that 'although the guilt of our birth-sin was blotted out at our baptism, yet the sin itself remains like a spark from hell-fire within us, which may be fanned into a flame . . . While we are in the flesh, we are all fallen and corrupt, but the Holy Spirit entering in at baptism mends our nature and opens the door both of the church and the kingdom.'

In contrast, we consider the view of a Baptist minister, Henry Cook, who belongs to a very different school of sacramental belief. He says that the phrase 'original sin' 'calls for a good deal more definition than it generally gets from those who use it,' and that it must not be 'confused with original guilt, a very different thing. That human nature has a bias to sin we cannot doubt, but actual sin cannot exist until there is a self-conscious, self-determining personality to create it; and this an infant cannot possibly have.'[43]

We turn now to a Methodist minister, W. F. Flemington, whose denomination officially supports infant baptism. He writes that 'since an infant cannot be guilty of actual sin . . . the common solution was found in the doctrine of original sin – the baptism of infants purified them from the sin of which they were guilty through their membership of the human race. This teaching', says Flemington, 'is supported by a long and impressive tradition, but many Christians today find grave difficulty in accepting it.'[44]

The origin of evil

The story of the Fall, with its disastrous consequences, raises the prior question as to why God should create a situation in which this could happen. The origin of evil is a very perplexing problem – a problem which, as far as we are aware, no religion or philosophy has ever been able to solve. The reality of evil in a world created by a God, who is believed to be all-wise, all-loving and all-powerful, presents an irreconcilable dualism – a dualism which solves one theological difficulty only to give rise to another. We will say more about this issue later.

In pre-critical times, Genesis provided the historical cause of original sin; and Romans the Christian interpretation. But scholarly criticism shows that the Genesis account of the Fall of Adam is an aetiological myth. In an article on the Fall, Bruce Vawter says that 'in company with other Near Eastern myths of primordial man, it presents immortality not as a gift that has been lost, but as an opportunity missed.'[45] The story aims to show that it is imperfect humanity, not God, which accounts for the evil and hardship in the world.

Biblical criticism in the nineteenth century ruled out the historicity of the Adam and Eve story. Moreover, the increasing acceptance of evolutionary theories favoured belief in the ascent of man from a primeval state rather than his descent from a higher level of perfection. Christian theology in the nineteenth century tended to take an optimistic view of man's potential for good; but a more realistic estimate of man's moral and spiritual condition has taken over in the twentieth century, inclining some people to give a measure of credence to the idea of the Fall and original sin, though few theologians recognize inherited guilt.

Truth has many facets. The story of Adam is not less true because it is in the form of a Hebrew 'allegory' – to use Alan Richardson's word – rather than a historical fact. The Hebrew word 'Adam' (= 'dust of the earth') is not of course an individual's name; but 'man' as a collective noun, representing, in the mind of the Yahwist, the human race in its struggle to overcome its sinfulness and to find an explanation of how it came to possess this innate tendency to choose the wrong instead of the right, the bad instead of the good. It was this tortuous dilemma with which Paul grappled in his letter to the Romans.

Criticism has been levelled against the doctrine of original sin on a number of counts. For one thing: Is the phrase itself satisfactory? If 'sin' requires the exercise of free-will against God's law, then this requires personality – a conscious being, which inanimate nature does not possess. It can be argued that no impersonal thing can properly be called evil – only its misuse by a responsible person endowed with freedom of action.

Original sin, if such there be, is not 'an evil substance transmitted by inheritance in the same way as physical peculiarities are transmitted.'[46] In the light of this observation, can we accept Article IX's judgment that original sin 'deserves God's wrath and damnation'? Dr Bicknell adds that 'neither charity nor common sense allow us to suppose that an infant who cannot choose between good and evil is personally exposed to the wrath of God.'[47]

Attention has been drawn to the fact that we cannot inherit 'sin' properly understood; but we do inherit dispositions and tendencies that contribute to sin. Moreover, when it comes to determining the causes of sin, it is difficult to draw the line between the influences of heredity and environment. Pelagianism erred in over-emphasizing the individual at the expense of the societary element in human life.

One must also consider further, a point we have already mentioned, that in human history since primitive times man has 'risen' rather than 'fallen'. This is the view which anthropology and the theory of evolution would hold. Science cannot envisage any alternative to the 'ascent of man'. It is said that 'man has never possessed the original harmony of . . . an unfallen state . . . Sin is derived solely from the individual will and cannot be inborn; and the discord between flesh and spirit . . . is no sign of a bias to evil, but the inevitable outcome of man's development.'[48]

Science may indicate the source of our animal nature, but sin is surely set on the higher level of moral and rational life – the level at which man sins in 'missing the mark' (ἁμαρτία) in the exercise of his volitional freedom and power. Sin presents a problem well expressed and personally illustrated by St Paul: 'I delight in the law of God in my inmost self, but I see in my members another law at war with the law of my mind and making me captive to the law of sin which dwells in my members.' (Rom. 7.22).

Philosophy and original sin

What light does philosophy throw on the doctrine of original sin? We look at four important representative philosophers.[49]

Spinoza, in regarding evil as essentially negative, echoed the view of some of the Church Fathers, especially Augustine, who gleaned this idea from Greek philosophy and sought to harmonize it with Christian theology. Spinoza saw evil as faulty knowledge and with non-being. For him, evil was mere appearance and therefore an enquiry into original sin was irrelevant.

Nor is it easy to find a place in the philosophy of Leibniz for the orthodox view of original sin. In fact, he came near to denying, as did Spinoza, the reality of evil. Yet he accepted a form of the doctrine of original sin, similar to that of Tertullian, in which he regarded all souls as existing germinally in Adam.

Kant gave serious attention to original sin. He held that the ultimate seat of sin is in the will alone – as did certain of the early Fathers – and sought an individualistic explanation of inborn sinfulness. This tended to exaggerate the volitional factor in sinful activity and to ignore the real solidarity of the race. He taught that sin arises when the impulses of sense are followed rather than the dictates of reason. Its origin must lie in our freedom – otherwise it would not be sin.

Schleiermacher shifts the emphasis from physical to social heredity. The guilt of what he calls original sin attaches to an individual only in respect of his membership of a guilty race and his making the common sinfulness his own. This, however, blurs the line between inherited disposition and acquired habit. A theory, associated with Schleiermacher, sees the Fall as part of God's purpose. God created imperfect beings, knowing that they would fall; but he decreed this, so that they might develop morally into a mature personal relationship with him. And so earth became a 'vale of soul making'.

It is clear from this very brief and selective survey that philosophy affords little support for the church's traditional doctrine of original sin.

The problem of evil

We end this chapter by looking more closely at a difficulty we raised earlier – namely the problem of the origin of evil. The story of Adam and Eve takes for granted the existence of an evil agent – the 'serpent' or the 'Devil', as Milton has it in Paradise Lost. It is a sort of personification or force of evil working against God and his purposes for the human race. In other words, it presents an inexplicable and irreconcilable dualism. It is a dualism which offers a superficial solution as to how sin could enter God's world. But, at the same time, it leaves unanswered the vexed question as to how such an evil power or person ever came to exist, in the first place, in a universe created by a wholly righteous and omnipotent God.

Perhaps, as humans, we lack the 'category of thought' – to use Kant's perceptive phrase – by which alone this seemingly illogical impasse can be resolved. In Paul's language, we can know only 'in part' and see only 'in a riddle'. It is not possible or relevant to pursue this intriguing and baffling problem any further here, but it needs to be borne in mind that it is part of the larger framework in which should be set any serious consideration of original sin and the origin of evil.

CHAPTER NINE

The Essence and Effectiveness of Grace

It need hardly be said that the subject of grace, not least in relation to baptism, has given rise to much disputation over the centuries. Dr F. L. Cross defines grace as 'the supernatural assistance of God bestowed upon a rational being with a view to his sanctification. While the necessity of this aid is generally admitted, the manner of it has been a subject of discussion among Christians since the fourth century.'[1]

The study of grace goes back to Bible times. God's grace finds expression in the Hebrew words for 'favour' and 'loving-kindness'. It is a divine grace, bestowed on Israel whether or not they deserved or merited such favour. Every blessing stems from this source. The grace of God is traceable in the eighth century prophets, especially Amos and Hosea, in the writings of Deutero-Isaiah and in the Psalms. Yahweh's grace is revealed as powerful and wonderfully forgiving.

In the New Testament, the two Hebrew words are brought together in the Greek term 'Charis' (*χάρις*). The deeper meaning of *χάρις* in early Christianity – the unmerited divine love that stoops to bestow its favour and forgiveness – inherits its quality partly from the Old Testament; but its richest elements come from Christ's redeeming love. 'Charis' is not a word that Jesus uses; but its essence is exemplified in his life and teaching – a divine grace that is seen to be greater than human sinfulness and the powers of darkness.

The grace of God is manifest throughout the New Testament. It created the redeeming and spiritual atmosphere in which the early Christians lived and moved and had their being. Their missionary message was all of grace. They went forth, having been commended to the grace of God (Acts 14.16), with prayers at the throne of grace (Heb. 4.16). It is in the letters of St Paul where grace is most fully treated. The apostle could have said with Robert Robinson (1735–1790):

'O to grace how great a debtor
Daily I'm constrained to be!
Let that grace, Lord, like a fetter,
Bind my wandering heart to Thee.'

Paul made his indebtedness plain enough in his own words: 'By the grace of God I am what I am, and His grace towards me was not in vain. On the contrary, I worked harder than any of them, yet not I, but the grace of God which was in me.' (1 Cor. 15.10). By grace, he means the free love of God, directed to undeserving humanity. It is the source of salvation, of righteousness and of every good and perfect gift.

J. G. Davies sums it up by saying that 'χάρις cannot be detached from Jesus Christ; and, therefore, for Paul it is not an energizing principle nor an infused quality, but the loving-kindness of a personal God in action.'[2]

As we move from the Biblical evidence and see grace as interpreted in its historical and theological setting, we realize how various are the theories formulated to explain the nature and activities of this gift of God.

The Early Church

Tertullian was the first to formulate a doctrine of grace – for whom it was essentially a divine energy in the soul. Grace was prominent in the controversy between Augustine and Pelagius – their divergence of view centring on human nature. In Augustine, grace was essential and indispensable, since fallen man could only sin. Sometimes he identified grace with the gift of the Holy Spirit, at other times with the Spirit himself. Grace was not indefectible, because salvation required perseverance. It was, however, irresistible since it always achieved its end.[3] Yet, he held that grace did not obliterate human free-will and responsibility; and to clarify this he attempted to distinguish between prevenient grace, subsequent grace and efficacious grace.

For Karl Barth the cross of Christ was vividly reflected in the baptismal waters. God's grace revealed on Calvary overshadowed the font. He wrote: 'Christian baptism is in essence the representation of a man's renewal through his participation, by the power of the Holy Spirit, in the death and resurrection of Jesus Christ.'[4]

Raymond Burnish draws attention to Schmemann's conclusion that grace for the early church was so linked to their experience of

Christ that they did not think it necessary to define it – hence the difficulty in finding a definition of grace in the early Christian era. It followed that the understanding of grace changed and became, as he says, an 'essence in itself.' It was divorced from its form.[5]

It is pointed out that the Western Church defined grace as a created substance, distinct from God and the world. Though the Eastern Church regarded 'created grace' as heretical, Schmemann says that it adopted a similar theological approach. So an abstract 'grace' replaced the concrete 'event' as the theological focus of the sacrament; and the function of the 'form' was to assure its validity. This approach involved no interest in either death or resurrection and the real purpose of baptism is regarded as the endowment of grace upon the person baptized. Schmemann concludes that the sacraments have been transformed by this thinking into mere obligations without meaning, and have become an 'incomprehensible means' of an equally 'incomprehensible grace'.[6]

Pelagius apparently recognized the need of grace, but his definition differed greatly from the orthodox view. He interpreted grace, not as an indwelling divine power, but as instruction, enlightenment, freewill, reason or conscience. It is clear that Pelagius undervalued the sacraments. He wrote: 'We are not by nature, but by imitation, sons of God.'[7] Unlike Jerome and Augustine, Pelagius maintained that freedom to accept or reject God's law was given by grace. Even the Mosaic Law was a means and manifestation of grace.[8] Moreover, despite his emphasis on the autonomy of the will, Pelagius held that in divine forgiveness there is an unmerited gift of grace.[9]

Ambrose, Bishop of Milan, in the fourth century, seems to have regarded grace as an impersonal element or essence, which was communicated in some indefinable mechanical way. This understanding of grace was far removed from the New Testament's conception of grace in terms of the personal and prevenient love of God. A further deviation from Scripture is associated with St Thomas Aquinas in the thirteenth century. He taught the permanence of baptism, since it conveyed divine grace; but, in a sense alien to the New Testament, he interpreted God's grace in terms of an impersonal power transmitted through the sacraments.[10]

In his doctorate thesis, T. F. Torrance was led, as he studied the literature of the Apostolic Fathers, to consider how and why there arose a doctrine of grace different from that of the New Testament. Torrance expresses the firm conviction that 'the misunderstanding of the Gospel which took place as early as the second century, with the consequent relapse into non-Christian ideas, has resulted in a doctrine that is largely unbiblical and that has been only partially corrected by the work of Augustine and the Reformers. The great mistake has been to detach the thought of grace from the person of Jesus Christ.'[11]

Later in this published work, Torrance states that grace in the New Testament is the predominant factor in faith or it is not faith. He maintains that, in the Fathers, grace did not have this radical character. What took precedence was God's call to a new obedience to revealed truth. Grace was subsidiary to that. So religion was viewed as man's acts towards God rather than God's acts for man.[12]

Torrance sums up his examination of grace in the early Fathers by making three observations:

(1) Grace became related to the continuance of the Christian life rather than to God's love as the presupposition of the whole Christian experience.
(2) Grace was regarded as pneumatic and was associated with the Holy Spirit. But there was a parallel change in thought about the Holy Spirit. The Spirit had lost his connection with Christ and was regarded in a sub-personal way as pneumatic power (*δύναμις*). The early Christians lived in a demonic world of superstition and worship of the mysterious and the occult. So the Spirit of God was seen as the divine energy that overcomes evil powers. Grace was a spiritual energy within the heart of the believer. It was a pneumatic energy implanted in the soul. 'Thus the relation of grace and man came to be thought of sub-personally as cause and effect instead of as word and faith . . . This idea of grace as ghostly potency was not very different from the deifying *δύναμις* of Greek mythology or the mystery religions.'[13]
(3) The Church was considered the depository of pneumatic grace, which might be used in a sacramental way after the pattern of the mystery religions. The church possessed the means of grace. Ignatius (early second century) linked this with the episcopate. Grace resided in the Bishop and could be transferred through the Spirit by the church. *χάρις* fell into line with the current pneumatic tendencies in the Hellenistic world and so lapsed from its New Testament theological use into a psychological use. *χαρις* always had a sensuous substratum in Hellenic

thought and this tended to alter the doctrine of grace. It came to be regarded as a pneumatic and divinising power and at times was hypostasised and made into a distinct divine or supernatural entity.[14]

The tendency traceable in the early Fathers to put forward sacramental views, influenced by their pagan environment and alien to the general tenor of the New Testament, prompts Maurice Wiles to write: 'Sacramental language is inevitably dangerous language. That which is adequate to express the vital religious purpose of the sacrament is always in danger of falling over into superstition. The line between the two is not easy to draw. There are times when the Fathers do appear to cross that line; there are many more times when those who built upon their ideas in succeeding centuries have undoubtedly done so. The Fathers must bear their share of the blame, but not the full responsibility for those who came after them. Moreover, there is much of rich and positive value that could not have been there without that risk. Like the utterances of a prophet, you can remove the dangers from sacramental language and render it safe only at the cost of removing its great evocative power for good also.'[15]

Grace and magic

On another page, Wiles explains that the physical character of sacraments makes them vulnerable to the charge of making salvation available in a magical or automatic way. 'This is not a necessary concomitant of sacramental practice, though it is a real danger against which the sacramentalist has always to be on his guard.'[16]

In an article on Grace, A. S. Martin says that the Primitive Church did not regard the rite of baptism as magical or mechanical or ex opere operato and held that the visible elements and the ministerial action derive their validity from the Holy Spirit. Martin proceeds to point out, however, that 'soon pagan and superstitious elements were to enter in, to alter this free spiritual idea of sacramental grace into "another grace" altogether – a lapse from personal to sub-personal categories, in perfect consonance with the new and attractive idea of the church in its visibility and authority as the exclusive custodian of grace.'[17]

Whiteley ventures to raise the question as to whether there is anything 'magical' about St Paul's doctrine of baptism. He points out that 'magic' is a complex concept and 'shares with all forms of sacramentalism and ritual that it believes certain physical acts to have results which lie outside the sphere of normal physical causation; but to say that Pauline sacramentalism *shares* something with magic is not to say that it is "magical".' Whiteley further observes that the person being baptized, unlike the magician, does not compel an unseen power to act on his behalf. He is the recipient of a gift. Pauline baptism is closely identified with Christ and this is not typical of magical thought. Moreover, St Paul does not interpret baptism in terms of a mechanical act.[18]

Rudolf Bultmann expresses a more extreme view in no uncertain way. He is among the scholars who claim to trace pagan elements in the sacramentalism of the early Church. He holds that a sacrament involves supranatural powers that are bound to natural objects and to spoken words as their vehicles. 'If the conditions are fulfilled,' he says, 'the act . . . is itself a supranatural ceremony which works a miracle.' He concludes that 'it is clear that in earliest Christianity the sacrament was by no means a symbol, but a miracle-working rite.'[19]

Von Hugel says that 'magic begins only when and where things physical are taken to effect spiritual results apart altogether from minds transmitting or receiving.'[20] In scholarly circles, it is generally held that in 1 Cor. 10.1ff Paul gives clear warning against a magical – superstitious view of the sacraments and that 1 Peter 3.21 denies that external elements of baptism are its essence or its power.

It is said that the insistence in the early centuries on the objective efficacy of the sacrament of baptism is mainly the result of pagan presuppositions. It may be that no parts of the Christian ceremonial are borrowed from the mysteries, but the tendency to add to the solemnity of initiation, which is implied in the ceremonial development, is one of the characteristics of the mysteries. 'If the bestowal of grace through visible objects be a primitive Christian conception, the emphasis on the material means was largely evoked by pagan feeling . . . It may be doubted whether certainty about God for which men longed intensely could have been mediated . . . at that time except through . . . sacramental means of grace.'[21]

Dr C. Ryder Smith, formerly professor of theology at the University of London, and a supporter of infant baptism, writes as follows: 'If I understand the sacerdotalist answer aright, it asserts that by the act of baptism itself, if properly administered by a right person, grace is given to the child and by this grace it becomes a child of God. It seems to me', he says, 'that this doctrine has no warrant either in the New Testament or in psychology. I cannot but think that it crept into the church from the so-called mystery religions and other such heathen sources in the days when the church was far too susceptible to their influence. If the word "magical" be used in the popular and not in the scientific sense, it seems to me difficult to refuse it this concept. The doctrine has no analogies in the rest of human life . . . The only refuge for the theory . . . is to postulate a miracle in every baptism and to postulate it . . . in an outworn and non-Christian sense.'[22]

Various aspects of grace

Raymond Burnish points out that Schmemann has to define what he means by baptism because of the effect of centuries of theology which has separated the 'form' of what is done in baptism and the 'essence' of what the church believes to happen. He is concerned that much post-patristic theology fails to explain the relationship of baptism to the death and resurrection of Christ. While it is scriptural to define 'essence' as 'grace', Schmemann believed that the term 'grace' has become self-sufficient because of its identification with what the church believes to happen rather than what actually happens. In the apostolic church, the grace of baptism was linked to Christ's death and resurrection.[23]

Various aspects of grace, including its association with the Holy Spirit and with the baptismal water, appear in the Catechetical Lectures of Cyril of Jerusalem. He writes: 'Neither does he who is baptized, but has not been deemed worthy of the Spirit, possess perfect grace.'[24] As Burnish points out, Cyril referred to baptism in terms of grace or a free gift, and associated this baptismal grace with God's grace in forgiveness.[25] The idea of sacramental grace in the Catechetical Lectures was twofold – of water and the Holy Spirit – these two being inseparable in a valid baptism. 'It rests with God to bcstow gracc, but with you to accept and cherish it. Do not despise the grace because it is freely given.'[26] Cyril combined sacramental grace and prevenient grace.[27]

Another aspect of grace appears in the theology of Hugh of St Victor, leader of Catholic mysticism in the twelfth century. In his 'De sacramentis', he claimed that we had three organs of vision. (1) The natural eye; (2) The eye of reason; and (3) The eye of contemplation by which we see God. The first was not impaired by the Fall of Adam; the second was disturbed; and the third was destroyed. Happily, however, the eye of contemplation was restored by divine grace.[28]

Another feature of grace is brought out by Dr C. R. Smith. He says that 'some of the old theologians rightly used the word "grace" of the Godward side . . . and, to distinguish it from grace of other kinds, called it "prevenient grace". It comes in some degree to every man, whether baptized or not. The use of the word "grace", however, suggests the word "sin", for grace is love at work for sinful man.'[29] The idea of 'prevenient grace' – a grace that 'goes before' (praevenire) – appears in one of our Prayer Book Collects[30]: 'Lord, we pray that thy grace may always prevent and follow us and make us continually to be given to all good works.' In the Oxford Dictionary, 'prevenient grace' is defined as 'preceding repentance and predisposing the heart to seek God.'

The 'First World Conference on Faith and Order', held at Lausanne in 1927, 'decided to concentrate attention on the doctrine of grace and the problems connected with the ministry and the sacraments.' It was an agenda that would have commended itself in some respects to St Augustine of Hippo. He regarded the Catholic Church as the only channel of salvation and its sacraments and the means of grace as essential. Grace was given through the sacraments – hence his support for infant baptism. He accepted heretical baptism as valid, but he also believed that there was no salvation outside the church! He reconciled the seemingly irreconcilable by claiming that baptism (no matter who officiated) left an indelible mark, but that grace is received only when a believer baptized in schism is received into the Catholic Church by the imposition of hands. One is inclined to ask, however, whether or not some degree of grace was present when schismatic baptism imparted the indelible character. We are not alone in finding some elements of Augustinian doctrine difficult to understand or to defend.[31]

Freedom is seen by Augustine as dependent on grace – grace being regarded as an internal operation of the Holy Spirit that energizes the will and achieves good works. Grace overcomes the inner conflict between flesh and spirit. Augustine classifies grace as (1) prevenient; (2) co-operating; (3) sufficient; (4) efficient.

Let us now look at the problem presented by predestination in its relationship to grace. G. W. H. Lampe defines predestination as 'the foreknowledge of God and the fore-ordaining of the means by which those who are to be saved will be saved . . . Those who are elect can respond to the Gospel; the rest . . . cannot act upon it

. . . . It is given by grace to those who are predestined.'[32] Lampe points out that this attempt to push the logic of grace to extremes provoked a considerable reaction in the Early Western Church. The Eastern desert Fathers – Cassian and Vincent of Lerinum – interpreted the operation of grace in terms of assistance. Criticism was particularly directed to Augustine's doctrine of prevenient grace on which predestination depended. Some questionable support for the doctrine has been found in John 15.16: 'You did not choose me, but I chose you.'

Calvin held that 'when we cannot receive the sacraments of the church, the grace of God is not so inseparably annexed to them that we cannot obtain it by faith according to his word'.[33] Calvin's conviction here found expression in his condemnation of the baptism of infants in extremis.[34] He regarded this practice as unnecessary and superstitious. It was unnecessary because, as Calvin said, the child whom God has elected is assured of salvation whether or not he is baptized.

Richard Hooker (c. 1554–1600) questioned Calvin's claim that it was not essential for elected infants to be baptized. While Hooker did not consider that unbaptized children are necessarily eternally lost, he nevertheless referred to them as those 'whose safety we are not absolutely able to warrant.'[35] While many Anglicans held to the stricter view, there were those who, though appreciating the value of baptism, were reluctant to insist on its indispensability.

With these references to predestination in mind, we recall how Lampe, in his study 'The Seal of the Spirit' speaks of some writers who regard the seal as the inward stamp of the divine image by which the believer is recognized as one of the elect, the medium being baptism. He goes on to say that among the various patristic ideas of the seal are instances where the seal is the presence of the Holy Spirit or baptism itself.[36] Constantine the Deacon puts an imaginary speech into the mouth of the martyrs. It deals with the seal of the Spirit as a protection against evil forces and sets the sealing of the elect with Christ's blood alongside the marking of the door-posts with lamb's blood at the first passover in ancient Israel. (Exodus 12).[37]

Lampe points out that many patristic instances refer to baptism in water (the 'laver' or the 'font') as the medium of the sealing of believers with the Holy Spirit. It appears, therefore, that the seal means baptism in water, but in some cases it seems to refer to the whole rite of initiation, including the final consignation. Constantine referred to his baptism as a sealing and sees baptism in water as superseding all other channels in the complex rite and gives to the whole its meaning and title.[38] Since the seal was generally believed to be given in baptism, the words 'unbaptized' and 'unsealed' became interchangeable terms.

This evidence shows that the Fathers regarded baptism, not only as the means of receiving the seal, but itself as the seal which marks a person as belonging to Christ. The baptismal seal was viewed not merely as formal and mechanical, but as spiritual, an impress on the soul stamped by the Spirit of God, restoring man to the primal 'likeness', leading to an idea of the seal as an imprint on man of the 'imago Dei'.[39]

In a chapter dealing with 'The Disintegration of the New Testament Doctrine of the Seal of the Spirit', Lampe suggests that 'the increasingly widespread acceptance of infant baptism as a normal practice may have raised the question as to what gifts and graces the baptized infant might properly be said to have received.' Asking this question would itself tend to weaken 'the New Testament doctrine of the positive significance of the putting on of Christ in Baptism.'[40]

We conclude our consideration of the link between the seal and baptism by observing that from the third century onwards the terms 'σφϱαγις', 'signaculum' may mean any of the following: (1) The inward stamp of the Spirit on the Soul; (2) The impress of the imago Dei; (3) Baptism by which the inward stamp is received; (4) Unction by which the Spirit's presence is known; or, more often (5) The 'consignatio' with the sign of the cross.[41]

Our aim so far in this chapter has been to isolate grace, as far as that is possible, and to consider its nature and purpose. Let us now look briefly at its involvement in the sacraments generally, and then more fully at its connection with baptism in particular.

What is a Sacrament?

Perhaps we should remind ourselves of what a sacrament is – not forgetting, and certainly not despising, the well-known definition that a sacrament is 'an outward and visible sign of an inward and spiritual grace'. Gustaf Aulen says that the sacrament objectifies the Gospel. 'As pure actions the sacraments are nothing apart from the Word. But the sacrament serves as a guardian of the Word.' He adds that 'Evangelical theology speaks of the sacraments as a verbum visibile, a visible Word', but this is said to overstress the visual element and neglects the essential character of the sacraments, namely the action.[42]

Dr J. N. D. Kelly defines sacraments as 'those external rites, more precisely signs, which Christians believe convey, by Christ's appointment, an unseen sanctifying grace. Their number has been reckoned differently at different times . . . for which some circumstantial evidence survives from the second century.' While *μυστήριον* (Greek) and sacramentum (Latin) became the technical terms for a sacrament, there is no certain trace of their use before the time of the Alexandrian Fathers and Tertullian.[43] Bishop Colin Buchanan, in a booklet on 'Adult Baptism', points out that 'the defining of "seven sacraments" and the systematizing of "grace" attributable to each is usually traced to Peter Lombard in the twelfth century, though the fullest medieval elaboration came with Aquinas in the thirteenth.'[44]

This observation by Buchanan had been dealt with more fully by Williston Walker in his exposition of 'High Scholasticism and its Theology'. He says that the ancient view that all sacred actions were sacraments was qualified by Hugh of St Victor and Abelard, who ascribed sacramental quality to five ordinances, while Peter Lombard listed seven: baptism, confirmation, the Lord's Supper, penance, extreme unction, ordination and matrimony. Lombard held that all were instituted by Christ, directly or through the apostles and all convey grace from Christ. They were indispensable for union with God.[45] Beasley-Murray humorously assesses the difficulty when he says that the term 'sacrament' has lent itself to so many interpretations that 'it is like a nylon stretch-stocking: it can fit limbs of many shapes!'[46]

Our study of grace in this chapter calls for a clear understanding of what constitutes a valid sacrament. Whether we can meet this demand is, of course, another matter. As to the rite of baptism, it has been widely accepted over the centuries that water and the Trinitarian formula ensure the validity of the sacrament; despite the involvement of undesirable elements. In the minds of many, these 'undesirable elements' undermined the genuineness of the sacrament. This is illustrated by the colourful conflict between two distinguished bishops in the third century. Cyprian, Bishop of Carthage, rejected schismatic baptism by arguing: 'How can he who lacks the Spirit confer the Spirit's gifts?' The Donatists agreed with Cyprian, maintaining that the character of the officiant affected the value and soundness of the rite. To admit this, however, would undermine the validity of past-sacramental ritual and would make the efficacy of the rite depend on the administration. The reaction, therefore, of Stephen, the Bishop of Rome, was predictable. He maintained that the sacrament belongs, not to the church, but to Christ, and is validated, not by the worthiness of the officiant, but by the correctness of the form. The rite of baptism was of inherent value and efficacy. Half a century had to pass before agreement was reached – in favour of Rome.[47]

In later times, Augustine raised the subject of Schismatic baptism, insisting that, though it was validly performed, it did not convey salvation as long as the recipient remained outside the church. In this way, he preserved his belief in the objective efficacy of the sacrament and at the same time maintained his conviction that only in the church could baptismal grace ensure personal salvation.[48] Elsewhere, Augustine said that it was wrong for a layman to baptize when there is no urgent necessity, yet the baptism is valid.[49] This emphasizes the unimportance of the officiant and the all-importance of the ritual act. Augustine's teaching here regarding the relevance of the officiant's character to the conveying of God's grace was echoed by the Council of Trent in the sixteenth century. Article VII decreed: Administration by an authorised minister 'with the intention of doing what the church does' is mandatory, and even a minister in 'mortal sin' who observed all the essentials of the sacraments 'effects and conveys it'.

McGiffert points out that the nature and effects of baptism were settled long before the Middle Ages. The 'matter' was water, and the 'form' was in the name of the three Persons of the Trinity. Without this triune form, the sacrament was invalid. The officiant was generally the 'minister'. Heretical baptism was considered valid, provided the correct formula was used.[50] Writing also on the validity of the sacrament, but in a somewhat different way, Walker turns his attention to the Schoolmen and especially to Thomas Aquinas. He says that every sacrament consists of two elements defined in Aristotelian terms of form and water – a material portion (water, bread, etc.) and a formula conveying its sacred use ('I baptize you . . .' etc). The officiant must have the intention of doing what Christ and the Church appointed. The recipient – at least for one with years of discretion – must have a sincere desire to receive the benefits of the sacrament.[51]

Gustaf Aulen, under the heading of 'Misrepresentations of the Christian Idea of Baptism', mentioned two: (1) The interpretation which speaks of the effect of baptism as mechanical and deals in ideas below the spiritual plane; and (2) That which speaks of the human prerequisites for the reception of the grace of baptism in such a way that it abrogates the primacy of grace. On an earlier page, Aulen had written: 'Baptism reveals the character of divine love as spontaneous and prevenient: it is the sacrament of prevenient grace.'[52]

The Reformers did not see the gifts of grace as being inseparably connected with the outward form of the sacraments. They emphasised rather the subjective side of the rite, and the relevance of the Word for the believer. In this respect, Calvin was more emphatic than Luther. Calvin wrote: 'not that such graces are included and bound in the sacrament, so as to be conferred by its efficacy, but only that by this badge the Lord declares to us that He is pleased to bestow all these things upon us.'[53]

The Reformers and grace

Luther identified grace with the mercy of God revealed in Christ, a grace which sinners experience as forgiveness. To have faith is to have grace – wer glaubt, der hat. This divine favour, this grace of God, is conveyed by the Holy Spirit through the Word. The sacraments are efficacious signs of it. With seeming inconsistency, however, Luther goes beyond this and teaches that the sacraments convey an additional grace beyond that which is made ours in Christ. Yet for Luther, 'the certainty of forgiveness in Christ was for him the sum of religion.'[54]

The Administration of Baptism in Hermann's 'Consultation' requires the priest to say immediately after the child's baptism: 'The almighty everlasting God . . . who hath begotten thee again with water and the Holy Ghost and hath forgiven thee all thy sins, confirm thee with his grace unto everlasting life.'[55] In the form for the Public Baptism of Infants in the Book of Common Prayer (1549), the act of baptizing is followed by the giving of the chrisom: 'Take this white vesture for a token of the innocence which, by God's grace in this holy sacrament of baptism, is given unto thee.'

Another aspect of grace that we now need to consider is the question whether baptism as a means of grace is essential. Dr W. Walker says that the Reformation broke the dominance of the sacramental system which had controlled Christianity for many centuries. Baptism and the Lord's Supper were preserved and highly valued, but they were now regarded more as seals to the divine promises, not as exclusive channels of grace.[56]

Gustaf Aulen assesses the sacrament as a medium of divine grace in a somewhat similar way. For Aulen, to regard the baptismal rite as a means of grace does not deny that God's love could save in other ways. Faith does not ration the grace of God. The Reformers' emphasis on the Word was not intended to depreciate the sacraments. Christ is present in both. The sacraments do not mediate a special kind of grace, different from the grace that comes through the Word.[57]

During the Reformation, the sacraments apparently were not considered to be the only, or even the principal, means of grace. According to Harnack, the sacraments for Luther were not ranked higher than 'a peculiar form of the saving Word of God.'[58] Sacrament and preaching belonged together in wielding a comparable influence. Calvin, in the 'Institutes', deals first with prayer and faith, as though giving them priority, before he turns his attention to the Sacraments. This tendency is traceable also in Puritan dissent in distinction from most areas of Anglicanism. It is said that whereas the Puritans wanted sermons, Archbishop Laud preferred an altar. While not speaking for all Reformers, Calvin appeared to represent many of them when he wrote: 'It is an error to suppose that anything more is conferred by the sacraments than is offered by the Word of God and obtained by true faith . . . Assurance of salvation does not depend on participation in the sacraments, as if justification consisted in it. This, which is treasured up in Christ alone, we know to be communicated, not less by the preaching of the Gospel than by the seal of the sacrament, and it may be completely enjoyed without this seal.'[59]

Some of these views as to the channels along which the grace of God can be communicated are echoed in the 'Westminster Confession', drawn up by an Assembly of Divines in 1643–47. This 'Confession' stated that the efficacy of the sacraments did not depend on the piety of 'him that doth administer them' but upon the work of the Spirit. Baptism was to be administered only once to believers and their children; but it was made clear that 'grace and salvation are not so inseparably annexed unto baptism that no person can be regenerated or saved without it.'[60]

In chapter three, we looked at the question as to whether or not Cornelius was baptized (Acts 10). Critical scholarship has suggested that his being baptized was added to the text later by a redactor in order to regularize the story. It seems certain, however, that he received the gift of the Holy Spirit first – as Acts 10 states – a rare instance in the New Testament where the Spirit was received prior to water-baptism. On this episode, W. F. Flemington makes the significant comment that 'the grace of God is not bound by the observance of any particular ordinance.'[61]

Baptism – only a sign?

Mindful of our aim, stated earlier in this book, of attempting to make this an objective study – of a very subjective subject! – we consider now the important question whether baptism is simply a sign or symbol, or something much more substantial than that. Perhaps no question has given rise to more divisive answers. Let us look at some of the views held, in the hope of gaining a clearer understanding of what the rite essentially is and how it is related to the grace of God.

Augustine believed that a sacrament was a 'sacred sign' (signum sacrum) or 'the sign of a sacred thing' (signum rei sacrae). Some held that the sacraments were no more than 'signs'. Others maintained that they were 'efficacious signs' and imparted the grace which they signified. Peter Lombard defined the sacrament as the 'visible form of invisible grace'. He goes on to explain that a sacrament is properly so called because it is a sign of the grace of God and the form of invisible grace 'in the sense that it bears its image and exists as its cause.'[62]

Thomas Aquinas interpreted grace, not as a mystical experience nor as a personal influence, but as a substance. This meant that the sacrament, not simply symbolized grace, but contained and communicated it.[63]

In 1525 Ulrich Zwingli wrote a sentence that is said to sum up his doctrine of baptism: 'Baptism must be an outward sign that we have been engaged to a new life and incorporated in Christ'.[64] He rejected the view that the sacrament communicated the grace which it signifies.[65] For Zwingli, baptism was not in itself a means of grace or its ritual a necessity. It was no more than a covenant sign or symbol pledging discipleship. Baptism represented, but not effected, an inward change. It was a public testimony.

The symbolic view of baptism in the Reformed Churches has been encouraged by Calvin's definition of a sacrament as 'an external sign, by which the Lord seals on our consciences his promises of goodness towards us, in order to sustain the weakness of our faith;

and we in turn testify our piety towards him.'[66] Calvin also held that Baptism is primarily the sign and seal of the remission of sins and more than a mere outward mark. Yet the water has no inherent spiritual power, but serves mainly 'to fasten our minds on Christ alone'. The objectivity which Calvin attaches to the sacrament does not include any ex opere operato.[67]

Reference should be made here to what the Anglican Articles say on the sacraments. Article 25 states that the sacraments are 'not only badges or tokens of Christian men's profession', but they are 'effectual signs of grace'. Prof H. A. Woodhouse quotes Richard Hooker as saying that the sacraments have 'generative force and virtue', are 'visible signs of invisible grace' and are 'powerful instruments of God to eternal life'. This does not mean that they contain 'in themselves vital force or efficacy', for they are rather instruments of salvation. 'They really give what they promise and are what they signify'.[68] We need to bear in mind the words of Article 27: 'As by an instrument they that receive baptism rightly are grafted into the church. The promise of forgiveness of sin, and of our adoption to be the sons of God by the Holy Ghost are visibly signed and sealed; faith is confirmed, and grace increased by virtue of prayer unto God.'

Dr Beasley-Murray, a Baptist theologian, has written of his concern that members of his own Denomination have not always shown enough appreciation of the sacramental importance of Baptism – particularly in times past. In 1966, he quoted J. M. Ross, a Presbyterian layman, who after a study of Baptist theology, wrote that 'From about the middle of the seventeenth century until quite recent times, the main tendency of Baptist thought has been to regard this ordinance as having no more than symbolic value.'[69]

There is, however, more to be said on the positive side. On a later page, Beasley-Murray raises the question: Does anything happen to the baptized at his baptism? In reply, he says that one who is not a sacramentarian will say that the symbolism relates to events and spiritual processes independent of the act of baptism. Baptism is a witness, not a means of bestowal. The Baptist sees the sacrament as testifying to salvation already attained by faith; whereas the Paedobaptist stresses a future realization by faith of what has been vouched for by his sponsors.[70]

In order to give more 'substance', as it were, to his presentation of the baptismal rite, Beasley-Murray calls on H. J. Wotherspoon who writes: 'Whoever says sacrament says grace, for grace is the differentia of the sacrament, by which it is more than a symbol'.[71] Beasley-Murray says that he is bound to conclude that the understanding of baptism as 'a beautiful and expressive symbol' and nothing more, is irreconcilable with the New Testament. With some frankness, he adds that he hopes his Baptist brethren will now see this and appreciate that, as the hymn says, 'The Lord hath yet more light and truth to break forth from his Word'.[72]

With equal frankness, Neville Clark writes: 'If Paedobaptists have sown theological confusion by the introduction of infant baptism . . . the persistent myopia in respect to the prevenience of grace, so far as infant blessing is concerned, has been scarcely less disastrous . . . Paedo-baptist practice has made use of the wrong rite and Baptist practice has enshrined the wrong emphasis.'[73]

Before we move away from Baptist circles, let us consider A. C. Underwood's observation that believers can be 'carried beyond symbolism' to an experience in which God does something for them in response to their repentance and faith. They receive from him a further endowment of the Spirit and further power to walk in newness of life. 'It makes their surrender to Christ more absolute and enhances their union with him . . . and brings them a profounder experience of that divine grace they had already embraced by faith at their conversion.' Underwood acknowledges that baptism is more than a sign – a material medium used as a vehicle of God's grace.[74]

In support of his belief that 'a sacrament is more than a sign', John Macquarrie quotes the Anglican Article 25, which states that sacraments 'are not only badges or tokens' but 'effectual signs'. He points out that the word 'effectual' implies that the sacraments do not simply represent reality, but are themselves a part of the reality, the vehicle by which the reality comes to be, the means by which God works.[75] We conclude our study of this aspect of grace with a balanced statement by C. T. Craig: 'Sacrament and symbol need to be held together. Where the objective gift is emphasized, there is always the danger of falling into the misinterpretation of an automatic result. Where the symbolic nature is stressed, the tendency is to look upon baptism as a superfluous addition which supplies nothing important. A complete view of baptism will hold together symbol and sacrament and dissolve neither in the other.'[76]

It is said that, in the Middle Ages, Pope Innocent iii (1160–1216) believed that, as original sin was inherited by infants 'sine consensu', so they could be freed from it 'per vim sacramenti' before they were old enough to be aware of what was happening. Similarly, he thought that baptism would be effective if administered to men asleep or mad, provided they had previously shown an intention of receiving the sacrament. Only a definite resistance at the time of baptism could render it inoperative.[77] In a serious study like this, perhaps we are not permitted to smile!

The view that the baptismal rite itself effected a spiritual change in the person baptized led at times to the initiation of heathen people into the church simply by the act of baptism. This involved a lowering of Christian standards, not least in the case of the widespread practice of infant baptism, which was seldom followed up by 'the nurture and admonition of the Lord' and was often based on the belief in the mechanical and automatic power of the outward form to effect regeneration.

Grace and *ex opere operato*

Let us now focus our attention more directly on the belief that the baptismal rite has within itself the power to effect a change in the recipient summed up in the phrase 'ex opere operato'. This Latin phrase has been translated 'through the performance of the work' and has been contrasted with 'ex opere operantis', which means 'through the work of the performer'. In a comment which some people may regard as too limited or one-sided, Prof E. L. Mascall says: 'Although its meaning is often misunderstood, the purpose of the phrase is simply to emphasise that sacraments are primarily the acts of God and not of men; it does not deny the fact that the grace given in the sacrament will only be morally effective in the life of the recipient if he has the right dispositions and co-operates with it.'[78]

Aulen is more aware of the difficulties than Mascall appears to be. He says that from the beginning of Christian history difficulties have arisen regarding the mechanization connected with the sacramental idea. The most serious danger, he says, attaches to ex opere operato, i.e. the mere performance of the act. The theory is that sacraments work in a physical way; so that sacramental grace belongs to a level below personal and spiritual fellowship with God.[79]

In the 'Bull Exultate Deo' of 1439 and in the decrees of the Council of Trent (1545–1563), the sacraments are said to contain and confer grace ex opere operato, i.e. by the power of God at work in the sacrament. The baptismal rite is efficacious by virtue of what it inherently is and not because of the character of the administrator or the faith of the recipient.[80]

Dr Donald Lake points out that very early in the history of the Christian Church, baptism came to be regarded as a means of grace, or a sacrament, in the sense of an instrumental means of regeneration. Schism within the church and heresy outside compelled the church to consider and, if possible, to determine the validity of baptism. This discussion or contention – sometimes acrimonious and lacking Christian charity – has lingered on down the ages and is still with us, though now considerably 'sweetened' and qualified by ecumenical contacts. The arguments in the early church, intensified by the Novatian and Donatist controversies, gave rise to this concept, if not the phrase, ex opere operato.[81]

The Reformers tended to attach little value to the outward elements in the baptismal rite and to deny that the sacrament conferred grace ex opere operato. Luther at one time believed that grace is conveyed 'not certainly by the water, but by the Word of God, which is with and beside the water, and by the faith which trusts in such Word of God in the water.'[82] It should be borne in mind, however, that Luther, in order to counter over-much emphasis on feeling modified his earlier view by stressing 'the objectivity of the means of grace' and the outward element of water.[83]

John Calvin held that the sacrament could impart no benefit to the unbeliever. The Tridentine view that the right use of the elements conveyed grace upon all, without the recipient having the personal prerequisites of baptism, was not acceptable.[84] The Westminister Confession (1643–46) – a very influential Calvinist Creed – also states that 'the grace which is exhibited in and by the sacraments rightly used is not conferred by any power in them', but by 'the work of the Spirit and the word of institution which contains . . . a promise of Benefit to worthy receivers.'[85]

Dom David Knowles takes us back to Thomas Aquinas and his contemporaries, pointing out that one feature of sacramental grace was its certainty. 'With the sacraments the performance of the correct act, with the suitable inward disposition, gives certainty of the reception of sacramental grace, ex opere operato.' For Aquinas, this transaction is governed by a spiritual condition on the part of the recipient. 'The soul', says Knowles, 'if it is to receive actual sacramental grace, must be right in its relationship to God. Otherwise . . . the grace remains inoperant. The recipient, if not an infant, . . . explicit sorrow for sin is required.'[86]

We conclude our consideration of this aspect of sacramental grace with a brief observation by Jürgen Moltmann – a German theologian. Different as his doctrine is from that of Dr Knowles, yet there is common ground to be seen here. 'Baptism,' says Professor Moltmann, 'points to the liberation of man which took place once and for all in the death of Christ . . . In this context there can be no talk about the efficacy of baptism ex opere operato. Baptism is efficacious ex verbo vocante . . . It is a creative event, but it creates nothing without faith.'[87]

Grace and the baptismal water

Perhaps no element in the sacramental ritual has attracted more comment than the baptismal water. What is its precise relationship to the transmission of grace? This question has been variously answered in the past and in the present. Let us look at a representative selection of interpretations.

Ignatius, bishop of Antioch, early second century, wrote a letter to the church in Ephesus in which he says that Christ was baptized so that 'he might purify the water by his passion' (*τῷ πάθει*).[88] One interpretation of this statement is that it anticipates the death of Jesus and so gave a purifying quality to the water of baptism. This view finds support in the 'Excerpts of Theodotus': 'Regeneration is by water and spirit . . . For this reason the Saviour was baptized . . . in order that he might consecrate the whole water for those who were being regenerated'.[89] A. W. Argyle writes that 'here we see already the unscriptural teaching that the baptism of Jesus gave a mystical sanctifying potency to the baptismal water itself.'[90] He also points out that a similar explanation appears in the writings of Tertullian[91], Clement of Alexandria[92], and Ambrose[93], except that they trace the efficacy of the water, not to the cross of Christ, but to his sinlessness.

Tertullian appears to have been the first person to mention the consecration of the water. He eulogized the sanctified qualities of the baptismal water, which he held conferred eternal life.[94] According to Cyprian, the water must be sanctified by a priest who has the Holy Spirit;[95] while Cyril of Jerusalem speaks of the sacred efficacy of water, which has received the invocation of the three Persons in the Trinity. Cyril of Alexandria goes further and says: 'By means of the operation of the Spirit, the natural water (*αἰσθητον ὕδωϱ*) is transelemented to a quasi-divine and mysterious power.' Not surprisingly, the question has been raised as to whether Cyril here is teaching that the water is changed into a divine 'material'.[96]

On the origin of the blessing of the water, J. D. C. Fisher observes that 'the custom of formally consecrating the water to be used in baptism can be traced back to the time of Tertullian (AD c.200) and seems to have been introduced when the church ceased to baptize out of doors in living or 'running water'.[97] Fisher writes: 'In a somewhat harsh judgement G. R. Beasley-Murray says that Tertullian unwittingly links the saving efficacy of the baptismal waters with downright animism.'[98]

The long prayer in the Gelasian Sacramentary is designed to ensure the presence of the Holy Spirit: 'May the power of the Holy Spirit descend into all the water of this font and make the whole substance of this water fruitful with regenerating power.'[99] Fisher draws attention to some of the many ancient writers – Eastern and Western – who attribute the spiritual benefits of baptism to the effective presence of the Holy Spirit in the consecrated waters. Here are two testimonies: (1) Ambrose says, 'If there is any grace in the water, it is not through the nature of the water but through the presence of the Holy Spirit.'[100] (2) Cyril of Jerusalem wrote: 'Do not regard the laver as mere water, but regard the spiritual grace given with the water.'[101]

E. C. Whitaker, a recognized authority on baptismal liturgy, shows that from the time of Tertullian the blessing of the water was believed 'to invest it with power to effect the purposes of baptism which it did not otherwise possess.'[102] The elaborate prayers in the baptismal liturgy dwelt on the symbolism of water in all its rich variety and drew largely on the Old Testament for the imagery.[103] These prayers show that baptismal benefits come, not from the water itself, but from Christ's passion and resurrection. That is why the prayers liken baptismal water to the water that flowed out of Christ's side on the cross (John 19. 34). From the fourth century onwards, a baptismal prayer offered by the bishop asked that the Holy Spirit would 'give fecundity to the water, to purify the water and to dispense all evil spirits which might infest it.'[104]

In dealing with the baptismal rites in the fourth and fifth centuries, E. J. Yarnold refers to the blessing of the baptismal water. He writes: 'Although in an emergency ordinary water could presumably be used, proper practice required that the water should be consecrated.' Indeed it was commonly held that 'not all waters have a curative power; only that water has it which has the grace of

Christ.'[105] According to Chrysostom, it is the power of the Holy Spirit which makes the baptismal water effective.[106] The Emperor Constantine believed that his death-bed baptism – though inevitably an attenuated form – would remit his past sins 'through the efficacy of the mystical words (*λόγων ἀποῤῥήτων δυνάμει*) and the salutary waters of baptism.'[107]

From the sixth to the eighth century, the initiatory rite in Rome included the blessing of the font. It was believed that the consecration of the water was essential in order to convey the spiritual blessings and efficacy of the sacrament.[108]

With reference to the baptismal rite in the second Prayer Book of 1552, it is pointed out that after the opening exhortation there comes a revised version of the Flood-prayer, which, however, retains the statement that by his own baptism our Lord sanctified the flood Jordan and all the waters to the mystical washing away of sin, although Bucer had alleged that it was unscriptural and encouraged the 'superstitious belief that a kind of power of sanctifying in the waters is imposed upon the baptism of Christ.'[109]

In John Keble's view the efficacy of baptism largely depended on the consecration of the water. He also reiterated the belief that there was a causal connection between the baptism of Jesus and the sanctity of the baptismal water. 'We may consider it,' he says, 'as an act of our great high priest and saviour, applying by the church's prayer to the particular water that is in the font, the sanctifying virtue, which in His own baptism he had conferred upon all the waters of the earth.'[110]

Water-baptism and Spirit-baptism

In this chapter on sacramental grace, it is relevant to move on now and consider briefly the relationship between water-baptism and Spirit-baptism, though we shall have more to say about this in a later chapter.

G. W. H. Lampe in 'The Seal of the Spirit', held that 'water-baptism' and 'Spirit-baptism' were inseparably linked in the Apostolic Church. He writes: 'The indwelling presence of the Spirit, a Person and not a donum gratiae, is mediated to the believer through baptism as the sacrament of conversion.' Lampe questions the view that links the gift of the Spirit with confirmation and the laying-on of hands. In his Catechetical Lectures, Cyril of Jerusalem linked together baptism by water and baptism by the Spirit. In his own words: 'Baptism purges our sins and conveys to us the gift of the

Holy Spirit.'[111] According to Hans Conzelmann: 'From the beginning onward, baptism was administered and experienced as baptism of the Spirit.'[112] We need only add that this is not how many other theologians see it.

Dr J. R. C. Perkins is quoted as saying that for the Baptists of the eighteenth and nineteenth centuries the greatest problem lay in determining the relationship between baptism and the doctrine of the Holy Spirit. We appreciate their difficulty! This is said to have led them to a more 'sacramental' view of the rite. Some held that in baptism God really acts – a God-to-man rather than a man-to-God relationship.[113]

In the increasingly elaborate baptismal ritual, clearly designed for adults, in the 'Apostolic Tradition', it is stated that the bishop lays his hands on the candidates and prays for the Holy Spirit and grace to be given to the newly-baptized. Here it is plain that the Spirit and grace are endowments that follow the act of water-baptism rather than being concomitants of it.[114]

Attention has been drawn to the similarity in the theory and practice of baptism revealed by John Calvin and John Knox. For these two theologians water-baptism is a demonstration and proof of the benefits which God wills to confer rather than the instrumental means by which he confers them. In view of the prominence which Origen gave to the 'Name' in baptism, Lampe reckons that this early Father would agree that 'the Christian convert is marked with a seal of God's ownership through the invocation over him of the threefold name.'[115] According to Lampe, if Origen had studied the implications of the seal of the Spirit, he would have distinguished between water-baptism as a means of forgiveness and chrismation as an instrument of conferring the gift of the Spirit or the seal of the divine image – thus anticipating the views of later Fathers and of modern theologians of the Puller-Mason-Dix schools of thought.[116]

Our study of sacramental grace has made us aware of the indefinable relationship between what is 'outward and visible' and what is 'inward and spiritual'. It is clear that the more we delve into some religious mysteries the greater our empirical knowledge may become, but not necessarily our ability to give a rational explanation. As the Psalmist of old would say, it is so high we cannot attain unto it. Yet the very attempt to ponder the nature of the relationship in the baptismal rite between the object and subject, the material and non-material, the earthly and heavenly, serves to bring home to us the reality and effectiveness of the sacrament.

Grace has sometimes been interpreted as 'an indefinable power, and the Spirit, operating through this grace, as an indeterminable potentiality separated from Christ'. This has led to the conclusion that when the rite itself is solely regarded as producing the spiritual change in the person baptized, then there is a false objectivity. When exclusive attention is given to the change in the recipient of baptism, the result is a false subjectivity.

Professor Anthony Hanson has a relevant word for us here when he wrote that 'Christianity is an incarnational religion. This means that God does not repudiate matter, the visible, the sensible, space-time; but actually uses it as a means of manifesting and communicating himself.' D. M. Baillie quotes C. S. Lewis in this connection: 'God likes matter; he invented it'.[117]

It has been pointed out that, although the Jews did not separate the physical and the spiritual, as did the more dualistically minded Greeks, yet they did distinguish between the 'inward' and the 'outward'. A. W. Argyle holds that this biblical distinction must not be confused with the distinction between physical and non-physical, which the Bible does not separate. The 'outward' and 'inward' are disparate in a moral, not a metaphysical, sense.[118] Dr Whiteley draws attention to the fact that when we think of 'an outward and visible sign of an inward and spiritual grace' we tend to conjure up mental pictures of two realms of being, linked by some kind of psycho-physical parallelism. In Paul's doctrine of baptism there is a distinction, but no opposition, between 'outward' and 'inward', which for the apostle were harmonized in Christian baptism.[119]

In a chapter on 'Material, Spiritual and Sacramental', Gilmore says that some members of his Baptist Denomination have tended to minimize the connection between the material and spiritual world. Hence they are said to have undervalued the baptismal rite, preferring to regard it as an 'ordinance' rather than as a 'sacrament'. Gilmore writes of Baptists who have questioned whether God does anything at baptism. He quotes R. L. Child: 'Some good Baptists apparently think not. Indeed, at times, they almost give us the impression that they rather hope not'![120]

Henry Cook, in his book 'What Baptists Stand For', emphasizes the distinction between the spiritual and the material and states that the sacramental ritual is merely symbolic, and that Christ is found, not in the material elements, but in the soul of the believer. This prompts Gilmore to ask whether we should drive so big a wedge between the spiritual and the material.[121]

In replying to his own question, he makes the point that science no longer draws so firm a division between matter and spirit. In support of this view, he quotes Prof C. A. Coulson, who concludes that science today is seen by many as a religious activity.[122] Facts cannot be fully known and the observer cannot be completely independent of the thing he observes. Science and philosophy show that material things can properly be said to 'exist' only in so far as they impinge on the human spirit and perception. 'To the scientist the worlds of matter and spirit are not nearly so clearly distinguished as formerly.'[123] The closing of the gap between the material and the spiritual spheres appears to have had its effects in Christian circles and especially in an increasing appreciation of the sacraments.

Finally, we turn to the early Fathers to see what light they can throw on the relationship between the material and the spiritual in the sacramental means of grace. Maurice Wiles says that the Fathers never made the mistake of putting the whole weight of the positive meaning of the sacraments on the outward form alone. Baptism by itself could not save; it was not magic. Though they never regarded the outward form as sufficient, they nevertheless considered it absolutely necessary. Salvation was not secured by baptism alone, nor was it secured without it, except in the event of 'baptism in blood' (martyrdom) or 'baptism of desire'. The latter, though outside the visible church, was regarded as virtually equivalent to baptism and an anticipation of sacramental grace.[124]

Grace and infant baptism

Following what we have already said in this chapter about various aspects of grace in relation to the sacrament, we now consider the relevance of this to infant baptism. According to Gustaf Aulen, the infant rite is 'directly in line with the Gospel proclamation of grace.' He argues that those who reject the validity of this practice make the gracious will of God dependent on human qualification. The Reformers, to guard against mechanistic ideas, maintained that the gift of baptism was only through faith. But how does this relate to infants? Aulen offers the explanation that infant baptism is the act of election by divine grace – the 'objective' gift which exists before, and independently of, faith.[125]

It has been said that 'Luther thought that infant baptism best expressed the true relationship of the sinner to God in the matter of salvation. The helpless child symbolized how the grace of God alone saves man . . . Since he believed that man in matters of faith was absolutely helpless even as an adult . . . it was not difficult for him to accept infant baptism.'[126] Alongside this, we would recall the observation that, in order not to contradict his statement that sacraments could not confer grace without faith in the recipients, Luther held that infants could have faith! – but this involves an objective efficaciousness inconsistent with his previous insistence on personal faith.[127]

In support of infant baptism, Calvin uses the story of Jesus blessing the children (Mat. 19) to show how the grace of Christ is conveyed to children – thus rescuing them from the peril imposed upon them by Adam's transmitted sin. 'To exclude from the grace of redemption', he says, 'those who are of that age would be cruel . . . And if they were partakers of the spiritual gifts, which are represented by baptism, it is unreasonable that they should be deprived of the outward act.'[128] Basing his baptismal teaching on 'the priority of grace', Calvin ruled out Luther's 'colourful speculations about the unborn baby's spiritual capacity' and the Anabaptist stress on pre-baptismal Christian experience.

It is God, says John Macquarrie, who takes the initiative in reconciliation and grace – an act of divine love which can involve infants without their being conscious of it. 'Moreover, as the child's life is moulded by divine grace mediated through the community of faith, he enters into the vocation of the Christian . . .'[129] Dr Bethune-Baker draws attention to the fact that this passivity in the person baptized appeared in Augustine's teaching when he maintained that an infant in baptism is a passive recipient of grace – grace which is 'irresistible and indefectible, but which enables the will to choose the good.'[130]

This reference to Augustine reminds us how, in his Confessions, leaving aside the problem and peril of post-baptismal sin, he reflects on whether it would have been better if his mother, Monica, had agreed to his being baptized as an infant. His reflections on this hypothetical question incline him to the view that baptism in infancy would have endowed him with the divine grace by which he could have lived a better life and resisted evil ways.

The idea that infant helplessness reveals the necessity and enabling power of God's grace is touched upon by W. F. Flemington. He writes: 'The sacrament of baptism is "verbum visibile", the Gospel manifest in action, and pre-eminently so when the subject of baptism is an infant. The very helplessness of the child, when seen against the whole background of this sacrament of the Gospel, is eloquent of man's universal need for the divine grace and of the answer God has made to that need in Christ.' Flemington concedes, however, that this need of divine grace and the recognition of how Christ meets that need 'are not things of which an infant can . . . himself be conscious.' That does not mean, however, that infant baptism has no direct significance for the subject of the rite.[131]

Jürgen Moltmann points out that Karl Barth 'has stressed the saving event completed and perfected in Christ, thus denying to baptism the character of a means of salvation which is sacramental, or necessary for salvation, or which supplements or prolongs salvation.' It is this cognitive element involved which leads Barth to reject infant baptism in favour of the baptism of believers.[132] Heinrich Schlier differs from Barth and holds that baptism is a sacramental action, which effects the salvation of the person baptized. It is instrumental in bringing about what it symbolizes. Schlier maintains that baptism is a necessary means of salvation, and that it is therefore essential to include infants.[133]

It is argued by R. E. O. White that if infant baptism is held to bring the infant within the kingdom of God, to initiate him into the sphere where grace operates, to impart spiritual life or regenerate the soul, 'then plainly the whole of Christ's teaching on the conditions of discipleship and the way into life is rejected.'[134] In support, P. T. Forsyth is quoted as saying that it is 'as if baptism made a soul a Christian at some subliminal depth.'[135]

It seems to us that the elements of truth in White's interpretation as to the essence and validity of baptism suffers from imbalance and over-statement. An assessment of his reasoning and conclusions might be made in the light of our study in earlier chapters, not least in chapter three dealing with the question of infant baptism in the New Testament and particularly in our consideration of grace in this chapter.

Moreover, we should not overlook the fact that on an earlier page White himself offers a more satisfactory interpretation of the baptism of Jesus. He writes: 'The descent of the Spirit in the baptism of Jesus marks a supreme turning point in the development of the Christian rite. From this moment, the negative, ritual, purificatory aspect of Jewish and Johannine baptism is overlaid with the positive and enriching character of Christ's baptism. The renunciation of the past is taken up into the reception of grace and power for the future; and the rite which had expressed mainly what man does to fulfil God's will, becomes now also a rite expressing something God does to make man's obedience effective.'[136]

CHAPTER TEN

Relating Repentance and Faith to Infant Baptism

The World Council of Churches in 1982 in a study of 'Baptism, Eucharist and Ministry', issued a Faith and Order Paper which stated that 'while the possibility that infant baptism was also practised in the Apostolic Age cannot be excluded, baptism upon personal confession of faith is the most clearly attested pattern of the New Testament documents.'[1]

Beasley-Murray says that several years ago he was assigned the task, in an ecumenical Faith and Order group, of investigating the relation of baptism to faith – and adds humorously that it was 'a dangerous assignment to hand to a Baptist!' The line that he took was to tabulate the associations of baptism in the New Testament writings and those of faith and see to what extent there was a correlation between the two. He considered the Biblical evidence that linked, first baptism then faith, to (1) forgiveness, (2) union with Christ, (3) possession of the Holy Spirit, (4) membership in the church, and (5) inheritance of the Kingdom of God.

From this study of the Scripture correlation of baptism and faith, Beasley-Murray drew the conclusion that 'God's gift to baptism and to faith is one . . . There is no question of His giving one part in baptism and another to faith. He gives *all* in baptism and *all* to faith . . . It is all of God, who brings a man to faith and to baptism.'[2]

The New Testament

According to Dr N. P. Williams, formerly professor of theology at Oxford, 'We have originally in the New Testament only adult and believers' baptism. Baptism takes place upon the confession of personal faith.'[3] In another book, Williams maintains that the scriptural references to initiation assume that the recipients are adults who have consciously and deliberately renounced sin and have professed personal faith in Christ.[4]

W. F. Flemington interprets Baptism in the New Testament in terms of the proclamation of the Word – the 'kerygma in action' –

an objective interpretation designed to show the relation between baptism and faith. References to baptism in Acts are nearly always connected with 'hearing the word' or 'believing'. Men are able to believe only because they have first 'heard' or 'received the word'. The 'Word of the Gospel' is expressed and made visible in baptism.[5] But it is argued that if baptism is the 'kerygma in action', then it should be received as the kerygma is received, namely in faith.

As for the view that 'baptism conveys its grace independently of faith', Dr Beasley-Murray points out that this is not acceptable to any of the Protestant traditions.[6] This view prompted the attempts to find a place for faith in infant baptism, either in the infant himself or in the sponsors or in the church. Beasley-Murray also observes that there is ample evidence in the New Testament that the Gospel of grace calls for faith and is effective through faith. He points out that in the Apostolic church 'the response of faith was made in baptism . . . an embodiment of the whole Gospel – of grace and faith alike. This, he says, infant baptism can never be.'[7]

It is maintained that if baptism involves 'repentance and faith, acceptance and surrender, then it is . . . congruous with the whole message of the Master, and . . . such baptism carries His authority and inherits His promise.'[8] 'It seems incredible,' exclaims R. E. White, 'that the church should ever be found denying, or obscuring for a moment, these conditions of repentance and faith so clearly enunciated by Jesus – yet such a denial is a commonplace of paedobaptist apologetic.'[9]

In weighing White's argument, we need to bear in mind that nowhere in the Gospels does Jesus directly link repentance with baptism. The only place where he combines faith with baptism is in Mark 16.16: 'He who believes and is baptized will be saved'; but, as textual criticism makes plain, this verse was not originally part of Mark's Gospel. Moreover, as we saw in chapter three, there is little in the Gospels that associates Jesus with baptism itself either in his teaching or practice. Even Matthew 28.19, with its Trinitarian formula, lacks corroboration in the rest of the New Testament.

Lampe sees a significant connection between the baptismal rite and the baptism of Christ. He says that 'baptism is a sacramental rite which looks back to the Messiah-Servant baptism of Jesus . . . the external symbol through which the atoning work of Christ was applied to the believer . . . and in the union with Christ effected by faith . . . he found the realisation of the forgiveness of sins.'[10]

Turning now to the Book of Acts, K. W. Noakes suggests that

the author intended the imperative of Peter's command in 2.38 – 'Repent and be baptized . . . and you will receive the gift of the Holy Spirit' – to establish the pattern and norm for entry into the church. He writes: 'There are three important and directly related elements in this process of entry into the church: repentance, baptism in water and reception of the Spirit.'[11] One wonders how Noakes would relate these elements to infant baptism.

According to the 'Acts of the Apostles', the Samaritans were baptized in water without receiving the Holy Spirit (Acts 8) and Cornelius and his relatives and friends were baptized in Spirit without being baptized in water (Acts 10). But, in an attempt to explain this divergence, it is said that they are different aspects of one great initiation complex which includes the inward attitudes of repentance and faith; the outward marks of water baptism and the laying-on of hands; and the declaration by God of sins forgiven and heart renewal.[12]

John Macquarrie says that 'baptism includes the moments described . . . as conviction of sin and repentance.' He adds that it is clear from the evidence in the early chapters of Acts that the Christian baptismal rite resembles the baptism given by St John the Baptist in being a baptism of repentance for the remission of sins.[13]

Flemington also gives close attention to the Book of Acts and draws attention to much evidence in which Christian belief and baptism are linked.[14] After St Paul's encounter with Christ and his conversion experience, the Apostle finds himself in Damascus. There Ananias lays his hands on him – an administration by which Paul regains his sight and receives the Holy Spirit. It is significant that on this occasion baptism is preceded not only by a belief in, and experience of, Christ but also by the gift of the Holy Spirit. Elsewhere this endowment of the Spirit usually either accompanies or follows baptism.

Turning to another episode in Acts, we note that the Western Text inserts a verse (37) into chapter eight, which reads: 'And Philip said, If you believe with all your heart, you may' (be baptized). 'And he replied, I believe that Jesus Christ is the Son of God.' It is widely held that this verse does not belong to the original account of the conversation between Philip and the Ethiopian 'on the road that goes down from Jerusalem to Gaza'. But given that it is not part of the original text, it does at least show that, at the time of the interpolation, belief in Christ was held to be an essential prerequisite of baptism.

The reference in the New Testament to baptism 'in the name of Jesus' has led scholars to suggest that here we have the beginnings of later credal statements and catechismal instruction. Such passages as 1 Peter 3, 18–22 are thought to be the source of credal elaboration in baptismal confession, leading to the view that the first part of 1 Peter might have been a baptismal homily. An embryonic form of baptismal confession is held to be traceable in such New Testament references as Eph. 5.26, Heb. 4.14, 10.23, and 1 Tim. 6.12. The author of Hebrews also speaks of two complementary aspects of baptism, inward and outward – aspects we observed in the previous chapter; 'Let us draw near with a true heart in full assurance of faith, with our hearts sprinkled clean from an evil conscience and our bodies washed with pure water'(10.22).

The inward and outward of Christian initiation are made clear in Gal. 3.26f 'In Christ Jesus you are all sons of God through faith. For as many of you as were baptized into Christ have put on Christ.' As W. H. P. Hatch observes, 'faith and baptism . . . constitute a single act of which faith is the subjective and baptism the objective side.'[15] This scriptural evidence is taken to imply that the recipients of baptism were required to have faith in Christ as a prerequisite of Christian initiation.

With reference to Rom. 10.9, 10, it is pointed out that its significance lies in the widely held view that its summary of the Christian confession as 'Jesus is Lord' is taken from an early baptismal confession made by a candidate for baptism. Rom. 6, 1–11 has been interpreted in a somewhat similar way. It is suggested that 'Do you not know' in verse 3 implies that Roman Christians knew that baptism meant into Christ's death and that the use of 'we' implies the existence of a confession. It is also held that the words 'raised from the dead by the glory of the Father' are not Pauline language, but are derived from a confession. With reference to Rom. 6, Beasley-Murray says that 'this chapter has the convert in mind and all that Paul says of baptism presumes a faith responsive to the grace of God operative in it.' On a later page, he writes: 'When we consider the existential nature of baptism as described by Paul and the importance of faith for its efficacy . . . on the basis of Paul's own declarations, the idea of baptizing infants involves a departure from his baptismal theology'.[16]

The leading question is whether grace is dependent on faith or whether it is the other way round. Two reasons are put forward for not regarding faith as a condition for the reception of grace, namely:

(1) Laying down conditions for receiving grace and salvation makes the Gospel too legalistic. (2) Faith cannot be produced by man, it is God's gift. In reply, we recall how Paul pronounced faith the only condition of salvation as opposed to works. Romans 3.23ff says that sinners are saved by the gift of God's grace mediated through the cross of Christ – 'an expiation by his blood, to be received by faith' (RSV), or, keeping closer to the Greek, 'an expiation through faith in his blood' (*ἱλαστήριον δια πίστεως ἐν τῳ αὐτοῦ αἵματι*). This makes clear the necessity of faith – at least in Pauline theology.

It would appear that Judaism demanded from proselytes both faith and repentance and that this background of religious thought and experience was related to the message of John the Baptist and Jesus. According to Luke, John sternly challenged the crowds that came to be baptized, with the words: 'Bear fruits that befit repentance' (3.8). St Mark's account is unusually smooth and mild; 'John the baptizer appeared in the wilderness, preaching a baptism of repentance for the forgiveness of sins.' (1.4). Jesus, while not mentioning baptism, began his ministry with the exhortation: 'Repent, and believe in the Gospel' (Mark 1.15).

Some who subscribe to the view that baptism is the 'kerygma in action' may perhaps see here in the word 'Gospel' an implication of the baptismal rite. It seems to us, however, that in this verse the link between Gospel and baptism is too slender a thread to carry this interpretation.

The Early Church

Michael Ramsey, formally Archbishop of Canterbury, pointed out that it was the practice of the Apostolic church to admit adults into the Christian society and by the closely linked rites of baptism and confirmation through faith to receive the Holy Spirit. Ramsey adds: 'The church must be loyal to this apostolic fact in its totality, including the words "through faith".'[17]

Erich Dinkler says that in the early church, following the resurrection of Christ and the delay in the parousia, the sacramental meaning of baptism became no longer exclusively dependent on the recipient's faith, but attained 'a quality in itself as a magically operative rite.' He says that this development begins as early as the time of Luke's 'Acts' and is influenced in general by Gnostic-Christian practice. It is referred to in Hermas.[18] Dinkler points out that faith in Christ is no longer the only 'conditio sine qua non', but is seen as an outcome of baptism. As soon as this was acknowledged, infant baptism had its dogmatic justification.[19]

D. F. Neil expresses the view that, for the early church, baptism developed from belief in Christ – an experience which included the four stages of repentance, faith, baptism and incorporation into the 'body of Christ'. Neil stresses the connection between faith and baptism by using Denney's well-known words: 'Baptism and faith are but the outside and inside of the same thing.'[20]

The teaching of Irenaeus appears to assume believers' baptism. The recipient is expected to have faith and to be a committed Christian. At baptism, the candidate receives the Rule of Truth – the confession of Christian belief at baptism – a confession involving the Trinity, the incarnation, passion and resurrection.[21]

A fuller description of the early baptismal rite, in which faith features, is given by E. C. Whitaker. He points out that in the account contained in Tertullian's 'Treatise Concerning Baptism' and Hippolytus's 'The Apostolic Tradition', when the candidate entered the water, he was questioned in the triple interrogation on the faith, out of which the Apostles' Creed was later to grow, and to each question he answered: I believe. After each response the deacon laid his hand on the candidate's head and baptized him in the water. We note that no form of words is provided other than the credal interrogation and its responses. This was to be the way in the Western church for some years. The formula which is familiar to us today was introduced into the West from the Syrian Church only gradually over the centuries.[22]

In the fourth century, we find bishop Basil the Great, of Caesarea, saying that we are saved by faith and by regeneration effected by grace conveyed in baptism. He held that faith and baptism are two ways of salvation, cognate to one another and inseparable.[23] Raymond Burnish says that the relationship between baptism and faith in the fourth century came across in the stress which was put on the need for the candidate to be sincere about his desire for baptism. He then adds that 'the faith of the candidate was plainly the gift of the grace of God and the candidate had to affirm his faith in, and commitment to, Christ before he was baptized.'[24]

However much the necessity of faith in baptism may have been widely recognised in theory, there were divergences in practice. As Herbert Wood put it: 'The church opened her doors to infant and Barbarian, partly because only so could she influence them, and partly because she believed that baptism could of itself confer benefits before faith was instructed or even existent.'[25] This opening of her doors by the church – judged by many nowadays as indiscriminate baptism – could not have commended itself to St Cyril of Jerusalem who, in his Catechetical Lectures, warns candidates for baptism against hypocrisy and makes clear the need for faith. He says, 'If you pretend, men will indeed baptize you, but the Spirit will not baptize you. If you approach with faith, men will minister to you visibly, but the Holy Spirit will bestow upon you what is not visible.'[26]

The prerequisites of baptism

Maurice Wiles, in his book on The Early Fathers, points out that Cyril of Jerusalem, lecturing to his catechumens, recalls the story of Simon Magus (Acts 8. 13–24) to illustrate the uselessness of baptism where the heart is not right. Wiles says that when the Fathers speak of the saving power of baptism, it is never the bare rite that they mean; it is baptism and faith together as an inseparable unity which they intend. This point is re-iterated by Maurice Wiles on a later page. He writes: 'Sign and meaning belong together. It is the unity of baptism and faith with which the Fathers are primarily concerned.' Wiles adds the qualification, however, that in practice the two have not always gone together. 'It is this fact which lies at the root of so many of the problems we encounter in trying to think clearly about the sacraments.'[27]

Following our reference to the Paulicians in chapter five, it is relevant to recall here that a sect holding Paulician beliefs settled in Russian Armenia in 1828, having the manual The Key of Truth, which claimed to date back a thousand years. This 'key' refers to three divine mysteries – repentance, baptism and holy communion. 'These three He gave to adults and not to catechumens, who have not repented or are unbelieving.'[28] The Paulicians condemned the baptism of non-Christian adults and infants who were unable to have a personal belief. This means that they rejected infant baptism and urged believers' baptism, preferably for people aged thirty – the age when it was thought Jesus was baptized.

The Anabaptist Movement, which began in 1523 in Zurich, arose as a result of the questioning by the Reformation of the traditional interpretation and practice of baptism. The Anabaptists regarded 'believers' baptism' as the only way into the Christian life. Bernard Reardon says that they attached no sacramental meaning to baptism and that they laid less emphasis on the positive attestation of faith –

even on the capacity to believe – than on repentance and the need for forgiveness.[29]

With reference to early Protestant baptismal theology, Jürgen Moltmann says that when the efficacy of baptism is based on its performance in accordance with its ordinance, when non-resistance is presupposed on the recipient's part, when we speak of the vicarious efficacy of the faith of the parents or of the church, or even about a 'seed of faith' in infants – then this sacramental objectivism is ministering to the practice of infant baptism. 'For this practice,' reasons Moltmann, 'requires the proof that baptism can not only follow on faith but that it can also precede faith and the profession of faith and can bring about both.'[30]

Gustaf Aulen observes that in order to avoid the mechanistic ideas associated with baptism, the Reformers insisted that baptism is valid only if received in, and through, faith. He recognizes that difficulties arose when this requirement was applied to infant baptism, influenced by the one-time view of Luther that some form of faith in the child validated the infant rite. This idea, however, led back to 'those conceptions, below the personal and spiritual level, which it was intended to avoid – even in the most sensitive matter of all, namely the concept of faith itself.'[31]

Luther is believed to have valued the sacraments mainly for two reasons: (1) First as a safeguard against legalistic attempts to achieve salvation; and (2) Secondly to counter over-much stress on inward experience.[32] Fisher says that Luther considered that the form of baptism was of far less importance than the faith of the person to be baptized. Luther maintained that 'the virtue of baptism lies not so much in the faith or practice of the administrator as in the recipient.'[33] Fisher goes on to state that Luther put a new emphasis on the subjective element in the reception of the sacraments, the efficacy of which depended on the recipient's faith in the divine word of promise. To quote Luther again: 'The sacraments are not fulfilled by the ritual, but only when they are believed . . . When faith is indubitably present, they most assuredly and effectively impart grace.'[34]

In Luther's thought, the Word constituted the sacrament; but in the absence of personal faith the benefits of sacraments are lost, because they are not perceived by the senses or provable by reason. It followed, therefore, that for Luther faith was essential to sacramental efficacy. As Gilmore shows, Luther used faith in two senses: (1) Historic faith or what we believe; and (2) Saving faith, by which the believer is one with Christ. It is not clear how Luther related this second meaning of faith to infant baptism, which he supported partly because the infant rite revealed our utter dependence on God. And since his theology of baptism required faith in the recipient, it followed that faith must somehow be found in the child.[35]

Central in the teaching Luther and Zwingli was God's grace in Christ, received by the exercise of the believer's faith. This tenet is seen in their sacramental theology. Luther, in his 'Concerning the Babylonian Captivity of the Church' (1520), shows how God's endowments are dependent on the recipient's faith.[36] This emphasis on personal faith, as an essential qualification, was more evident in their approach to the eucharist than to baptism. Hence their hesitant acceptance of the infant rite – a reluctance more particularly applicable to Zwingli.

Infant baptism – a dilemma

Infant baptism for Zwingli was indeed a dilemma. He was in two minds. In his 18th Article, he refers to a time when those who were baptized had previously been instructed in Christian belief and confessed their faith.[37] Bucer, a Strasbourg Reformer and theologian, held that the sacrament had instrumental efficacy, but dependent on the recipient's faith. Calvin, who theologically speaking had sat at Bucer's feet, also believed that the sacrament was a means of grace in which repentance and faith were essential. By faith, Calvin meant the intellectual acceptance of Christ as Redeemer, leading to trust in God's salvation, without interpreting faith as a purely human entity.[38] He saw repentance as conversion to God from fear. Calvin held that repentance and faith were inseparable and were the work of the Holy Spirit. He believed that our salvation was entirely due to God's initiative. The recipient's awareness of this makes Calvin's recognition of infant baptism all the more inexplicable. The explanation is that he and other Reformers combined two incompatible elements. They believed infant baptism need not undermine the link between faith and baptism.[39] Calvin taught that 'baptism gave man an assurance of pardon and of participation in the gifts of Christ, but that it was efficacious only for the elect, since they alone have the faith without which the rite is worthless'.[40]

Reardon draws attention to the Dutch theologian, Menno Simons, who in the first half of the sixteenth century taught that faith does not follow from baptism, but baptism follows from faith.[41] Menno opposed infant baptism partly because faith cannot be received by infants; to confer baptism upon 'those who at birth have less sense than irrational creatures is as idolatrous as it is futile.'[42]

Oscar Cullmann relates faith to baptism in three ways: (1) Faith must be present *after* baptism; (2) Adults are required to exhibit faith *before* baptism; and (3) Baptism must be accompanied by the faith of the congregation, which Cullmann considered to be essential in any valid baptism.[43]

Cullmann supported the view that baptism was vicarious and this view is used to support infant baptism. The baptism of Jesus was 'an initiation into his passion' – vicarious sinbearing – a general baptism which we can enter by individual baptism. It is argued that as Christ's vicarious baptism was accomplished prior to, and apart from, our faith or response, it can therefore be applied to infants *before* they have faith or understanding.[44] This interpretation has been deemed forced and illogical. There does not appear to be any evidence or support for this idea in the New Testament.[45] It would be reasonable to ask – if Christ's baptism was vicarious – why do we need to be baptized?

We must not overlook the fact, however, that Cullmann did recognize a connection between faith and baptism, but it was post-baptism faith as far as infants were concerned. In the case of adults, faith is required before baptism as well.[46] And, as we saw in the previous chapter, personal faith whether before or after baptism is widely regarded as being preceded by prevenient grace. So the initiative is God's; and once again we are made aware of the seemingly inexplicable or irreconcilable dichotomy of determinism and free will, with the related theological concept of divine election.

P. T. Forsyth (1848–1921) maintains that believers' baptism and infant baptism, despite differences, have in common the Word and its setting in a faithful church. He held that believers' baptism is baptism *on* faith, whereas infant baptism is baptism *unto* faith, yet each of these two rites is validated by faith alone.[47]

Daniel Jenkins offers a carefully reasoned defence of infant baptism in which he considers Karl Barth's rejection of the rite. He argues that Barth's disapproval of re-baptism implies that he recognized his own baptism as an infant as having some validity and that this recognition was inconsistent – 'inconsistent because, if the infant lacks faith the rite is meaningless, so that no repetition is involved if he is "properly" baptized when he makes the profession of faith in maturity.'[48]

Baptism administered with the right intention, writes Burkhard

Neunheuser, is always valid, even when it remains fruitless for want of the proper dispositions in the baptized. 'Such a case does, of course, presuppose a minimum of faith and goodwill, without which no salvation at all can be possible.' On a later page, he adds that baptism is in a special sense both the sacrament of faith in Christ and the embodiment of that faith. 'That is why, should circumstances make baptism impossible, faith alone can impart fellowship with Christ and redemption through what is called "baptism of desire".'[49]

Donald Bridge, a Baptist, and David Phypers, an Anglican, got together from opposite sides regarding infant baptism to produce a book called 'The Water that Divides'. It is an attempt, as the back cover says, to 'explain the views of Baptists and infant Baptists, subjecting both to the New Testament in an equally ruthless way.' An illustration of this frankness appears in a section headed The Nature of Baptismal Grace. One paragraph reads: 'For our salvation we are dependent on the grace of God. On that, all Christians agree. But how and when and where is that grace supplied? The extreme sacramentalist view links it with external religious rites (and especially with baptism) in an almost automatic manner which obscures the need for repentance and faith . . . This is held to be sufficient, quite regardless of the state of mind and will of the candidate for baptism either at the time or subsequently. It is startling both in its exclusivism and in its inclusivism. It excludes from the kingdom of God all who have not received baptism, regardless of their faith; it counts as Christians all who have been baptized, regardless of their lack of faith.'[50]

Vicarious faith

Let us now look more closely at an aspect of baptism to which we have already referred, namely the idea of 'vicarious faith'.

Aquinas recognized that baptism was a sacrament requiring belief and that an infant did not possess the necessary faith. He held, however, that the faith or intention of the parents and the church availed on behalf of the child. E. C. Whitaker senses how artificial it may seem for sponsors to answer for infants, but he supports the practice by stressing that the Church's concern is with the faith of the recipient, whether he is an adult or an infant, whether his faith is in the present or in the future.[51]

Despite Luther's emphasis on faith in the person receiving the sacrament, he supported infant baptism by saying that 'infants are helped by vicarious faith: the faith of those who present them for baptism.' He reinforced his argument by claiming that all things are possible in response to the prayers of a believing church when it presents the infant and this is changed, cleansed and renewed by their infused faith.[52]

In support of the view that sponsors can be effectively linked to infants at their baptism by supplying a vicarious faith, reference has been made to the healing miracles in the Gospels, where the faith of relatives or friends is thought to have contributed to the healing process. Instances quoted include the healing of the Centurion's servant (Matthew 8.5ff); the cripple (Matthew 9.1ff); Jairus's daughter (Matthew 9.18ff); and the epileptic boy (Matthew 17.14ff). There does not appear, however, in the New Testament to be any instance of vicarious faith being responsible under God for another person's salvation. Moreover, often in modern times, a sponsor's undoubted repentance and faith, witnessed at an infant's baptism, have not been noticeably transmitted or realised in the child either in the present or in later years.

So we do well to ask: Can one exercise faith for another? Can one's repentance and faith effect a change in another person's life while the supposed recipient is passive and unresponsive? Some supporters of infant baptism would seem to think so. To press the point: Can a sponsor's repentance and faith condition an unwitting infant to receive the blessings of salvation? No question is more likely to polarize the answers that Baptists and Paedobaptists could give. It is not the aim of this study to dogmatize in either direction, but as objectively as possible to consider the evidence.

The question: 'Can one exercise faith for another person?' calls for careful consideration. It is linked with another question: 'Is it psychologically or spiritually possible for one mind to influence another person's mind without the other person being aware of it?' We are now in the sphere in which intercessory prayer and telepathy are thought to be relevant – the sphere in which religion and psychology would appear to overlap. In this connection, a Christian psychologist has suggested that perhaps there is a depth at which all minds can meet, as do all lands beneath the sea, or (to change the metaphor) as each telephone line can be linked to all the other lines in one vast telephone exchange.[53]

If intercessory prayer can condition another person to receive the help which God, on Christ's authority, waits to bestow, or if telepathy represents an interaction of minds that is more than coincidence, then we are dealing with a spiritual or mental experience no less inexplicable than the suggested transference of faith from the sponsor to the infant at baptism. We have developed this line of thought partly to give pause to those who would deny too summarily that vicarious faith has any credence in the practice of infant baptism.

The idea that an infant at baptism is dependent on the faith of others is touched upon by Colin Buchanan. He says that nobody would dream of baptizing an unbelieving adult to attest 'the primacy of God's grace'. Baptism is given to an adult only when he shows signs of believing and of being drawn by God's love. 'The warrant for baptizing adults should be a professed desire to belong to Christ and to join his people and the equivalent warrant for infants should be the existing status in Christ and his church of the parents.'[54]

The psychological theory that God in baptism influences the subconscious mind of the infant is dealt with by Hugh Mackintosh, a Scottish theologian, when he wrote: 'It certainly will not commend the Christian religion to thoughtful men with a keen ethical sense if infant baptism should come to be defended by reference to the subliminal consciousness.'[55] With reference to this so-called subconscious faith, Peter Forsyth observes that 'theologically such a notion is fatal to the evangelical idea . . . It leads to all kinds of theosophic theories about an implanted germ affecting unconsciously the child's human nature.'[56]

It is pointed out that in the early centuries of the church the growth of the practice of infant baptism broke in on the natural connection between instruction, conscious faith, and sacrament. The prescribed order rested on the assumption of conscious faith in the subjects. H. G. Wood says that the ritual is frankly unsuitable for infants, but it is retained because the tradition that instruction and faith precede baptism is undeniably primitive. He therefore concludes that the evidence of the ritual is against a very early date for the practice of infant baptism. 'It was never supposed,' says Wood, 'that baptism apart from faith would suffice to secure eternal life.' Faith was still essential; but whereas faith had generally preceded baptism, it became increasingly accepted that baptism would be as effective if it preceded faith. 'And even so,' Wood argues, 'a vicarious faith was required for the valid baptism of infants.'[57]

In his book, The Theology of St Paul, Whiteley sets baptism in the larger biblical setting of Christ's cross and rising again, and sees faith as central to the sacrament. He says that 'the effects of Christ's work are communicated to us in baptism' – we should never, of course, say 'baptism' without also thinking 'faith' – and that this communication can be described as incorporation or sonship by adoption or as sharing in the death and resurrection of Christ.[58]

Repentance and faith feature in John Macquarrie's theological interpretation of the baptismal rite. He says that the inward spiritual content to which baptism gives a visible expression includes the awakening of faith through the agency of the Holy Spirit. 'This awakening . . . includes conviction of sin, the turning in penitence from sin to a new life, the response of commitment to the calling of God and acceptance by God in Christ.'[59]

Flemington interprets the sacrament in somewhat similar terms to those used by Macquarrie. He writes that baptism is the external counterpart of that inward attitude of repentance and faith to which forgiveness and the endowment of the Holy Spirit could be imparted. 'Baptism was the means whereby all who thus repented and believed . . . could be made members of the new Israel.'[60]

As we have seen, it is widely accepted that the evidence in the New Testament points to faith as a prerequisite of baptism and appears to provide no support for the view, inherent in paedobaptism, that the rite produces faith. Nevertheless, assuming the person baptized is spiritually qualified, it is generally held in all the churches that baptism, either at the time or later, can be expected to deepen the faith which the recipient already possessed. This is thought to imply that faith has a threefold involvement in baptism: (1) *Before* baptism, so that the candidate is equipped to confess Christ in the rite; (2) *In* baptism in order to receive God's blessing; (3) *After* baptism in order to ensure that the person baptized continues in the Christian life, empowered by the grace received in the sacrament.

The role of the sponsor

E. C. Whitaker has pointed out that for a thousand years before the Reformation the questions regarding faith and renunciation, drawn from Hippolytus, were put to the infant as though he were a believing adult! The ritual assumed that 'the child is capable of, and has experienced, a present faith and a present repentance . . . And the sole function of the godparent . . . is to supply the child's lack of articulate speech. The child is thus treated as a responsible but inarticulate person.'[61]

Not surprisingly, commenting on Whitaker's observations, Beasley-Murray says: 'If we lifted this issue out of "the baptismal debate", most people would admit that one cannot morally pledge another to repentance, faith and obedience to God.'[62] The sheer logic and common sense of this judgement must not prevent us from recognising that there is another side to consider – namely that, since it is within 'the baptismal debate', there may be elements in the sacrament that cannot be assessed in purely human or earthly terms.

A distinctive feature of the role of a sponsor at baptism appears in an ancient initiatory rite dated by Lowe in the eighth century, but by tradition a century earlier. This document is the Missale Bibbiense (or 'Bobbio Missal'). Fisher says it was 'named after the monastery in the Apennines where Mabillion found it.'[63] Its relevance and interest for us here lie in the way in which the sponsor replies to the Trinitarian interrogations. The question: 'Dost thou believe in God . . . ?' is answered by 'May he believe' (Respondet credat).[64] The response is presumably a prayer that in the future the personal faith, experienced by the sponsor, will find fulfilment in the life of the infant when he grows up. The implication of 'credat' (May he believe!) seems to be that, whereas the sponsor's belief is a matter of present fact, in the case of the infant it can be only a matter of hope for the future. Some people may well question whether this role of the sponsor in relation to an infant at baptism is authenticated by scripture and by a proper understanding of baptismal theology.

Fisher draws attention to the fact that, in the time of John the Deacon (c. 500), Christian initiation in Rome involved the baptism of infants and included in the ritual the recital of the Creed (the redditio symboli). The presbyter recited the creed with his hand upon the infant's head. This was understood to represent the confession of faith of the infant![65]

According to Alan Richardson, infant baptism, understood as the first part of the whole action of Christian initiation, symbolizes an essential New Testament truth. He goes on to say that 'faith is the response to God's saving act in Christ, not the condition of it . . . When I was weak and helpless, God Chose me . . . my faith is God's gift; it is called into being by the knowledge that God through the mediation of my parents or godparents . . . has called me to be his son. I am not justified by my faith . . . I believe because I am justified by God's action in Christ . . . This is the truth enshrined in the symbolism of infant baptism. The important thing in baptism is what God does, not what we do, whether we are infants or adults.'[66]

In a booklet entitled A Case for Infant Baptism, Bishop Colin Buchanan sums up the Baptist argument against paedobaptism as follows: Baptism requires repentance and faith on the part of the recipient. Infants cannot have repentance and faith, therefore whatever rites or forms are used in connection with infants these cannot rank as baptism; and lest through a resemblance to baptism in their outward form they mislead those parents, and indeed the whole people of God, we ought not to pretend by word or action that we are in fact giving baptism to infants.[67]

It has been said that paedobaptism implies that an infant may be a church member, though lacking conscious faith. When he grows up, he may still lack belief, but in view of his baptism when a child, he is a member of the church. In the final analysis, is it baptism in water or faith in Christ which saves? And might not baptism in infancy become a hindrance to faith in maturity?[68] We recall Tertullian's exhortation that children should come to baptism 'when they are growing up, when they are learning, when they are being taught what they are coming to; when they have become competent to know Christ.'[69]

Is faith essential?

Aulen argues that this notion of faith given to, or infused into, the child through baptism undermines the real significance of infant baptism. He holds that the infant rite is an act of election by divine love through which the baptized person receives, and is assured of, his right of membership in the church. This is the 'objective' gift of baptism which exists before, and independently of, faith.[70]

Flemington claims that the validity of the Gospel does not depend on faith. The church's practice of infant baptism witnesses to this 'objective givenness' of the Gospel. 'God has done something for the child.'[71] Flemington recalls some words of Bernard Manning: 'Your own baptism . . . ought to mean all the more because it happened before you knew, or could know, anything about it.' We find this reasoning questionable, if not illogical. Are we to conclude from this premise – which seems to us to beg the question – that adult baptism means less because we are aware of it? In our view, Manning does not offer a very convincing reason why the sacrament should mean more because as infants we were unaware of it happening. He attempts to justify his argument by saying that as Christ died for us without our knowledge, so without waiting for any faith or desire from us, baptism was bestowed upon us.[72]

In an article on baptism, A. J. Maclean puts forward an interesting argument, if not a convincing or logical one, in support of the claim that personal faith in the recipient is not required to validate infant baptism. He reasons as follows: If an adult coming to baptism has not faith, he puts the barrier of non-faith between God and himself; he cannot be in a neutral condition, but, if he does not believe in God, must disbelieve in him. With an infant it is not so. In the age of innocence, he cannot put a barrier between God and himself, and therefore the fact that he has not yet learnt to have an active faith does not preclude the working of the grace of God within him.[73]

Another viewpoint as to what constitutes the essential element which validates infant baptism is advanced by Dr C. R. Smith. He develops his argument by saying that 'in adult baptism, the individual consciously and willingly undertakes the service of God, consciously and willingly confesses Christ, consciously and willingly enters into fellowship with the Holy Spirit. A child cannot do these things. If, therefore, confession be the fundamental thing in baptism, baptism ought to be for adults. But what if fellowship with God, and not confession of faith, be fundamental? It seems to me,' says Dr Smith, 'that it is. A child may partake of a fellowship long before it chooses for itself – long before it clearly conceives what fellowship is. While, therefore, the fellowship of a child begins in infancy, it is not complete until the child himself consciously and freely consents with Christ.'[74]

Summing up

Both Scripture and Tradition see repentance and faith as essential elements in baptism. The ancient baptismal liturgies required the candidate to renounce the devil, and all his works. The application of these demands to innocent infants, who have no awareness or experience of this 'wicked world', has seemed inappropriate and unrealistic to many people over the centuries. To meet this anomalous situation sponsors were provided therefore in order to speak, not for themselves, but for the inarticulate child.

The theological application is clear. Repentance and faith are recognized as indispensable features of baptism – a recognition that carries the authentication of Scripture and of a long-standing liturgical tradition. But the increasing elaboration of the baptismal ritual since Apostolic times has tended to make the sacrament all the more remote as far as infants were concerned. As has often been observed, the infant was somehow fitted into the adult rite instead of a rite being designed especially for the young child. The question of a realistic and appropriate application of repentance and faith to infants presents a problem that goes far back in history – a problem that is still with us.

CHAPTER ELEVEN

Is Confirmation Essential?

Our enquiry in this chapter oversteps denomination boundaries, for the question of the relationship between baptism and confirmation concerns nearly all the churches in Western Christendom. It is also a matter of interest to the Orthodox Churches, even though they have retained at the infant level the wholeness of Christian initiation – an arrangement giving rise to questions considered in this book.

A Roman Catholic liturgist, E. J. Yarnold, in a Preface to a book by Austin Milner, says that 'in recent years the meaning of the sacrament of confirmation has been keenly debated in the Catholic Church.' Yarnold sets out the debatable issues by asking: (1) Is it merely the last stage in initiation? or (2) Is its purpose to strengthen the Christian? or (3) Is it a sacrament of the lay-apostolate? or (4) Is it primarily an opportunity for mature commitment to the church? Yarnold goes on to observe that the Apostolic Constitution of 1971, with its rite of confirmation, provides some of the answers.[1]

Austin Milner follows this up in the 'Introduction' to his book. He says that traditional theology has been challenged from two sides: (1) For some people, confirmation is a meaningless duplicate of baptism; (2) For others it is no less than the baptism of the Holy Spirit, promised by Christ, for which water-baptism is only the preparation.

Milner goes on to state a widely held view, namely that we still lack an adequate theology. Historians, he says, are agreed about the development of the rite, but disagree about its interpretation. Theologians remain inordinately attached to the limited medieval view which rests on very dubious foundations. Milner reckons that the charismatic movement has stimulated new and vital interest in the Holy Spirit.[2]

In a public lecture delivered at Oxford University in 1946, Dom Gregory Dix stated that the instrumental cause for the renewed interest in confirmation was a document entitled 'Confirmation Today' issued in 1944 as a Schedule attached to the Interim Reports of the Committees of the four Houses of Convocation. Dix points out that only one seventh of the Report surveys 'Confirmation in History and Doctrine' and criticises the Report for ignoring such books as Mason's 'Relation of Confirmation to Baptism', published in 1891, which he says has never been answered.

Dix is impressed by the views put forward by H. V. Martin, a Congregationalist in S. India, who states that 'there is not a shred of evidence in the New Testament that water-baptism was essential to joining the Apostolic Church.'[3] While Dix does not share this depreciation of water-baptism, he accepts Martin's conclusion that 'baptism in the Apostolic Church was primarily and fundamentally baptism in the Spirit' – an interpretation in line with Dix's understanding of confirmation in relation to water-baptism.[4] This leads us to a consideration of the New Testament evidence.

The New Testament

According to John Macquarrie, the first confirmation of which we have record is in Acts 8 – the conversion of the Samaritans by Philip, followed later by the visit of Peter and John, who laid their hands on them, accompanied by the gift of the Holy Spirit.[5]

This incident is often taken to imply that Philip, being of no higher status than a deacon, was qualified only to administer the baptismal rite and that the gift of the Holy Spirit had to await the apostolic laying on of hands, which Peter and John were qualified to supply. It is sometimes maintained that the Holy Spirit here should be understood to involve the endowment of such gifts as speaking with tongues or miracle working – an interpretation which would throw light on the Simon Magus episode.

Schlier adopted this viewpoint, saying that Luke found it unnecessary to mention that the Samaritans had received the Holy Spirit at their baptism by Philip and that the imposition of hands by Peter and John conveyed only the charismata.[6] Prof Lampe, who inclines towards the charismatic interpretation, holds that the Samaritan incident can best be considered as exceptional. He says that after the baptism of the first Samaritan converts, the leaders of the Church's mission came down from Jerusalem, and by the sign of fellowship and 'contact' incorporate them into the apostolic (i.e. missionary) church, with the result that there occurs a Samaritan 'Pentecost', at least to the extent that visible signs are manifested of the outpouring of the Spirit.[7]

A two-source theory has been put forward to explain the events at Samaria as presented by Luke in Acts. It is suggested that one source contained the story of Philip baptizing the Samaritan converts, and the other source included the account of the apostolic visitation. Acts 8.14 is regarded as the editorial link. The highlighting of these two visits reflects the importance of these Gentile conversions in the early expansion of the church.

Bearing in mind the view that the Samaritans did not receive the Holy Spirit from Philip's ministration because he was a deacon, we turn to the episode of the Ethiopian eunuch, in which Philip also figures. Our reason for doing so relates to the Western reading of Acts 8.39: 'When they came up out of the water the Holy Spirit fell upon the eunuch, but the angel of the Lord carried away Philip.'[8] This version may be textually questionable, but it is theologically important in that it represents the Holy Spirit being bestowed in baptism, with Philip, a deacon, officiating, and without any additional ceremony, such as the imposition of hands or anointing. This emendation of the original Greek text does at least reflect the mind of the church in the early part of the second century.[9]

As one would expect, Gregory Dix recognizes the significance of this textual emendation. He says that this Western text of Acts 8.39, if accepted, would be 'the only piece of New Testament evidence . . . which might suggest that the gift of the Spirit could on occasion be given by water-baptism alone.'[10]

W. F. Flemington, a distinguished Methodist scholar, says that this statement by Dix can be accepted only if we fail to understand at least three New Testament passages in their most obvious meaning. Of the first, Acts 2.38, Flemington says: 'It is hard to see how "be baptized" can mean: submit yourselves to a double rite, the first stage being water-baptism and the second stage a rite "with matter unspecified".' He also points out that there is no reference here to imposition of hands, anointing or sealing. 'Repentance and baptism in the name of Jesus Christ unto remission of sins will be followed by the reception of the Holy Spirit.'

The second passage, to which Flemington draws attention, is 1 Cor. 12.13: 'For in one Spirit we were all baptized . . . and were all made to drink of one Spirit.' Here too the obvious meaning seems to be that baptism is in the closest way linked with the Holy Spirit. Flemington quotes Abrahams as saying that in the Old Testament and Rabbinic usage it was common to link with the Spirit verbs related to water. 1 Cor. 12.13 illustrates this: '. . . we were all made to drink of one Spirit.'

The third passage which Flemington quotes to challenge Dix's statement is Acts 10.44–48 – the puzzling and unusual story of Cornelius. Here the Spirit precedes baptism. 'The "matter" of baptism . . . is not "chrism" but water.' Peter asks 'Can any one forbid water for baptizing these people who have received the Holy Spirit?' Is there a link here with the later Syrian pre-baptismal gift of the Spirit?[11] Flemington draws the conclusion that 'the endowment of the Spirit was associated . . . not with one of the rites in which it is customary today to find an antecedent of confirmation, but, on the contrary, directly with water-baptism.'

Flemington makes the observation that even if Cornelius was not baptized in water, as some take Acts 11.16 to imply, it would appear that 10.47f at least reflects the mind of the church in the latter part of the first century.[12]

We left the story of the Eunuch in order to follow Flemington's challenge to Gregory Dix's statement based on the Western text of Acts 8.39. We now return to consider Lampe's exegetical comment on Luke's observation that the Ethiopian 'went on his way rejoicing'. Lampe holds that the word 'rejoicing' (*χαίρων*) indicates that the eunuch possessed the Spirit after his baptism, because 'joy' (*χαρά*) is associated with the Spirit in Acts 13.52, in 1 Thess. 1.6 and elsewhere in the New Testament. For Lampe, therefore, this means that there is evidence of the eunuch possessing the Holy Spirit independent of the Western text of Acts 8.39. He reinforces his argument by reference to the conversion of the Philippian jailer. Here, while there is no direct mention of the Holy Spirit in connection with his baptism, yet it does say that he afterwards 'rejoiced' (*ἠγαλλιάσατο*), which Lampe takes to signify 'spiritual joy' – an experience stated by Paul in Gal 5.22 to be a 'fruit of the Spirit'.[13]

The story of the twelve 'disciples' at Ephesus (Acts 19.1–7) also presents problems. They tell St Paul that they had been baptized by John the Baptist and that they had neither experience nor knowledge of the Holy Spirit. Doubt attaches to the use of the word 'disciple' (*μαθητής*). Some take the view that the context suggests that they are disciples of John, others point out that the frequent use of the term 'disciple' in Acts indicates that they were early followers of Christ, possibly converts of Apollos.

As to the difficulty arising from the re-baptism of these Ephesian believers, Markus Barth tries to resolve the difficulty by a textual re-alignment. He suggests that verse five should be added to verse four as being included in what Paul says to the 'disciples', and that Luke's description of events was not resumed till verse six. This means that Paul represents John the Baptist – who pointed his followers to Jesus – as having baptized his hearers 'in the name of Jesus Christ'.[14]

This exegesis would solve the problem of Paul's having re-baptized the group of 'disciples' at Ephesus. But, as often happens, a theory that solves one problem tends to create another. It is not otherwise here; for almost certainly many of the '3,000' who were baptized on the Day of Pentecost had been baptized previously by John. Moreover, it is argued that it would be incredible for John to baptize Jesus in the Jordan 'in the name of Jesus'.[15]

Running somewhat parallel with the Ephesian narrative is the story of Apollos (Acts 18. 24–28), a Jewish native of Alexandria, resident in Ephesus. He too had received only the baptism of John; but, unlike the twelve 'disciples' at Ephesus, there is no record of his having been baptized 'in the name of Jesus' or receiving the laying on of hands. Nevertheless, after having been given Christian instruction from Priscilla and Aquila, he was well received in Church circles. Did he obtain a direct endowment of the Holy Spirit, as in the case of Cornelius? Some believe that a gift of the Spirit is indicated by his being described as 'fervent in Spirit' (ζέων τῷ πνεύματι). While this interpretation is not without scholarly support, we are not able to find in the text sufficient warrant for this conclusion.

The narrative describing the visit of Ananias to Paul in Acts 9.10–19 also presents problems. Assuming that Luke's account accords with historical fact, we can draw some conclusions. One is that the assurance given by Ananias to Paul that he will receive the Holy Spirit is not included in the Lord's previous commission to Ananias. Another is that the account does not state that Paul actually received the Holy Spirit – though the context may suggest that he did. Assuming that he did receive the Holy Spirit, does the laying on of hands relate to the recovery of Paul's sight and the endowment of the Spirit or only to the former? If Paul received the Holy Spirit, then this endowment preceded his baptism – another instance anticipating the later pre-baptismal Syrian rite.

Not the least significant feature of this Damascus event is that the imposition of hands and the gift of the Spirit are administered by one who is not an apostle – another feature, as we shall see, that will recur in the later history of 'confirmation' – the word used of

Ananias's action by Dr W. K. L. Clarke.[16] This episode has clearly proved an embarrassment to some theologians and has prompted the suggestion that Ananias was able to perform this 'apostolic office' because God had temporarily given him an apostolic commission – an interpretation which does not seem to us very convincing.

The laying on of hands

The laying on of hands was used in commissioning men for the holding of some office or missionary enterprise. One instance is the appointing of the 'seven' in Acts 6. 1–6. The arrangements made for their selection and appointment are interesting. The twelve apostles take the initiative by calling on the 'body of the disciples' to choose 'seven men of good repute, full of the Spirit and of wisdom, whom we may appoint to this duty'. The 'body of the disciples' choose the seven 'whom they set before the apostles and having prayed they laid their hands upon them.' It appears to be generally assumed that it is the apostles whose hands are laid upon the chosen seven. This seems to be assumed on the grounds of spiritual status, not on the basis of the biblical text, which could equally well refer to 'the body of the disciples'.

As these men were chosen on the understanding that they were already 'full of the Spirit', it is clear that the imposition of hands on this occasion was not designed to convey the Spirit in a sacramental sense, but rather as a spiritual endowment for a specific task.

Dr G. B. Caird holds that the laying on of hands was not an apostolic monopoly. 'In the New Testament', he writes, 'the laying on of hands accompanies healing, baptism, the commissioning of missionaries and ordination. If we insist on finding a rationale for this practice, the only one that covers all the cases is that of Augustine: "What else is the laying on of hands but prayer over a man?"'[17]

In response to the claim put forward by Dix and Thornton that confirmation is more important than baptism, W. F. Flemington asks what New Testament support is there for such a claim. He argues that there is very little evidence in Scripture for such an additional rite as confirmation. Admittedly, there is reference in Acts and Hebrews to 'the laying on of hands' as a rite linked with, yet distinct from, water-baptism. Flemington points out that, although hand-laying in Acts is connected with the gift of the Holy Spirit, it is hardly mentioned elsewhere in the New Testament. If the imposition of hands is rightly regarded as the medium of the

Holy Spirit – an essential element in Christian initiation – it is surprising that Paul does not mention this association, even when he makes specific reference to those who have been endowed with the Spirit – e.g. Rom. 5.5; 8.9; or when he lists the gifts of the Spirit in 1 Cor. 12. The safe conclusion seems to be that in some areas in the Primitive Church the Holy Spirit was bestowed by the laying on of hands.[18]

Flemington's position is somewhat endorsed by Lampe, who holds that there is little evidence in the New Testament that the imposition of hands was widely practised in the apostolic church either separately from water-baptism or as part of the initiation ceremony. He says that most of the information about hand-laying comes from St Luke who relates it to the church's mission empowered by the Spirit. Lampe sees it as an instrument of ordination by which one becomes 'a sharer in the apostolicity of the apostles of Christ: it is the sign by which he receives a special endowment of the Holy Spirit' equipping him for Christian witness.[19]

In describing the coming of the Holy Spirit into the lives of the apostles, with its charismatic effects, St Luke in Acts 2 omits any reference to the laying on of hands. After all, who would lay hands on the apostles? Moreover, would it be possible for the apostles to baptize and to lay hands on 3,000 people in one day? This would not be the only occasion in the Book of Acts, as we have seen, that the Holy Spirit has been received without reference to any imposition of hands – a situation which has prompted the suggestion that this symbolic act may have been performed, but was omitted by Luke as an action that could be taken for granted.

Another way of accounting for this omission has been put forward. These instances where the Holy Spirit has been received without any hand-laying have been explained by pointing out that baptizein (*βαπτίζειν*) and baptisma (*βάπτισμα*) signify more than water-baptism and denote the whole act of Christian initiation, including the imposition of hands. As Dr E. J. Bicknell writes, commenting on Acts 8.12–17, 'Beyond all doubt, in the customs of the Early Church, baptism, unction and the laying on of hands formed a single sacrament.'[20]

The laying on of hands has a history that goes far back before New Testament times. It is not difficult to trace it in the Old Testament. Often this symbol was used as a means of conveying a blessing, as when Jacob laid his hands upon his son's head (Gen. 48.14ff). It formed part of the sacrificial ritual as when the priest placed his hands on the head of the scapegoat and confessed the sins of Israel (Lev. 16.20f). Joshua is commissioned for his high office as Moses' successor by the priest who 'laid his hands upon him' (Numbers 27.22f). There is also an instance of hand-laying whereby the meritorious spirit of one man is conveyed to another (Deut. 34.9). This ancient and traditional custom was taken up by Jesus and his disciples in a ministry of healing and helpfulness, and later by the Christian Church in a variety of ways – some sacramental – over subsequent centuries.

Anointing

Confirmation has been associated, not only with the laying on of hands, but also with anointing. We now, therefore, consider to what extent anointing can be traced in the New Testament. In his scholarly book on 'Baptismal Anointing', Dr Leonel Mitchell traces the history of the subject from its earliest appearance to its later forms in the rites of East and West, and expresses the hope that, in any reunion of the separated elements of Christian initiation, anointing will occupy its rightful place.

Mitchell admits that there is no unambiguous reference to anointing in the New Testament, but considers the most relevant texts, the first at which he looks being 2 Cor. 1.21f: 'But it is God who confirms (*βεβαιῶν*) us with you in Christ, and has anointed (*χρίσας*) us; he has sealed (*σφραγισάμενος*) us and given us the earnest (*ἀρραβῶνα*) of his Spirit in our hearts.' Here Paul uses the technical terms of the initiatory rites – 'confirmed', 'anointed' and 'sealed'.

The next passage Mitchell quotes is 1 John 2.20: 'You have an anointing (*χρῖσμα*) from the Holy One' and points out that 'the Holy One' is a title for Christ as Peter's confession in John 6.69 makes clear. Another reference to anointing appears in 1 John 2.27, which says that Chrisma (*χρῖσμα*) remains in you and will teach you all things – an echo of John 14.26.

Mitchell points out that the background to these texts is the Baptism of Jesus; when 'God anointed' (*ἔχρισεν*) Jesus of Nazareth with the Holy Spirit and power' (Acts 10.38) – an event which finds expression when Jesus applies to himself the words of Isaiah 61, 'The Spirit of the Lord is upon me, because he has anointed (*ἔχρισεν*) me . . .' (Luke 4.18). There is a further allusion in Acts 4.27 where reference is made to 'thy holy servant (*παῖδά*) Jesus, whom thou didst anoint.'(*ἔχρισας*)

Mitchell admits, however, that many scholars do not regard these texts as referring to an external rite of anointing, but are to be understood in metaphorical terms. Nevertheless, some people, including Thornton and Dix, interpret the anointing in a concrete form as in Exodus 30.25ff.[21] Mitchell says that the evidence does not appear to him conclusive enough to make a firm stand on either side of this controversy. He adds that 'whether the New Testament passages quoted refer to an actual anointing or not, there can be no reasonable doubt that Christians who did have a liturgical anointing used these passages as Scriptural justification for the practice.'[22]

Dr Thornton finds 'confirmation' in the New Testament, especially in such passages as 2 Cor. 1.21f; Eph. 1.13; 4.30, where a Christian is said to be 'anointed' or 'sealed' by the Holy Spirit.[23] These texts are taken by Thornton to signify that unction goes back to the beginning of the church – a conclusion which Flemington – who belonged to a different school of theological thought – is unable to accept.

Flemington regards the references to 'anointing' or 'sealing' as 'alternative ways of describing the gifts associated with water-baptism;'; and in support of this view quotes Hermas writing – in the middle of the second century – 'the seal, then, is the water.' Flemington also argues that those who stress the connection of the Holy Spirit with 'anointing' or 'sealing' or 'imposition of hands' appear to neglect the New Testament evidence that links the Holy Spirit with water-baptism.[24]

Henry VIII and Confirmation

It is interesting to have reason to think of Henry VIII in theological and biblical terms! His chapter 'On the Sacrament of Confirmation' – assuming that he actually wrote it – may be considered thoughtful and entertaining. In response to Martin Luther's statement that this rite is not supported by Scripture, the King argues that the criterion is not whether a sacrament is explicitly spelt out in Scripture, but whether it represents the mind of Christ or of his apostles as revealed by the Holy Spirit. Henry makes the perceptive observation that, if a sacrament cannot be sustained without explicit Scriptural evidence, then, assuming that only St John's Gospel had come down to us, we would have to rule out the sacrament of the Lord's Supper in the absence of any biblical evidence. As the King points out, the writer of this Gospel had omitted 'many other things which Jesus did'. (John 21.25)[25]

We are not aware that Lampe or Dix were influenced by Henry's stout defence of confirmation, but they both express views somewhat in harmony with the King's argument. Lampe says that we cannot be sure that the practice of much later times represents a continuous liturgical tradition from the primitive church; but, as we know very little of how things were done in New Testament times, it is possible that liturgical practice was more fully developed than the New Testament shows.[26]

Dom Gregory Dix states, as we saw earlier, that besides Scriptural evidence, we have two other sources, equally enlightening, about the original rites and meaning of Christian initiation in the formative age of the church. These are: (1) the early liturgical practice of the churches in conferring it; and (2) the comments upon this of early writers. Scientifically, he says, the liturgical evidence is primary because it is older in its substance and was formative of Christian thought before the New Testament documents were canonised.

We can now, says Dix, shake ourselves free from the sixteenth century – or rather medieval – delusion that primitive Christian worship and church order must have been drawn up in the light of the New Testament, which did not exist! He does not question the authority of the New Testament as a written doctrinal standard for us today. He simply argues that there is available another source of information on the original and apostolic interpretation of Christianity, which the Scriptures presuppose and which must be used to interpret Scripture.

Dix sums up by saying that the liturgical tradition is older in some respects than the New Testament and till the end of the second century it had an apostolic authority independent of the Scriptures.[27]

James Bulloch points out that the word 'confirmation' does not appear in the New Testament nor in the writings of the Fathers for the first three centuries.[28] Dr J. N. D. Kelly says that the belief that baptism conveyed the Holy Spirit was widely held, and that there is no trace at this time of a separate rite, such as unction or imposition of hands.[29]

The Epistle to the Hebrews (6.4) might be taken to imply that 'the laying on of hands' was regularly practised in some areas in association with baptism and that it was among the basic features of Christianity. It is pointed out, however, that the absence of any clear evidence of hand-laying in the century after Paul's death throws doubt on a rite of 'confirmation' being widely practised in the primitive church – though we should not expect baptismal uniformity and should allow for local differences.

It would appear that, outside the New Testament, the earliest information we have on baptism is in the Didache, where there is no reference to oil or imposition of hands. Around the middle of the second century, Justin Martyr, in his 'First Apology', describes Christian initiation in terms of baptism and the eucharist, but he says nothing about oil or laying on of hands. It is suggested that we should treat with reserve the view that the rites of the early church were simple until they were complicated and adorned in later practices. Perhaps the Didache and Justin simplified their accounts, for political reasons, in dangerous days for the Christian community, when some of their ceremonies were viewed with suspicion in the Roman Empire.[30] K. W. Noakes comments that, in the New Testament, baptism means entry into the body of Christ and hence baptism conveys the right to participate in the eucharist. 'This link,' he says, 'can perhaps be observed in the Didache (9.5; 10.6) and is made explicit in the initiation-rite described by Justin, where initiation leads directly to the eucharist.'[31] The question of administering communion after baptism and before confirmation will be discussed in the next chapter. (See also pages 193ff and 253f).

Tertullian and Hippolytus

Tertullian's 'De Baptismo' is one of the two earliest accounts of Christian initiation – the other being the 'Apostolic Tradition' by Hippolytus. Whitaker considers that Tertullian's account is not so precise as that of Hippolytus, but summarises their accounts of what followed water-baptism as follows:[32]

1. Anointing with oil in the name of Jesus Christ.
2. When dressed, they appear before the Bishop and the Church.
3. The Bishop lays his hand on them (individually? or corporately?) and says a prayer.
4. The Bishop then pours oil on each person's head or forehead, lays his hand in the oil and says: 'I anoint thee with holy oil in God the Father Almighty, and Christ Jesus, and the Holy Ghost.'
5. The Bishop seals each candidate with the sign of the cross, probably in oil.

Both accounts involve three actions: (1) Hand-laying; (2) Anointing; and (3) The Sign of the cross. We should bear in mind that the baptismal three-fold questioning on the faith – the basis of the Apostles' Creed – remained unchanged in the Western church until the Syrian formula was gradually adopted.

With regard to the pattern of initiation indicated by Tertullian and Hippolytus, Noakes says that 'this initiatory rite is a unity, although we can see clearly within it the elements which will in time become "Confirmation" (anointing, laying on of hands, signing with the cross). According to Tertullian the Holy Spirit is active throughout the whole rite; baptism in water by the operation of the Holy Spirit gives cleansing and remission of sins, while the ensuing hand-laying imparts the gift of the Spirit.'[33]

Attention has been drawn to the inconsistency that characterises Tertullian's teaching on Christian initiation. Kelly says that in one place he links the Holy Spirit with baptism and elsewhere says that it is in response to the Bishop's hand that the Spirit comes.[34] Lampe says that we must hold his confused thought on baptism and the laying on of hands responsible in no small measure for the difficulties and ambiguities which have continued from his day to our own to hamper the working out of a reasoned theology of the operation of the Holy Spirit in baptism and confirmation.[35]

It is suggested that a partial explanation for this 'confusion' may lie in the failure of second century writers to interpret the Book of Acts in terms of its missionary context and their tendency to relate to their own day the hand-laying in Acts as a description of confirmation.

The 'Apostolic Tradition'

In his preface, Gregory Dix says that 'the Apostolic Tradition of St Hippolytus is the most illuminating single source of evidence extant on the inner life and religious policy of the early Christian church.' Dix goes on sadly to say: 'It is an unfortunate fact that its text has reached us in a more deplorably battered condition than that of any other important early Christian document.' Yet he sees it as the fullest account of the liturgy of Christian initiation – a record of the authoritative paradosis of practice at a time when, with the increasing recognition of the New Testament Scriptures, its authority was beginning to be discarded. The 'Apostolic Tradition' reflects the liturgical practices at Rome and beyond the city in the late second century. Dix holds that some of its features can be traced back to the Apostolic Church prior to its separation from the Synagogue.

Following Dix's translation and including the uncertain bracketed phrases, we quote section 22 entitled 'Confirmation'.

1. 'And the Bishop shall lay his hand upon them invoking and saying: O Lord God who didst count these they servants worthy of deserving the forgiveness of sins by the laver of regeneration, make them worthy to be filled with thy Holy Spirit and upon them thy grace, that they may serve thee according to thy will; for to thee is the glory, to the Father and to the Son with the Holy Ghost in the holy Church, both now and ever and world without end. Amen.'
2. 'After this, pouring the consecrated oil from his hand and laying his hand on his head, he shall say: I anoint thee with holy oil in God the Father Almighty and Christ Jesus and the Holy Ghost.'
3. 'And sealing (*σφραγιζειν*) him on the forehead, he shall give him the kiss of peace and say: The Lord be with you. And he who has been sealed shall say: And with thy Spirit.'
4. 'And so he shall do to each one severally.'[36]

E. C. Whitaker observes that, in the 'Apostolic Tradition', there is early evidence of those ceremonies which in the Western Church came to be regarded as confirmation. He draws attention to the fact that, after the bishop has offered prayer for the Holy Spirit and had anointed the baptized with the sign of the cross, there followed the receiving of first communion. This meant that baptism, the post-baptismal ceremonies and the eucharist formed one complete liturgical event. 'It is important to note,' says Whitaker, 'that children and infants were baptized with their parents, received the anointing and laying on of the hand after baptism, and then with their parents received Holy Communion.'[37]

After outlining the ancient rite of initiation according to Hippolytus, Lampe regards it as an unwarrantable assumption that it is confirmation, not baptism, which here admits a man into the church. Confirmation, says Lampe, 'if we are so to designate the final stage of the initiatory rite, appears to be, at least according to the Latin text of the Apostolic Tradition, a complex of subsidiary ceremonies expressive of the bishop's blessing given by him as the head of the congregation to its newly baptized members.'[38]

In the third century, as Kelly points out, increasing attention was given to the subsidiary rites connected with baptism – chrismation, anointing with the sign of the cross, and the imposition of hands.

There was a tendency to regard baptism as effecting remission of sins and regeneration, and to associate the gift of the Spirit with these other rites.[39]

In the Western Church, confirmation was usually identified as the sacrament of the Holy Spirit. Yet to deny the Holy Spirit to baptism tended to deprive this essential sacrament of its positive content and to reduce it to a 'baptism of John'. To imply that the Holy Spirit is given in different forms or for different purposes leads to false distinctions of a quantitative kind – between internal and external operations. This may well give rise to the question as to how one becomes a member of the Church by baptism without receiving the Holy Spirit – a question Clement and Tertullian had reason to consider.[40]

With reference to the rite of Christian initiation in the ancient city of Rome, Prof W. H. C. Frend says: 'Confirmation, the laying on of hands, was coming to share with baptism an equal importance in a Christian's life.' In this crowded city, he says 'baptism signified the formal entry into church membership, but reception of the Spirit was delayed until confirmation'.[41]

Bishop J. W. C. Wand saw the situation somewhat differently. He wrote that confirmation followed immediately upon baptism and was indeed part of it. He described how the baptized received the imposition of the Bishop's hand and were anointed with consecrated oil. He says: 'This represents the Roman use. Elsewhere in the West there seems to have been no unction; while in the East it was the imposition of the hand that disappeared.'[42]

Arising from his valuable liturgical studies, Canon Whitaker observes that the practice of confirmation was very varied. He describes how, in fourth century Rome, the candidate dressed in white was presented to the bishop, now enthroned, who laid his hand on him and offered the prayer for the sevenfold gifts of the Spirit – a prayer included in the modern Anglican rite of confirmation. The bishop then signed the baptized on the forehead with chrism and said: 'The Sign of Christ unto life eternal'. The candidate is called a 'neophyte' ('newly born') and receives his first communion.[43]

As we consider the evidence associated with baptism and confirmation in the early centuries, we do well to keep in mind another relevant statement by Whitaker. He says that as baptisteries and churches were built and prayers, hymns and other liturgical forms were added, the earlier 'simple' patterns became overlaid with a massive structure of accretions and elaborations; with the result that their original simplicity is not easy to trace under the developed rites of Rome and Milan, of Antioch and Byzantium. Whitaker adds that the communications between different regions produced cross-fertilization of liturgies in various areas. There was, for instance, the adoption by the Western church of the Eastern form: 'I baptize you in the name of . . .' and the adoption by the Eastern church of the addition of an anointing after baptism from the West.[44]

In the fourth century, the growth and spread of the church meant that many baptized Christians had not been episcopally confirmed. Jerome (c. 354–c. 419) throws light on this problem. In his 'Dialogue of a Luciferian with an Orthodox', he agrees that there is no salvation in water-baptism alone. Baptism is 'of water' and 'of the Spirit'. When the Luciferian asks: 'What of the present practice of administering them separately?', Jerome replies that the bishop rushes round to those baptized by presbyters to call down the Holy Spirit by the laying on of hands. Jerome goes on to say that the bishop's much travelling is done 'for the glory of the bishop than from any pressure of necessity.'! 'The whole salvation of the church hangs on the bishop's self-importance.'![45]

This, says Jerome, is the only reason why no presbyter is permitted to baptize without chrism episcopally blessed. He seeks to support his argument by referring to the Ethiopian eunuch, quoting the questionable Western text at Acts 8.39, in order to prove that baptism in water alone, without a bishop, can impart the Holy Spirit. Has the 'Theologian' here taken over from the 'Text Critic'? – for in the Vulgate Jerome ignores this Western Text.

In his book on The Christian Fathers, Maurice Wiles says that water-baptism and laying on of hands at first went together in a single rite, 'as they do to this day in the Eastern Church, even with the practice of infant baptism.' Wiles points out, however, that in the West circumstances separated them and the problem arose of bestowing 'the Spirit in two halves' – 'an initial and a confirmatory giving; a coming in regeneration and a coming in seven-fold power. But for the most part the Fathers were content to associate the giving of the Spirit indiscriminately with baptism or with the laying on of hands, even where this appeared to lead them into inconsistencies in what they believed and taught.'[46]

Thornton somewhat qualifies the above depreciation of the Patristic writings. He says that if we attribute to the Fathers our modern habits of thought we are sure to misunderstand them. Thornton warns us against 'that sort of rationalistic criticism which tends to underrate what it has not learnt to understand.' This is a caveat relevant not least to the debates about the issues raised by this book.[47]

The unique Syrian rite

We turn from the early Fathers to consider one of the most interesting and significant rites in the early centuries – namely the Syrian rite of initiation. It is somewhat unique and certainly puzzling. In approaching this Eastern ritual we have the benefit of E. C. Whitaker as our guide.

He points out that the Syrian rite has no post-baptismal anointing. Basically, the rite consists of (1) anointing; (2) baptismal washing; and (3) eucharist. Early documents show that water-baptism was followed by Holy Communion and that there was no confirmation ceremony. The big question is: Did the Syrian Church's initiation include only water-baptism? – while the Western Church had two signs, water and oil. Did the Syrian Church believe that the Holy Spirit and other effects of initiation were conveyed solely by baptism? Or, in other words, what has become of confirmation in the Syrian rite? Father H. B. Green CR is quoted as saying: 'The accurate description of the Antiochene practice (and by implication that of the Syrian tradition in general) is not that it has a rite of confirmation in an unusual place, but that it lacked it altogether.'[48]

The 'Apostolic Constitutions' – eight books drawn up by an Eastern Arian in the late fourth century – contains a significant passage relevant to our discussion. 'Thou shalt first anoint the person with holy oil and afterwards baptize him with water, and finally shalt seal him with chrism; that the anointing with oil may be a participation of the Holy Spirit, and the water a symbol of the death, and the chrism a seal of the covenants. But if there be neither oil nor chrism, the water is sufficient both for the anointing, and for the seal, and for the confession of him that is dead.'[49]

Whitaker says that the teaching of this passage supports the view that the origin of confirmation is in the oil which accompanied the baptismal bath. It is not surprising that in some places the gift of the Holy Spirit was early associated with the oil. It is also not surprising if the connection of oil with the Holy Spirit was not made, or sometimes made, or, as in the 'Apostolic Constitutions', not regarded as important.

Commenting further in this passage, Whitaker observes that 'the water is sufficient' because it is primary and embodies the full meaning of initiation. 'The oil was an adventitious and optional addition.' It would be relevant here to recall our discussion on 'The Essence and Effectiveness of Grace' in chapter nine. Whitaker goes on to say that there is no evidence to prove the theory that confirmation originated in a development within the early church by which the oil at the baptismal bath came to share the sacramental associations of the water, any more than there is evidence to prove the theory that confirmation originated in the institution of our Lord.

It seems certain that in the early centuries the Syrian Church did not have any rite separable from baptism such as 'confirmation'. In the light of the evidence, which he has so competently assembled and considered, Whitaker concludes that 'by a tradition no less real and apostolic than that which we have received in the West, the early Syrian Church had no second sign, no rite of confirmation, in their forms of Christian initiation; for them water was sufficient'.[50]

On British soil

When St Augustine of Canterbury, towards the end of the sixth century, at the behest of Pope Gregory the Great, landed apprehensively in Kent, England was a 'heathen' land, except for the areas covered by the Celtic Church in the West and the North. From the beginning of the mission, episcopal confirmation, presumably according to the Roman rite, was regarded as an indispensable feature of Christian initiation. It is said that crowds of converts were baptized – as many as ten thousand in one day! Most of this baptizing was no doubt carried out by presbyters, but the Roman ritual would not allow them to administer confirmation. The laying on of hands was associated with the gift of the Holy Spirit, but there were too few bishops to administer confirmation to so many converts. One can only conclude that several people were never confirmed.

J. D. C. Fisher's scholarly book on 'Christian Initiation: Baptism in the Medieval West' has as its significant subtitle 'A study in the disintegration of the primitive rite of initiation'. Beginning in the seventh century, he shows how in the following thousand years the rite was divided into three distinct parts – baptism, confirmation and communion – except in the Orthodox Churches. This formed the background to the liturgical work of the Reformers, at which we shall look presently, and is relevant in considering any future revision of Christian initiation, as we shall see in the next chapter.

Fisher points out that the oldest baptismal liturgy emanating from any part of the British Isles is found in the Stowe Missal, 'an Irish book dating from around AD 800, though possibly containing older material.' The rite in the Stowe Missal has the 'pedilavium' (feet washing) but no episcopal imposition of hands. It has one unction only after baptism, performed by a presbyter, who follows a rubric direction: 'in cerebrum in fronte', which signifies conferring the Holy Spirit. This rite, therefore, includes confirmation by a priest – a rite which may have been practised in Ireland until the twelfth century.

In 1172 the Synod of Cashel ruled that the Roman rite as used in England be adopted by the Church of Ireland. 'Hence,' says Fisher, 'there arose in Ireland the same situation which we have encountered in Gaul, Germany and England, in that the presence of a bishop is henceforward indispensable, if the initiatory rite is to be celebrated in its entirety.'[51]

Faustus's famous sermon

People living in remote areas miles away from a bishop might well have asked what was to be gained by confirmation. Such sentiments prompted Faustus (late 5th century) – a semi-Pelagian bishop, probably of British origin, Abbot of Lérins from 437 – to deal with this issue in a Pentecostal sermon, a sermon destined to have an unexpectedly great influence on the later theology of confirmation in the West. Faustus declared: 'Someone may ask, "What good can the ministry of him who confirms do for me after the mystery of baptism? I see," he may say, "that we do not receive so much from the font if afterwards we have need of something else in addition."'

Faustus replies by using a military metaphor to show that confirmation supplies the baptized person with weapons for spiritual conquest in life's battles. He says: 'The Holy Spirit who descended upon the baptismal waters bearing salvation, gave at the font all that is needed for innocence; at confirmation he gives an increase for grace . . . In baptism we are born again to life; after baptism we are confirmed for battle. In baptism we are washed; after baptism we are strengthened.'

Confirmation does not provide the initial gift of the Holy Spirit – for the Holy Spirit was effective in baptism, which is not 'incomplete in its kind'. But there is a gift of a different nature conferred by the

Holy Spirit – the help essential for the battle of living. Milner observes that 'the distinction between new birth from water and the Holy Spirit, and the assistance of the Spirit for the subsequent growth, goes back to Irenaeus and beyond and is probably the basis on which the Western distinction of the two rites has always rested.'[52]

The events in the time that followed the delivery of Faustus's sermon did not favour the development of confirmation as an independent rite. All the evidence in Gaul and Northern Italy during the next two and a half centuries shows that the separate episcopal rite – called confirmation – was unknown. The liturgical books from these areas include simplified ceremonies of initiation – baptism, chrismation and Holy Communion – administered by a priest. The Holy Spirit was believed to be conveyed through chrismation, which had been previously consecrated by the bishop.

This famous sermon by Faustus is said to be the first known attempt to base a theology of initiation on a disintegrated rite. He interpreted confirmation in terms of Pentecost. In this ceremony, the Holy Spirit completed and sealed baptism. It would appear that Faustus was the first person to use the noun 'confirmatio' as a liturgical term. The corresponding verb was used by the Council of Riez in 439 with regard to confirming neophytes, an expression understood in South Gaul, where baptism was by the presbyter and confirmation by the bishop. Faustus, however, used a different verb (roboramur) when referring to confirmation as strengthening. When 'confirm' was first used, confirmation was a sacramental act conveying grace – it did not include the renewal of baptismal promises.

This teaching of Faustus on the relationship between baptism and confirmation was accepted as standard doctrine by the medieval church because of its inclusion in the 'False Decretals' which were considered genuine by such church leaders as Thomas Aquinas and Gratian, the compiler of canon law.[53]

The False Decretals

The 'False Decretals' make an interesting and astonishing story – a story that can hardly be condoned by the suggestion that perhaps the ends justified the means. The ends envisaged included the restoration of the bishops' exclusive right to administer confirmation – an episcopal administration that was opposed by the secular rulers. It was known that the only religious authority the rulers would respect was the ancient decretals of the Roman Pontiffs. Leading clerics, therefore, decided on an ingenious forgery which proved more successful and influential than they could ever have imagined. A canonical collection was produced and inserted in an earlier genuine collection of Conciliar acts edited by Isidore of Seville (c. 560–636) – a collection of ancient texts adaptable to the current subordination of bishops by the secular powers. These 'False Decretals' (called also 'Pseudo-Isidorian Decretals') deceived not only the state rulers but canonists and theologians of later times. They were included in the Decretals of Gratian and made an impact on the belief and practice of Christian initiations for many years – indeed throughout and beyond the Middle Ages.

Gregory Dix goes so far as to say that 'the debate on "Confirmation Today" in the Upper House of Canterbury in May 1945 revealed that its members . . . still stand staunchly by the doctrine first promulgated in the Forged Decretals.'[54] Their genuineness was first questioned by Nicholas of Cusa and Juan Torquemada in the fifteenth century.[55] Dix sums up the situation by saying: 'It is not only that these pseudo-decretals are cited as authoritative in every discussion . . . or in dispute about essentials . . . as to whether confirmation is a sacrament at all; . . . they are even cited again with respect in the discussion at Trent, and by Catholic and Protestant controversialists later still. But what is far more serious is that the limitations of their treatment became permanent for Western theology' – including the whole content and meaning of confirmation.[56]

A. T. and R. P. Hanson in their book 'Reasonable Belief' point out that in the West, during the reformation of church life in the reign of the Emperor Charlemagne, bishops in their diocesan travels laid hands on older children in what was considered to be a sacrament of strengthening for Christian living. From this form of confirmation the Anglican Reformers were led to abolish anointing with oil in baptism and to develop the imposition of hands in preparation for a mature Christian life and in readiness to receive the Eucharist. Such is the background to the service of confirmation in the Church of England, the administration being carried out solely by a bishop.[57]

Rabanus Maurus (c. 776–856) and his former tutor, Alcuin, held that the first post-baptismal unction by the presbyter conferred the Holy Spirit, but they needed to determine the meaning of the chrismation and hand-laying by the bishop, which by tradition also conferred the Holy Spirit. They concluded that the episcopal imposition of the hand conveyed the Spirit of sevenfold grace to strengthen the baptized. Their interpretation led to the later view that the grace of confirmation should be understood as strengthening.

During Rabanus's time, the Carolingian bishops reasserted their part in confirmation – thus forming a separate ceremony of the laying on of hands and so avoiding any duplication with the chrismation performed by the presbyters, which was the traditional form of confirmation in Gaul. Rabanus defines the theological meaning of this second rite by saying that the Holy Spirit is given in confirmation so that the recipient 'may be strengthened to preach to others the same gift which he himself received in baptism.'[58]

In the latter part of the eighth century, the Carolingian bishops, in restoring the episcopal imposition of hands, seem to have been influenced by the events in Samaria and Ephesus as recorded in Acts 8 and 19. Rabanus is said to stand midway between primitive and medieval teaching. Primitive tradition appears in practice, but 'all the elements of the medieval theory – one might say of the modern Anglican theory – are now taking shape, though they have not yet been put together.'[59]

Thomas Aquinas (1224–1274) who had a great influence on Western theology, saw confirmation as the sacrament of growth, the rite by which the soul develops from spiritual infancy to spiritual maturity. Presumably unaware of the unreliability of his source, he quotes Pope Melchiades as saying: 'The Holy Spirit . . . in the font confers all that is needed to restore innocence, in confirmation he supplies a growth in grace; in baptism we are generated to life, after baptism we are confirmed for combat; in baptism we are washed, after baptism we are strengthened'. These words attributed to Melchiades were later traced to the Pentecostal sermon preached by Faustus, Abbot of Lérins, in the fifth century.

Thomas – like his contemporaries – was clearly misled by the interpolations of Pseudo-Isidore as to the sources quoted. Thus was his theological foundation undermined. He also faltered in his interpretation of the phrase 'augmentum praestat ad gratiam'. This meant 'supplies an addition to grace', but Aquinas rendered 'augmentum' as spiritual growth or maturity. However questionable his definition of the grace of confirmation, he attached importance to the rite, without making it essential to salvation.[60]

While still with Aquinas, we observe that he solved the problem – to his satisfaction – of ascribing the institution of confirmation to

Christ by saying that the Lord promised rather than presented it. This meant that Thomas traced the founding of this rite to the church, as inspired by the Holy Spirit.[61]

Confirmation – a neglected rite

The general subordination of confirmation to baptism in medieval times prompted the Council of Lambeth in 1281 to deplore the neglectfulness in the teaching and practice of confirmation and to rule that 'none shall be admitted to the Sacrament of the Lord's Body and Blood . . . unless he be confirmed or reasonably hindered from being confirmed.'[62] The last clause provided a means of evading the rite. The question of administering Holy Communion before confirmation is still very much a live issue. A motion from the House of Bishops that 'experiments in admitting people to communion before confirmation be discontinued' was turned down by the General Synod, meeting in York in July 1991. This debatable issue will be dealt with more fully in the next chapter. A regulation, requiring a person to be confirmed before receiving the eucharist, appeared in the Sarum Manual and in the 1662 Book of Common Prayer, which reads: 'And there shall none be admitted to the Holy Communion until such time as he be confirmed or be ready and desirous of being confirmed.' The exceptive clause recognised practical difficulties.

Dix says that the last official attempt he can trace of getting confirmation administered in close association with infant baptism is a Canon of the Diocesan Synod of Exeter in 1287, ruling that parents who do not have their children confirmed by the age of three must fast on bread and water every Friday unto they do![63] This prompts Dix to refer to the eucharistic doctrine of 'Concomitance' whereby one kind is as sacramentally effective as both; and then says that an equivalent theory of 'Baptismal Concomitance' is developing in practice whereby 'all the effects of the reception of both Baptism-in-water and Baptism-in-the-Spirit come to be ascribed to the reception of Baptism-in-water alone.'[64]

Moving into another area of church life in the Middle Ages, we note that there is some evidence of neglect or indifference with regard to the administration of confirmation on the part of some bishops and parents. It needs to be borne in mind, however, that certain bishops were pre-occupied with affairs of state.

Deanesly's book on Medieval Church history has pages that make rather depressing reading. It states that young children were confirmed, blessed and anointed with chrism by the bishop; but adds that at times, during the fourteenth century, no appointments were made and no records were kept. Deanesly adds that 'the administration of confirmation in the early medieval centuries must have been casual in the extreme, a careless bishop blessing the children without troubling to dismount.'[65]

Professor Anthony Hanson writes in a somewhat similar strain when he points out that confirmation, administered from seven years of age, usually depended on the bishop's uncertain visit. 'It is plain,' he says, 'that bishops would often confirm by the roadside, from horseback, or in a field; often blessing the children from afar rather than laying hands on each individual. There can be no doubt that a very great number of people were never confirmed at all.'[66]

This sort of situation raised the question as to how essential confirmation is. The view that one was not a full Christian until confirmed was taken to imply that baptism was defective. To meet this problem, Alexander of Hales (c. 1170–1245) argued that there was 'the fullness of sufficiency and the fullness of abundance; the first given in baptism, the second in confirmation. Or there is the fullness in essence and the fullness in strength.'[67] This distinction qualified the Canon Law statement that confirmation was essential, and supported the view that confirmation did not add anything indispensable to the grace conveyed in Baptism.[68]

The Reformation

The Reformation in the sixteenth century saw the following changes in the rite of confirmation:

(1) The ancient prayer for the sevenfold gift of the Holy Spirit was retained.
(2) The use of oil was abolished and replaced by the imposition of hands.
(3) The formula which had accompanied the unction was revised to fit in with the practice of hand-laying.
(4) The prayer at the end of the Sarum ritual was replaced by a prayer taken from Hermann.
(5) The 1549 Book of Common Prayer omitted the oil, but retained the sign of the cross immediately before the laying on of hands.
(6) The 1552 Prayer Book omitted also the sign of the cross and the 'formulary again changed to that which remains in use today.'

The purpose was to bring confirmation more in line with Scripture.[69]

On earlier pages, we raised the question whether the rite of confirmation was essential to salvation. This question is answered by the reformers in the 1552 Prayer Book, which says that it is safe to defer confirmation because 'it is certain by God's word that children being baptized have all things necessary for their salvation and be undoubtedly saved.' No subsequent Anglican Prayer Book has ruled against this judgement.

As for the reformers' preference for the episcopal imposition of hands, they saw this action as reflecting apostolic practice and in connection with the instruction of children. The 1549 Prayer Book rules that candidates for confirmation must know the Creed, the Lord's Prayer and the Ten Commandments. Whitaker follows this up by saying that already we see the confirmation service 'acquiring the two-fold character which it has today, consisting first of the renewal of the baptismal vows and then the laying on of hands with prayer.'[70]

Baptism in the New Testament and in the Didache is generally considered to have been a simple ritual but, as we saw earlier, it became increasingly complex, with exorcism, anointing and hand-laying, etc. From about the fifth century, infant baptism seems to have been universally practised and, with the unavailability of a bishop, was separated from the ceremonial parts which became known as confirmation. The Medieval Church regarded both parts as one rite of initiation. But, at the Reformation, Calvin and other leaders regarded the episcopal administration as merely repeating what had taken place at baptism. The implication was plain. Was confirmation really necessary? In the minds of some Reformers, it was a superfluous episcopal ritual. Never was confirmation more in search of a theology.

Another aim, evident in the Reformation, was to relate confirmation to baptism in a way that would evoke the requisite response of faith in Christian initiation. It was not an aim which infants could be expected to fulfil. Emphasis was placed on the catechetical rather than on the sacramental aspect of confirmation.

The Reformers' development of confirmation helped to meet the deficiency of infant baptism by providing a profession of faith (sola fide) followed by the bishop's blessing and prayer for the enabling power of the Holy Spirit. It is pointed out that the main stress in the Prayer Book is not on the gift of the Spirit but on the believer's increased experience of the Spirit already given at baptism. The Anglican service is designed so that the candidates can ratify their baptismal vows and for the church through the bishop to confirm their testimony.

Martin Luther

Martin Luther assessed and interpreted the rite of confirmation. He rejected the medieval ritual of confirmation because he believed that it was only a human invention, not divinely instituted, and therefore it was neither a sacrament nor a means of grace. He held that to say it conferred the Holy Spirit detracted from baptism. As for the apostolic laying on of hands in the New Testament, this, he argued, was designed to provide foreign tongues for preaching the gospel, but did not last. For this reason, Luther did not draw up a rite of confirmation as such, but produced a catechism for children to learn before being admitted to Holy Communion.[71]

Luther wrote at great length on confirmation in his 'Babylonian Captivity' (1520). In a significant passage, he questioned why the laying on of hands should give rise to the 'sacrament' of confirmation. He reckoned it had no foundation in Scripture and darkly suggested that it was a Romanist pretext 'devised to embellish the duties of bishops'! For Luther, confirmation was not a sacrament of divine institution; it was not accompanied by a divine promise, although Christ did lay his hands on people. He quoted the questionable ending of Mark: 'They shall lay hands on the sick and they shall recover' (16.18), and commented: 'No one has turned this into a sacrament, because it is impossible.'

Fisher points out that according to Luther the validity of a sacrament depends on whether the New Testament quotes Jesus as saying that a particular act was an outward sign of inward grace. By this criterion, he concluded that confirmation, whether by hand-laying or sealing with chrism, was not a sacrament and therefore was not essential to salvation.

In 1522, despite his reservations, Luther wrote: 'I allow that confirmation be administered provided that it is known that God has said nothing about it, and knows nothing about it,[72] and that what the bishops allege about it is false. They mock our God in saying that it is a sacrament of God, when it is a merely human invention.'[73]

Luther's position may be summed up by saying that he tolerated a form of confirmation that consisted merely of a sincere blessing of children who had been taught the faith. We should bear in mind that later Lutheran rites of confirmation were not drawn up by Luther.[74]

Ulrich Zwingli (1484–1531) denied that confirmation was a sacrament and practised no such rite at Zurich. He taught that Jesus instituted only two sacraments – baptism and the Lord's Supper. Zwingli considered that confirmation began when infant baptism became widespread; and he shared the view of other Reformers that in ancient times there existed a more perfect form of this rite.[75]

In 1538, Bucer (1491–1551) drew up the 'Ziegenhain Order of Church Discipline' in which children were questioned about the Christian faith by the pastor, who then asked the congregation to pray that the children might persevere and be given an increase of the Holy Spirit. Finally the pastor laid his hands on them, confirming them in the Lord's name, after which they were given Holy Communion. This is another instance of presbyteral confirmation.

In the 'Consultation' – produced by Bucer and Melanchthon in 1543 – Bucer says that since infants cannot confess their faith, they must do so when they are older and have learnt the benefits of baptism. Following the example of Christ and his apostles, the laying on of hands is used. Whenever possible, the bishop officiated, but in his absence a deputy took his place, in order to avoid having to postpone the confirmation. The officiant lays his hands on them and says: 'Confirm this thy servant with the Holy Spirit, that he may continue in the obedience of the Gospel and strongly resist the devil and his own weakness and not grieve the Holy Ghost.' The use of oil was given up because of its being associated with superstition. This is significant because of its influence on Cranmer and on the Book of Common Prayer.

In 1538 at Ziegenhain an 'Order of Church Discipline' was produced, including these rules regarding confirmation:

Children who have received catechetical instruction and are qualified for Holy Communion, shall on a high festival, e.g. Easter, be presented to the pastors in the congregation. When the children have answered questions and committed themselves to Christ, the pastor lays his hands on the children, confirming them in the name of the Lord and establishing them in Christian fellowship and admitting them to Holy Communion.

Calvin and Confirmation

John Calvin (1509–1564) had some very definite and disparaging views concerning confirmation. He rejected the medieval rite as a pretended sacrament that was not supported by Scripture. The idea that confirmation equipped the Christian for spiritual battles reduced the efficacy of baptism, by which we put on Christ, with his gifts. Moreover, he claimed that the imposition of hands in Acts 8 was a sign that ceased when its effects ended.

In the original edition of the Institutes in 1536, Calvin wrote that he wished the custom had been retained which was 'practised among the ancients before this abortive image of a sacrament made its appearance'. It was not such a confirmation as the Romanists pretend – an injury to baptism – but a catechetical exercise, in which children or youths professed their faith before the church.[76]

In the revised edition of 1543, Calvin enlarged on this view by saying that the ancient custom was for the children of Christians when old enough to be presented to the bishop who examined them by reference to the catechism. 'That this exercise . . . might have the greater dignity and reverence, they also practised the ceremony of the imposition of hands . . . This custom is frequently mentioned by ancient writers.'[77]

Fisher points out that early Church practice does not support Calvin's claim. Hippolytus's Apostolic Tradition (AD c. 217) and the Gelasian Sacramentary (sixth century) show that infants were baptized, confirmed and communicated at the same time; but, if no bishop was available, confirmation was deferred, sometimes indefinitely. There was a public confession of faith in primitive baptismal liturgies; but this was part of the catechumenate before baptism, known as the 'redditio symboli'. Adults confessed their faith in person, infants through sponsors.[78]

Calvin's belief in an original form of confirmation in Apostolic times – later corrupted – was widely shared in the sixteenth century, as shown in the writings of Bucer, Cranmer, Jewell and Whitgift. But Calvin did not introduce this supposedly primitive practice in his own church at Geneva.

In his severe criticism of confirmation, Calvin stated that it is 'one of the most deadly wiles of Satan . . . that this pretended sacrament is nowhere recommended in Scripture, either under this name or with this ritual or this signification.' Calvin goes on to ask how the Roman papacy will 'assure us that chrism is the vessel of the Holy Spirit. We see oil, a thick and vicious liquid, and we see nothing besides.' He asks: 'Who has taught them to seek salvation in oil? Who has taught them to attribute to it the property of imparting spiritual strength?'[79]

Calvin also sceptically questions how oil which man terms chrism can receive 'a new and secret virtue of the Spirit'. Oil, he says, is not mentioned by any ancient Christian writer, nor by anybody in the Middle Ages, 'wherein numerous errors abound'. Fisher adds a corrective comment: 'This is a wildly inaccurate assertion. Every Western rite of initiation from the time of Tertullian, at the end of the second century, included an anointing with oil after the act of baptism, and the Fathers frequently referred to it.'[80]

Calvin also speaks disparagingly of the rule that only bishops can administer confirmation on the ground that it is not biblical. He argues that 'if a reason be sought from Scripture, all confess that it makes no distinction between a bishop and a presbyter'.[81] He also makes the pertinent observation that, since only bishops are deemed qualified to administer confirmation, why does not the same limiting rule apply to the celebration of the Lord's Supper.[82] This raises the important issue as to why the eucharist which is of undoubted sacramental standing and which carries unquestionable Dominical authority should not have as high an episcopal standing as confirmation – a rite which, at least in Protestant circles, is not officially ranked as a sacrament.

Bucer's 'Consultation' (1543) – as it is briefly called – includes the observation that 'Forasmuch as . . . everyone cannot be visited by one bishop, we must needs procure that this office of examination and confirmation . . . be executed by more persons, seeing that it cannot be done by one.' The parish priest, having prepared the children for confirmation, shall lay his hand upon them and say: 'Confirm this thy servant with thy Holy Spirit that he may continue in the obedience of thy Gospel and strongly resist the devil and his own weakness, and not grieve the Holy Spirit . . .'

An additional note is added stating that 'the sign of oil was wont to be used in confirmation, but because they abused this sign most superstitiously, and forasmuch as . . . signs and shadows of spiritual things ought not to bc so much regarded as the thing and truth itself, the sign of laying on of hands shall be sufficient in this ministration, which the apostles and ancient fathers thought sufficient.'[83]

The 'Antididagma' strongly criticised the 'Consultation's' treatment of confirmation and maintained that the confirmation of the baptized, which is performed by the imposition of episcopal hands and the making of the sign of the cross with holy chrism on the forehead of the baptized, was celebrated from the time of the apostles in the Catholic Church as a great sacrament.[84]

In 1536, the 'Ten Articles' were issued by order of Henry VIII. These dealt only with the three sacraments of baptism, eucharist and penance, which meant that the king now accepted much of Luther's theology as expressed in the 'Babylonian Captivity' – teaching he opposed in 1521, some fifteen years earlier. The 'Ten Articles' led in 1537 to a special session of Convocation which revealed diverse views on whether confirmation was a sacrament instituted by Christ in the New Testament.

Cranmer expressed more radical views than any of the other bishops or theologians. He found no evidence in Scripture that confirmation was instituted by Jesus, or that the 'matter' was to be chrism. He favoured the Lutheran view that the imposition of hands in Acts 8 conveyed a gift that later was terminated. He held that this biblical passage was not related to the rite of confirmation of his day. The Bishops' Book, produced by a group of bishops in 1537, urged bishops and preachers to tell people how the Apostles, knowing that the early Christians at baptism had been regenerated and forgiven and had received grace and gifts of the Holy Spirit, 'yet they used to go unto the people after they were baptized and so, by their prayer and laying of their hands upon them, did give and confer unto them the Holy Spirit.' 'Yet it is not to be thought that there is any such necessity of confirmation of infants, but that they being baptized and dying innocent . . . shall be assured to attain everlasting life.'

In the Questionnaire of 1540, Henry VIII put some questions to a group of bishops and theologians. Fisher sums up their answers by saying that 'there is almost complete agreement that confirmation with the laying on of hands is Scriptural, being derived from . . . Acts 8, and that the use of chrism goes back to the primitive church, if not to the apostolic age itself.'

During the latter part of the King's reign, there were differences of opinion as to the matter, form and effect of confirmation. Cranmer's radical views were not generally accepted. He was probably chiefly responsible for the 1549 Prayer Book, including its order of confirmation, with the title: 'Confirmation, wherein is contained a catechism for children'. The use of the word 'Confirmation' is significant. The rite had been rejected by Zwingli and Calvin and by many of the Lutheran churches. It would appear that this order of confirmation was designed as a continuation of the rite in the Western church dating back to Faustus of Riez in the fifth century.

The 1549 Prayer Book

Commenting on the requirements stated in the First Rubric of the 1549 Prayer Book, Fisher says that 'the argument here put forward . . . to justify on theological grounds the refusal of confirmation to infants shows a singular unawareness of the practice of the primitive church, where normally candidates of any age from infancy upwards were admitted not only to baptism but also to confirmation and communion,[85] . . . and continued in the Western church until the late Middle Ages.'[86]

One wonders what Fisher meant by 'the primitive church' in this context. Is he referring to the church prior to the year AD 200. If so, we would recall our discussion in chapters three and four as to whether there was any direct or convincing evidence of infant initiation into the Christian Church in the New Testament or in the first two centuries. Our examination led us to question this possibility.

A later rubric in this 1549 Prayer Book says that, when the children can repeat the Articles, the Lord's Prayer and the Decalogue and can answer catechetical questions, they shall be presented to the bishop by a godparent for confirmation, which proceeds as follows:

> Minister: Our help is in the name of the Lord,
> Answer: Which hath made both heaven and earth.
> Minister: Blessed is the name of the Lord,
> Answer: Henceforth world without end.
> Minister: The Lord be with you,
> Answer: And with thy spirit.

The prayer that follows is a translation of the corresponding Latin prayers in the 'Sarum Manual', which in turn is derived from the sixth century 'Gelasian Sacramentary'. This shows that the purpose of confirmation is to convey the sevenfold gifts of the Holy Spirit.[87] A rubric says that the bishop shall cross them on the forehead and lay his hand upon their heads saying: 'I sign thee with the sign of the cross and lay my hand upon thee in the name of the Father and of the Son and of the Holy Ghost.' Here the use of one hand dates back to the time of Tertullian around AD 200.

Afterwards, the bishop says: 'The peace of the Lord abide with you', the response being 'And with thy spirit'.

At this point, the prayer in the 'Sarum Manual' referred to chrism and so is omitted. In its place there is a new prayer with elements taken from a collect in the 'Consultation', which includes a reference to the Apostolic imposition of hands.

Then the bishop gives the children the Trinitarian blessing. A final rubric adds: 'And there shall none be admitted to the Holy Communion until such time as he be confirmed'. Baptized persons are urged to learn the catechism and so be eligible to communicate. We recall that infant communion has always been allowed in the Eastern Church and in the West from the third to the twelfth century.

The 1552 Prayer Book

The changes in the 'Order of Confirmation' in the 1552 Prayer Book, as compared with the 1549 Book may be summed up as follows:

(1) The signing of the forehead and the peace are omitted.
(2) The omission of the prayer 'Sign them, O Lord . . .', which includes the words: 'Confirm and strengthen them with the inward unction of the Holy Ghost.'
(3) Instead of 'send down from heaven . . . thy Holy Ghost' in the 1549 Book, the 1552 Prayer Book has 'strengthen them with the Holy Ghost.'

Moreover, the prayer 'Defend, O Lord . . .', said by the bishop over each candidate as he confirms him, did not necessarily indicate an objective gift of the Holy Spirit at that moment. This prayer could be used in a general way apart from confirmation. It is derived from phrases in the long collect in Bucer's 'Consultation',[88] containing the words: 'increase in them the gift of the Spirit that ever going forward in the knowledge and obedience of the gospel . . . they may continue to the end . . . that thou wilt defend them with thy almighty right hand . . .'.

While the hand-laying with prayer in the rite of 1549 could be interpreted as a means of grace wherein the Holy Spirit was sacramentally imparted, the changes made in 1552 made such an interpretation less likely.[89]

Our survey in this chapter has brought together representative views on the relative importance of baptism and confirmation. We have considered the evidence presented in Scripture, the Early Church, the Medieval Church and the Reformation. The writers and theologians, whose views we have included in this enquiry, are not agreed in their assessment of confirmation. Some see it as essential, while others regard it either as merely a completion of baptism, or as an enabling blessing for mission, or as of such minor spiritual potency as to be dispensable. The consensus of opinion among the witnesses we have considered seems clearly to attach more sacramental validity and efficaciousness to baptism than to confirmation.

Some would see the essence of confirmation expressed in a verse written by Charles Wesley (1707–1788) in the eighteenth century:

> 'Jesus, confirm my heart's desire
> To work, and speak, and think for Thee;
> Still let me guard the holy fire,
> And still stir up Thy gift in me.'

Toronto Consultation (1991)

It so happens that, while this chapter was being written, the 'Fourth International Anglican Liturgical Consultation' was being held in Trinity College, Toronto. It took place in August 1991 and lasted five days. A Report has just been published under the title: 'Christian Initiation in the Anglican Communion'. The conference was truly international, consisting of sixty-four liturgical leaders from various parts of the world. It brought together representatives from East and West, North and South. The convenor of the Consultation was the Revd Prof David Holeton, of Trinity College, who also edited the report.

Selected statements from this Report on the relative significance and validity of baptism and confirmation serve as a fitting conclusion to this chapter on: 'Is Confirmation Essential?' The Report says that whatever the pastoral strengths of confirmation may be, 'this discipline has lent itself to theological over-valuation and misrepresentation. There is little warrant in Scripture, in the reformers, or in the Prayer Book tradition itself, to support the notion that the imposition of hands somehow completes baptism and concludes the process of Christian initiation. This widespread notion has resulted in the exclusion of baptized children from full participation in the eucharist.' It follows that this has tended to lower the age of confirmation and to produce a less mature participation in it.

The Report adds that in recent years various Anglican provinces have recognized baptism as admitting to Holy Communion, 'as surely as it admits to the body of Christ.' The Report also states that 'the administration of confirmation following adult baptism is unnecessary and misleading and should be discontinued.' Confirmation is 'a pastoral office in its own right, and not as a part of the initiatory process.'

The members of this Toronto Consultation 'produced seven recommendations which are offered to the Anglican Communion as basic principles for Christian initiation.' There was 'a high degree of consensus' – only four of the sixty-four members dissenting from the third of the Recommendations, which were as follows:

(1) The renewal of baptismal practice is an integral part of mission and evangelism. Liturgical texts must point beyond the life of the church to God's mission in the world.
(2) Baptism is for people of all ages, both adults and infants. Baptism is administered after preparation and instruction of the candidates, or where they are unable to answer for themselves, of their parent(s) or guardian(s).
(3) Baptism is complete sacramental initiation and leads to participation in the eucharist. Confirmation and other rites of affirmation have a continuing pastoral role in the renewal of faith among the baptized, but are in no way to be seen as a completion of baptism or as necessary for admission to communion.
(4) The catechumenate is a model for preparation and formation for baptism. We recognize that its constituent liturgical rites may vary in different cultural contexts.
(5) Whatever language is used in the rest of the baptismal rite, both the profession of faith and the baptismal formula should continue to name God as Father, Son and Holy Spirit.
(6) Baptism once received is unrepeatable and any rites of renewal must avoid being misconstrued as rebaptism.
(7) The pastoral rite of confirmation may be delegated by the bishop to a presbyter.

In this chapter we have been looking mostly at the relevant evidence in the past to see what light it throws on the question of the sacramental necessity or effectiveness of confirmation in relation to baptism. We carry over this enquiry into the next chapter where we shall consider the essential features and formulation of Christian initiation in the setting of ecumenism, with particular reference to infant baptism.

CHAPTER TWELVE

Future Prospects – Infant Baptism and Ecumenism

The year 2,000 seems to be much in the minds of some Anglican liturgists as they contemplate the possible revision of the 'Alternative Service Book' when its legal life ends at the turn of the century. This has provided the stimulus for the publication of at least two books on the changes that might be made. One is entitled 'Liturgy for a New Century', published in 1991, which is a sequel to an earlier book, 'Towards Liturgy 2,000', issued two years earlier.

The later book is edited by Michael Perham and consists of articles by various authors. Two of the contributions are of particular relevance to this chapter. One deals with 'Some Ecumenical Considerations' by John Fenwick, the Archbishop of Canterbury's assistant secretary for ecumenical affairs. The other article is concerned with 'Confirmation and its Future', written by David Stancliffe, Provost of Portsmouth and a member of the Liturgical Commission.

In his chapter on ecumenism, John Fenwick says that 'the amount of cross-fertilization that has taken place between various Western Churches' – Roman Catholic, Anglican, Methodist, United Reformed Church and Moravian – 'over the past decade has blurred the distinction between their rites to a remarkable degree.' Fenwick observes that this has had a profound effect on ecumenical attitudes. He illustrates this impact by pointing out that Christians who have attended the services of other denominations have expressed surprise at finding them so similar to the ritual of their own church.

Fenwick believes that *The Alternative Service Book 1980* has contributed to this end. Then, with 'ASB 2,000' in view, he says: 'Now that we have discovered . . . that liturgical revision can contribute to ecumenism, should we not undertake further revision with that aim more explicitly in view?' With this in mind, Fenwick holds that we should make better use of the liturgical traditions already available to us.[1]

The 20th century has seen an amazing moving together of the

Christian churches. Bigotry and a claim to possess a monopoly of the truth have diminished. The churches are not only talking but listening to one another. Our study has shown the extent to which Christians of different communions have gone in their mutual recognition of baptism as the entry into the church and into the kingdom of God. The problem lies in the diversity of view regarding the theology and practice of the baptismal rite and the interpretation of its relationship to confirmation.

Whatever the varying views or emphases with respect to baptism or confirmation have been, it is widely recognised that in the Early Church Christian initiation had a wholeness which subsequent centuries have tended to take apart. As the 'Apostolic Tradition' shows, water-baptism and what came to be called 'confirmation', as well as Holy Communion, belonged together. But, as we have seen, some writers question the necessity of reuniting these sundered parts and see salvation essentially either in water-baptism or in Spirit-baptism. As for the eucharist, we saw how this has not always been administered in the same place in the larger setting of Christian initiation.

In the Orthodox Churches, as we have already observed, this liturgical unity has been, and still is, already practised at infancy by a rite that combines the three elements of baptism, 'confirmation' and communion. But many people would rule out a re-unification at infancy despite precedents in the past. Adding to the child's passivity at baptism, the further rites of confirmation and communion, in which also the infant would not be personally responsive, would not be widely acceptable.

It seems to be generally recognised that the practice of infant baptism presents the chief problem in restoring the wholeness of Christian initiation. Some of the reasons for the tenacious hold that the infant rite has had in the past, and still has in the present, have been touched upon earlier in this book. The parental concern for emergency 'christening' lest a baby dies unbaptized appears to stem unwittingly from past beliefs regarding eternal salvation – beliefs which have long since shed their irrational and unbiblical presuppositions.

World Council of Churches

The 'Faith and Order Paper No. III' entitled *Baptism, Eucharist and Ministry* (BEM), issued by the World Council of Churches in 1982, aroused more world-wide interest and response than the writers of the report envisaged. The importance and centrality of baptism in the ecumenical movement is touched on repeatedly in this sensitively worded document. The same can be said of the sequel, consisting of a *Report on the Process and Responses*, the 'Faith and Order Paper No. 149', published by the World Council in 1990.

What we have just said was borne out by a statement on BEM issued by the Faith and Order Commission in 1989 to the effect that 'no one envisaged the impact which it would have within and among the churches of such diverse historical origins and such varying traditions. This fruit of many years of ecumenical discussion has become the most widely distributed, translated and discussed ecumenical text in modern times.'[2]

In anticipation of the attention we shall give later to the ecumenical significance of infant baptism in the mainstream churches, let us first look at some of the relevant features concerning initiation in the Lima statement (1982) and in the subsequent survey of the responses of the churches to BEM.

With reference to the desirability of the churches mutually to recognize their various practices of baptism as sharing in the one baptism, the commentary (6) says: 'The need to recover baptismal unity is at the heart of the ecumenical task as it is central for the realization of genuine partnership within the Christian communities.'[3]

In an earlier chapter, we considered the question of how the widely recognized baptismal prerequisites of repentance and faith can be related to a child below the age of reason and individual responsibility. The question will be raised again later in this chapter. On this subject the Lima text says: 'While the possibility that infant baptism was also practised in the apostolic age cannot be excluded, baptism upon personal profession of faith is the most clearly attested pattern in the New Testament documents.[4]

Another debatable and timely topic is touched upon when the Lima Commentary raises the question as to why confirmation has to be interposed between baptism and the eucharist, in view of the fact that baptism is incorporation into the body of Christ. The issue was raised at the General Synod of the Church of England in July 1991. The BEM document makes bold to say: 'Those churches which baptize children but refuse them a share in the eucharist before such a rite (confirmation) may wish to ponder whether they have fully appreciated and accepted the consequences of baptism.'[5]

The question of linking communion to baptism without confirmation is raised again in the BEM Report on the church responses. It says: 'According to many churches . . . baptized children should be admitted to eucharistic communion.' Three reasons are given:-

(1) 'Baptism has definite ecclesiological implications and is a basic bond and expression of the given unity in Christ . . .'
(2) 'There is theological content common to both baptism and the eucharist, such as the theology of the covenant; participation in the death and resurrection of Christ; their pneumatological aspects; and the remission of sins.'
(3) 'The Orthodox Churches admit infants, children or adults to the eucharist directly after baptism and chrismation; in the Roman Catholic, and some other traditions, when children and adults are baptized they are confirmed and admitted to the eucharist in the same celebration, after due preparation as catechumens.'[6]

It is remarkable what a rumpus an innocent remark can create – judging by the reaction of certain churches to the phrase 'apparently indiscriminate baptism'. The context, in which the phrase appears, is a brief paragraph which covers both believer baptists and paedobaptists. It reads: 'The first may seek to express more visibly the fact that children are placed under the protection of God's grace. The latter must guard themselves against the practice of apparently indiscriminate baptism and take more seriously their responsibility for the nurture of children to mature commitment to Christ.'[7] There seems to us to be ample evidence to support both statements. We shall consider this question more fully on later pages.

'Report on the Process and Responses'

The relevance of baptism to ecumenism is reiterated in the World Council's second BEM volume. With reference to the replies from the churches to the Lima text, it says: 'Many responses recognize the importance of the text's stress on baptism as the primary and fundamental sacrament of unity and the implications of this for the ecumenical endeavour.' This Report on the churches' Responses adds that they approve paragraph 6, which states: 'Therefore our one baptism into Christ constitutes a call to the churches to overcome their divisions and visibly manifest their fellowship.'[8]

This 'Report on the Process and Responses', in recording the divergent views of various denominations, provides evidence of how far the churches are from organic unity, despite their unanimity in recognizing baptism as the sacrament of entry into the body of Christ, the One Holy Catholic and Apostolic Church. The Baptists would seem to be the farthest from the centre of the ecumenical circle, with their emphasis on believers' baptism, their doubts about the validity of the infant rite and their interpretation of 're-baptism'.

There is, of course, an anomalous side to this situation. All churches responding to BEM agree that baptism is 'incorporation into the body of Christ'. But there remains the divisiveness of ministerial orders. The Roman Catholic Church in its Response says that 'a person is baptized within a particular fellowship in a divided Christianity . . . . The contradiction between one baptism and divided Christian communities calls for an overcoming of division and a visible manifestation of baptismal fellowship.'[9]

The BEM document also makes mention of two Christian groups whose belief and practice set them apart, namely the Society of Friends and the Salvation Army. The 'Quakers' state that 'however valid and vital outward sacraments are for others, they are not in our experience necessary for the operation of God's grace . . . The whole of our everyday experience is the stuff of our religious awareness, it is here that God is best known to us.' The Salvation Army responds by saying that 'the only distinctive and utterly unique Christian baptism is baptism with the Holy Spirit.'[10]

In a paragraph headed 'Conclusion', the Report says that 'the most remarkable fact emerging from the responses of churches to the baptismal section is the degree of convergence that exists in areas of previous dissension . . . The encouragement to pursue this work for the sake of the visible unity of the church, a unity grounded in baptism, is heartening.' The Report, however, recognizes that differences remain – differences in terms of conceptions of faith, of the Holy Spirit, of the Church and its membership, and of the Christian life itself. It claims that understanding such areas as 'ecclesiology, sacramentality, and the sources of Christian authority in Scripture, Tradition and traditions, will both influence, and be influenced by, our understandings of baptism.'[11]

A chapter, entitled 'Draft Clarifications and Comments on Critical Points', deals with the uneasiness and disagreement expressed by several churches 'with regard to the terminology "believers' baptism" over "infant baptism", because it seems to imply the suggestion that infants and children could not be called "believers" (fideles).' The BEM Report defended its terminology on the ground that these terms were 'used by Baptist churches and Disciples and meanwhile common in ecumenical dialogue.' The Report adds that the Lima text and its commentary (1982) explains that 'the terminology does not prejudge the theological problems implied', and that 'believers' baptism' in more than one place in the text, is circumscribed as 'those baptized upon their own confession of faith.' The Report says that 'such persons are not necessarily "adults" in a legal sense, but could also be children of a certain age after due preparation.'[12]

On the relationship between baptism and confirmation, the Report points to the 'remarkable agreement' in the Responses regarding the gift of the Holy Spirit 'to those who die and rise with Christ in baptism'. There is disagreement, however, as to how the anointing and sealing of the Spirit is expressed in the baptismal rite and how it relates to confirmation and participation in the eucharist. The Responses show that some churches see confirmation as signifying the gift of the Spirit in Christian initiation. Others regard the rite as the means by which those baptized in childhood can make later a mature and personal confession of faith. All the churches are agreed that baptism is the first initiatory sign and that the culmination of Christian initiation is 'nourishment in the eucharist'. The Report reveals that the churches see this initiation as a unitary and comprehensive process, even though spread over some years – a total process that embodies God's 'gracious initiative in eliciting our faith.'[13]

On the back cover of a book 'Why It Matters' by Dr Michael Kinnamon is the observation that 'no ecumenical document has received as much attention or generated as much excitement as the convergence statement entitled "Baptism, Eucharist and Ministry".' With reference to the BEM treatment of Baptism, he says that it is 'a textbook example of ecumenical methodology in that it employs such a wide variety of "techniques" and "approaches" in order to deal with these traditional divisions.'[14]

Kinnamon points out that this Lima text makes several fundamental affirmations which, when lifted from a polemical context, could enable the churches to live with the remaining diversity in closer fellowship. Paragraph 5 in the BEM document is quoted as an example: 'The Holy Spirit is at work in the lives of people before, in, and after, their baptism.' To claim otherwise would be to place human limits on the sovereignty of God's grace. Kinnamon says that another illustration is in paragraph 8: 'Baptism is both God's gift and our human response to that gift.' Our faith, however, is not held as a condition for receiving God's grace. 'On the other hand,' writes Kinnamon, 'baptism in infancy demands a personal response of faith at an age of discretion, if it is to be Christian initiation as the New Testament understands it.'[15]

Paragraph 12 of BEM and its commentary are considered to be 'crucial'. Here the debate over baptismal practice is set in the larger context of Christian nurture involving (1) the growth of the child within a supportive Christian community; (2) a confession of faith when old enough; and (3) a lasting commitment to Christ. For believer baptists this involves placing children under the protection of God's grace and the care of the church. Paedobaptists are urged to avoid indiscriminate baptism and to follow more closely the child's spiritual development. Kinnamon also draws attention to BEM's plea for the avoidance of 'any practice that could be interpreted as rebaptism' (paragraph 13), instead of which the churches are urged to hold services for the reaffirmation of baptismal vows. The Lima text moves into another sensitive area when it recommends the acceptance of believers' baptism and infant baptism as 'equivalent alternatives for entry into the church.' Precedents for such an arrangement are, of course, to be found in the United Reformed Church in Britain and in the Church of North India.

Another book arising from the Lima text, entitled *Ecumenical Perspectives on Baptism, Eucharist and Ministry*, contains an article by Lewis Mudge called 'Convergence on Baptism.' Writing as one who had a hand in drafting the text, he refers to it as a 'fragile bridge of words between worlds,' and observes 'how very precariously some of these sentences work their way between – and indeed in, with, and among – historic confessional positions, as well as the theological idiosyncrasies of individual drafters!' Mudge adds that 'it is not the ingenuity of the words themselves that counts. It is the proof they bear that Protestant, Anglican, Roman Catholic and Orthodox theologians can meet, write such sentences together, and call the result "mature" enough to invite their colleagues all over the world to consider steps towards each other which will require a new level of ecumenical confidence.'[16]

It is pointed out that BEM on 'Baptism and Faith' has been drawn up to refer to all types of baptismal practice, whether infant baptism, believers' baptism or some combination of the two. To quote the Lima text: 'When one who can answer for himself is baptized, a personal confession of faith will be an integral part of the baptismal service. When an infant is baptized, the personal response will be offered at a later moment of life. In both cases the baptized person will have to grow in the understanding of faith.'[17]

Lewis Mudge draws attention to Lima's significant commentary on paragraph 12, in which an attempt is made to justify the practice of both infant and believers' baptism in the one church and to recognize them as 'equivalent alternatives'. The text says that the differences between infant and believers' baptism become less sharp when it is recognized that both forms of baptism embody God's own initiative in Christ and express a response of faith made within the believing community. 'The practice of infant baptism emphasizes the corporate faith and the faith which the child shares with its parents . . . . The practice of believers' baptism emphasizes the explicit confession of the person who responds to the grace of God in and through the community of faith and who seeks baptism.'[18]

The problem posed by confirmation is recognized by Mudge who brings out the significance which the Lima text attaches to it. He says that the problem lies in the different ways in which the churches mark the moment of the gift of the Spirit. 'Do they liturgically signify that the gift is given in the act of baptism itself, or . . . with some rite performed at a later moment, such as confirmation or chrismation?' The commentary at this point, says Mudge, is most carefully articulated and one can do no better than quote the key sentences: 'When the signs occur within a single liturgy, they express the fundamental conviction that incorporation into Christ and participation in His Spirit are inseparable. However, when the sign of the Spirit becomes separated from water baptism and does not occur until later in the life of the recipient, a serious problem arises, since it seems that incorporation into Christ is separated from full life in the Spirit. This is the inherent problem of a sacramental interpretation of confirmation.'[19]

British and Irish Churches respond

The Lima Report made an impact on the British and Irish Churches, as their Responses to BEM reveal. The Division of Ecumenical Affairs undertook, on behalf of the British Council of Churches, an analysis of the Responses which the mainstream churches in Britain had produced. The BCC published this report in 1988, with a section on Baptism by the Revd Keith Clements.

The baptismal section of the Lima text appears from this BCC survey to have had a mixed reception from the British churches – what is called a 'general appreciation' and 'a shared unease'. The Roman Catholics, the Baptists, the Methodists, the Moravians, the Anglicans, the Quakers and the Salvationists are quoted in that order as expressing qualified approval. On the other hand, the BEM text has given rise to questioning or criticism in the church responses. The Reformed, Evangelical and Free Church traditions express concern regarding the way in which the word 'Baptism' is used.

The theological use of the term to mean 'incorporation into Christ', 'washing away of sin', 'new birth', etc., prompts the Methodist Church to ask whether it is being said that the rite *effects* these things or simply that it *signifies* them as being important elements in the Christian life into which the baptized person is initiated. 'Methodists to not wish to deny efficacy in the sacraments. However, they plead that the nature of this efficacy be clarified, believing that there are some interpretations of the notion which they must reject.'[20]

The response of the Baptist Union of Great Britain is expressed more tersely: 'We are told that baptism *is* . . . *gives* . . . *unites* . . . *effects*. It has to be asked what is meant by 'baptism' where this sort of language is constantly used. Is it the actual performance of the rite? If so, the language seems at best hyperbole and at worst objectionable. It may be strongly affirmed that the efficacious work of the Gospel can rightly be spoken of in this way, and that baptism relates scripturally to the heart of that Gospel . . . What is not clear is the extent to which the report *identifies* the actual performance of the rite with this vast penumbra of meaning and significance.'[21]

The BCC survey shows that several of the non-episcopal churches share the view that the Lima text, in places, is inclined to confuse the sign (baptism) with the thing signified (the new life in Christ). Some of these churches venture to wonder whether ambiguous or unclear language is being used in BEM to obtain inclusiveness and agreement, indicating lack of convergence between the historic approaches of evangelical and catholic Christianity.

Several church responses viewed favourably the BEM statement that all forms of baptism involve a personal profession of faith – the infant rite looking to a future fulfilment, while a mature person witnesses to his faith when he is baptized. The Church of England's reply to Lima is quoted in support of this position: 'The balance held in the text between God's gift and our response, together with the importance of the community of faith, are all important for the reconciliation between those who practice infant baptism and those who practice only believers' baptism.'

The Anglican response also draws attention to the fact that, in *The Alternative Service Book 1980*, the adult rites of baptism and confirmation are placed first, followed by the baptismal service for infants. This response then observes: 'The prevenient character of God's grace is clearly manifested in infant baptism. Yet there also renunciation, profession of faith, and vows remain essential and are made in the faith of the church by sponsors. To the grace and forgiveness of God, of which baptism is the sign and instrument, the believer must respond in personal profession of faith, through conversion of heart and the acceptance of the ethical implications of baptism.'[22]

The BCC survey lightens the subject with a turn of humour when it represents the Scottish Baptists as saying that the baptismal theology of BEM (paras 1–11) is acceptable – provided it refers to believers' baptism! They go on to say: 'The imposition of this impressive New Testament theology on an unaware infant we find very difficult. The question remains: if faith is necessary for the completion or wholeness of baptism, where does that leave infant baptism in and of itself where such faith does not follow? They conclude that BEM is trying to combine two different theologies.

Somewhat linked with this Baptist statement is a perceptive observation by the Presbyterian Church of Wales: 'Infant baptism is not successfully defended by attempting to transplant into it every element of adult baptism. Greater progress might be made in relations with Baptist Churches if both forms of baptism were defended each on its own grounds as alternative forms, neither form exhibiting *all* the characteristics of the other and yet both exhibiting sufficient characteristics to justify the term "baptism" to both.'[23]

It is not surprising that the complex relationship of baptism, chrismation, confirmation and admission to communion is not solved by the Lima text or by the later BEM Report on the Responses. The BCC survey quotes a rather dispirited statement in the Church of England response: 'Clearly the exact relation between baptism, chrismation, confirmation and first communion is not evident. There is confusion in both belief and practice in the Church of England about which the Lima text gives little guidance. However, the theological principles of the text together with the insistence on the process of initiation will, we believe, enable us to understand what is legitimate difference in practice within a united church.'[24]

On the subject of what rite qualifies a person for church membership, the Presbyterian Church of Wales, echoing the sentiments of some other churches, says that the emphasis upon baptism as incorporation into the Body of Christ raises the question, for us, of the meaning of subsequent 'reception into *full* membership.' In what sense is a baptized child not a full member of the church? 'We welcome the final sentence of para. 8: "Personal commitment is necessary for responsible membership in the Body of Christ", but whereas other churches have been reconsidering the relation of confirmation to baptism, the PCW has not seriously assessed the significance of reception into full membership in its relation to baptism.'[25]

So far in this chapter we have been considering the rite of Christian initiation in the larger setting of the 'One Holy Catholic and Apostolic Church', with particular reference to the baptism of infants. We now focus our attention in turn on each of the main Christian denominations, beginning with the Roman Catholic Church. We shall look at the two rites which are most in line with this enquiry, namely the 'Rite of Baptism for Children' and the 'Rite of Confirmation'.

The Roman Catholic Church

Father James Shaughnessy, in the Foreword to Mark Searle's book on *Christening: The Making of Christians*, says that the new 'Rite of Baptism for Children' in 1969 was the first to take into account the fact that those to be baptized were infants. He said that the rite also emphasised the need for 'a proper indoctrination and preparation of parents, godparents and others.'[26]

Mark Searle points out that the revision of the liturgy of initiation was carried out by a Commission, but that the Council of Vatican II laid down the guidelines. These called for a change of style, a reversion to the traditional celebration of initiation, requiring the return of the adult rites of initiation to their original shape, including the catechumenate. 'The rite of baptism for infants is to be adapted to their condition as infants and the role of parents and godparents . . . is to be made more explicit.' The connection of confirmation with baptism and the eucharist is also to be made clear.

As Searle sees it, the adult rites of initiation are normative and that the infant rite will always need to be understood as the first stage in a growth towards Christian maturity. 'The sacraments are not magic. Grace builds on nature, and the sacraments of initiation – baptism, confirmation, eucharist – are but milestones in the spiritual journey of the awakening child.'[27]

On a later page of his comprehensive study of initiation, Mark Searle says that 'in the case of children . . . confirmation and first communion are generally separated from baptism by . . . several years. Because of this, it is . . . difficult to explain the meaning of confirmation, or to decide at what age it should be conferred or indeed to know why it should be celebrated at all.'[28]

For a closer study of baptism and confirmation we now turn to the large comprehensive Roman Catholic volume described as 'The Rites of the Catholic Church as Revised by Decree of the Second Vatican Ecumenical Council and Published by Authority of Pope Paul VI.' The Preface adds that the 'Roman Ritual has undergone numerous revisions since the edition of Pope Paul V of 1614. Now, in response to the directives of the Second Vatican Ecumenical Council, a new edition has been undertaken by the Holy See. One of the animating principles that has guided the preparation of the new rites is to encourage the people of God to understand and participate more fully in these sacred celebrations.'[29]

Rite of Baptism for Children (1969)

The 'Rite of Baptism for Children' is introduced by a Decree headed 'Sacred Congregation for Divine Worship' and reads: 'The Second Vatican Council decreed that the rite of baptism for children in the Roman Ritual should be revised in order that: (a) the rite might be better adapted to the actual condition of children: (b) the role and responsibilities of parents and godparents might be more clearly expressed; (c) suitable adaptations might be made for the baptism of a large number of people; (d) suitable adaptations might likewise be made for baptism administered by catechists in mission areas or by others in circumstances when the ordinary minister is unavailable; (e) a rite might be provided for use when a child has already been baptized according to the shorter rite, to mark the fact that he has already been received into the Church.'

The rite for the 'Baptism for Children' is preceded by an 'Introduction', offering interpretation and guidance for administration.[30] We select what seem to us to be the more significant features. This 'Introduction' first says that children or infants are to be understood as those who have not reached the age of discernment and are therefore unable to profess personal faith. It is then stated that 'from the earliest times, the Church . . . has baptized children as well as adults' – (a debatable question which we discussed in chapters 3 and 4) – therefore 'children should not be deprived of baptism, because they are baptized in the faith of the church'.[31] The 'Introduction' adds that 'to fulfil the true meaning of the sacrament, children must later be formed in the faith in which they have been baptized', and adds that 'the faith in which the children are baptized . . . is the common treasure of the whole Church of Christ.'

It is also stated that 'parents have a more important ministry and role in the baptism of infants than godparents', and that they 'should prepare to take part in the rite with understanding' – preparation in which the church should help. Both parents are not only expected to be present, but to be meaningfully involved in the celebration, including their signing the child with the cross, their renunciation of evil and their profession of faith. The priest is also required to see that 'baptism is always celebrated with proper dignity.'

The 'Introduction' recommends that baptism is celebrated during the Easter Vigil or on Sunday, even during Mass, 'so that the entire community may be present and the necessary relationship between baptism and eucharist may be clearly seen.' It is also stated that 'except in the case of danger, baptism should not be celebrated in private houses.'

Baptism is by 'immersion or infusion' and by invocation of the Trinity. The sacrament ends with the anointing with chrism, [32] 'which signifies the royal priesthood of the baptized', then by the ceremonies of the white garment, lighted candle and Ephphetha (optional). The celebration ends with the Lord's Prayer and a threefold blessing over mothers, fathers and all those present.

One significant feature is the responsibility which the church places upon the parents and to an understandably lesser extent upon the godparents: 'You have asked to have your children baptized. In doing so, you are accepting the responsibility of training them in the practice of the faith . . . . Do you clearly understand what you are undertaking?' One of the responsive prayers says: 'Make the lives of their parents and godparents examples of faith to inspire these children.' This is far removed from 'indiscriminate baptism'.

One element that is distinctive in this celebration, in comparison with most other modern rites of baptism, is the explicit reference to Satan and to original sin.[33] The celebrant offers this prayer of exorcism: 'Almighty and ever-living God, you sent your only Son into the world to cast out the power of Satan, spirit of evil . . . We pray for these children, set them free from original sin, make them temples of your glory and send your Holy Spirit to dwell within them.'

Another feature, which is not universally practised ecumenically in baptismal liturgy, is the anointing with oil. Here it is said that the celebrant 'anoints each child on the breast with the oil of catechumens' and says: 'We anoint you with the oil of salvation in the name of Christ our Saviour; may he strengthen you with his power, who lives and reigns for ever and ever.'

On previous pages, the question has often been raised as to whether the gift of the Holy Spirit is associated with baptism or with confirmation or with both. In this rite it is clearly linked with baptism when the celebrant says: 'My dear brothers and sisters, we now ask God to give these children new life in abundance through water and the Holy Spirit.' In connection with the blessing of the baptismal water, the priest touches the water with his right hand and says: 'We ask you, Father, with your Son to send the Holy Spirit upon the water of this font. May all who are buried with Christ in the death of baptism rise also with him to newness of life.'

By questions and answers, the parents and godparents renounce evil and profess the faith, followed by the actual baptism, after which the celebrant anoints each child on the crown of the head with chrism. The priest introduces the anointing with the words: 'God the Father of our Lord Jesus Christ has freed you from sin, given you a new birth by water and the Holy Spirit, and welcomed you into his holy people. He now anoints you with the chrism of salvation. As Christ was anointed Priest, Prophet, and King, so may you live always as members of his body, sharing everlasting life.'

After the anointing, the children are clothed in a white garment. In explanantion of this, the celebrant says: 'You have become a new creation and have clothed yourselves in Christ. See in this white garment the outward sign of your Christian dignity. With your family and friends to help you by word and example, bring that dignity unstained into the everlasting life of heaven.'

The Rite of Confirmation (1971)

A Decree under the heading 'Sacred Congregation For Divine Worship' states:

'In the sacrament of confirmation the apostles and the bishops, who are their successors, hand on to the baptized the special gift of the Holy Spirit, promised by Christ the Lord and poured out upon the apostles at Pentecost. Thus the initiation in the Christian life is completed so that believers are strengthened by power from heaven, made true witnesses of Christ in word and deed, and bound more closely to the church.'[34]

With the authority of Pope Paul VI, it is said that 'the faithful are born anew by baptism, strengthened by the sacrament of confirmation, and finally are sustained by the food of eternal life in the eucharist.'[35] Tertullian is quoted as saying: 'The body is washed, that the soul may be cleansed; the body is anointed, that the soul may be consecrated; the body is signed, that the soul may be fortified; the body is overshadowed by the laying on of hands, that the soul too may be enlightened by the Spirit; the body is fed on the body and blood of Christ, that the soul too should be nourished by God.'[36]

The Second Vatican Ecumenical Council ruled that the sacraments of initiation be revised to make them 'more suited to the understanding of the faithful.' The rite of confirmation has been revised so that 'the intimate connection which this sacrament has with the whole of Christian initiation should be more lucidly set forth.' Confirmation is here set forth as the rite 'through which the faithful receive the Holy Spirit as a gift.'

'Therefore . . . by our supreme apostolic authority we decree and lay down that in the Latin Church the following should be observed for the future: The Sacrament of Confirmation is conferred through the anointing with chrism on the forehead, which is done by the laying on of the hand and through the words: Accipe Signaculum Doni Spiritus Sancti.' (Receive the sign of the gift of the Holy Spirit.)[37]

It is said that the Bishop's hand-laying is the biblical gesture by which the Holy Spirit is bestowed and that the anointing with chrism signifies the effects of the Spirit. Adults and older children may be baptized, confirmed and admitted to the eucharist at the same time.

This 'Introduction' to the rite of confirmation also says: 'This giving of the Holy Spirit conforms believers more perfectly to Christ and strengthens them, so that they may bear witness to Christ for the building up of his body in faith and love. They are so marked with the character or seal of the Lord that the sacrament of confirmation cannot be repeated.'

Emphasis is laid on the qualifications and responsibilities of parents and sponsors. Parents are required 'to form and gradually increase a spirit of faith in the children and . . . prepare them for the fruitful reception of the sacraments of confirmation and the eucharist.' Sponsors must be spiritually qualified, sufficiently mature and practising Roman Catholics.

While in the Latin Church confirmation is usually postponed until about the seventh year, episcopal conferences may choose a more mature age. This 'Introduction' goes on to say: 'Ordinarily confirmation takes place within Mass in order to express more clearly the fundamental connection of this sacrament with the entirety of Christian initiation. The latter reaches its culmination in the communion of the body and blood of Christ.'

'Confirmation outside Mass' takes the following form:

1. Entrance Song
2. Opening Prayer
3. Celebration of the Word of God
4. Presentation of the Candidates
5. Homily or Instruction
6. Renewal of Baptismal Promises
7. The Laying on of Hands
8. The Anointing with Chrism
9. General Intercessions
10. Lord's Prayer
11. Prayer over the People

The above information and observations drawn from 'The Rites of the Catholic Church' are based on the traditional Latin pattern of Christian initiation, with the sequence of baptism, confirmation and eucharist. The pastoral practice in many countries, however, since the early part of the twentieth century, has reversed the traditional order of confirmation and first communion. On earlier pages, we considered the argument that the eucharist can appropriately follow baptism, if baptism involves a sharing of Christ's death and resurrection and thus qualifies for entry to the Church, the body of Christ. We have already noted that in other denominatins also there has been an increasing movement in favour of admitting baptized adults and older children to communion without waiting for confirmation or 'reception into full membership'.

Mark Searle, a Roman Catholic to whose book we have already

referred, reminds us that in the Early Church 'even infants and small children were admitted to Holy Communion after baptism' a practice which 'continued in Rome and was universally accepted.' Searle further observes that 'the tenderness of the children's age was no more thought to be a reason for postponing Holy Communion than it was for postponing baptism.' But from the twelfth century onwards, infant communion practically disappeared due mainly to the fact that fewer and fewer people of any age received the eucharist. Moreover 'in the nineteenth and twentieth centuries, even the traditional order of administering the sacraments . . . was abandoned when the emphasis on early first Communion meant that children went to Communion before they were confirmed, not only in the exceptional case, but as a general rule.' Therefore, says Searle, Vatican II tried to ensure that the continuity of the sacraments of initiation should be restored.[38]

Confirmation before Communion

It was the restoration of the traditional sequence of the initiatory rites which prompted the Roman Catholic diocese of Salford to launch a campaign whereby confirmation would follow baptism and precede first communion. This 'experiment', as it has been called, is described in an article in *New Liturgy* by Father Declan Gallagher.[39]

The article says that the Bishop, Patrick Kelly, was unhappy that the Western Church had settled for confirmation as a sacrament of commitment, where the question of age dominates, rather than as a sacrament of initiation, where the order of sequence matters. It was a situation which had drawn various comments of concern from Rome in recent years – including the following: Vatican II says that the 'intimate connection which this sacrament has with the whole process of Christian initiation is to be more clearly set forth.'[40] In his introduction to the new rite of confirmation (1971), Pope Paul VI writes: 'The faithful are born anew by baptism, strengthened by the sacrament of confirmation, and finally sustained by the food of eternal life in the eucharist.' With reference to the new rite, the Congregation for Divine Worship states: 'Those who have been baptized continue on the path of Christian initiation through the sacrament of confirmation.' Pope John Paul, in 1985, challenged the youth of the world with these words: 'Rethink – and very profoundly – the meaning of baptism and confirmation . . . From these there begins the path towards the eucharist.'

Gallagher's article on 'reforming the sacraments of initiation' also brings out the following points: (1) Parents are chiefly responsible for bringing their children to the faith of the Church; (2) Parents should be supported by the local community, especially by catechists and sponsors; (3) The uniqueness of each candidate must be recognised as they develop in faith; (4) There is need to restore the traditional order of the sacraments. Therefore, says Gallagher, Bishop Kelly 'wishes to examine in his diocese how best to move from the dominant idea that confirmation was a sacrament of commitment or "coming of age" to confirmation as an element of the process of initiation, closely connected with baptism.'

Under the heading of 'A plan of action', this article says that after extensive consultation, involving all parishes and schools, a programme was recommended which incorporated the following points:

(1) The importance of parents, underlined by meetings with them, home visits and encouragement of active sponsorship.
(2) Co-operation between home, the school and the faith community.
(3) A re-ordering of confirmation which should be offered to children about seven years of age, so enabling the sacrament to fit John Paul II's expression 'the path towards the eucharist'.
(4) All preparation and celebration should be related to the liturgical year. This requires preparation to begin in Advent, with confirmation to be celebrated on Pentecost in every parish at a non-eucharistic liturgy.
(5) The children should be introduced to the sacrament of reconciliation during the following Advent in the spirit of the great call 'Prepare the way of the Lord'.
(6) First communion should then take place at the following Easter Sunday. The child would be accompanied by family and sponsors at a Mass of their choice. After several further celebrations of the eucharist, the parish community could decide to celebrate the eucharist with all first communicants.
(7) This would be seen, therefore, as a process involving a growth in the faith of each parishioner and, consequently, a deeper understanding of their role in the parish. This process should be extended to the on-going care of children in the various stages of their faith development.

Father Declan Gallagher concludes his article with this observation: 'A great deal of time and effort will be required in order to establish all of this as a normal part of parish life. The diocese has issued a series of guidelines to help to set up the structures in order that the burdens are shared and to avoid confusion.' The article ends with the words 'The eyes of the world are on Salford!'

The Church of England

Turning our attention to the Church of England, we note that the initiation services in the Alternative Service Book of 1980 were the culmination of demands for a revision stretching back over several years. E. C. Whitaker points out that as long ago as 1938 a joint committee of the Convocation of Canterbury reported that 'there is a great need for a revision of the service for the ministration of public baptism to infants' – a view subsequently endorsed by such reports as 'Confirmation Today' (1944), 'Baptism Today' (1949) and 'Baptism and Confirmation Today' (1955).[41]

These reports considered the question of deferring baptism; the theological relationship of confirmation to the infant rite; the pastoral opportunities presented by requests for baptism; the appropriate age for confirmation; and the role of sponsors. The reports also express concern regarding the Prayer Book's implication that baptism remits the sins of infants.[42] It is also suggested that parents should be personally involved in the vows made at infant baptism. The use of chrism is proposed, and Christ's blessing of the children in Mark 10 is omitted from the Scripture readings. In addition, the reports recommended more modern and simpler initiatory rites.

The way was paved for the realization of such proposals by the passing into law of the 'Prayer Book (Alternative and other Services) Measure' in 1965. Soon followed 'Series Two', then 'Series Three' and eventually the 'Alternative Service Book' of 1980, with its revised services of Baptism and Confirmation. These modern initiatory services were designed to meet widespread criticism and pastoral needs. A significant feature of the revision was the change from 'Thou' to 'You' in addressing the Almighty, and the replacing of various archaic expressions. It is held that such revision need not detract from quality of language or reverence in worship.

The baptism of children

Whitaker holds that a decrease in infant baptism has led to an increase in the baptism of adults. Moreover, since some children are being baptized beyond infancy, the rite for the 'baptism of infants' has become the 'baptism of *children*.' The initiation of adults has given rise to a service combining the three rites of baptism, confirmation and first communion. These new baptismal rites, as in the Roman Catholic ritual of 1969, lay increased emphasis on the personal commitment and responsibility of the parents and of the congregation.[43]

These new initiatory rites seek to preserve what is essential and permanent in the Church's ancient tradition and to express and interpret it in modern terms and in relation to the pastoral needs of today.[44] The ritual is new in expression, but basically ancient. Central in the service is the water-baptism, associated with the 'form' derived in the early church from a Syrian rite. Also preserved from the past is the threefold questioning of the faith, which belonged to the original Western liturgy. Prior to the sacrament is the section headed 'Decision', which includes the ancient renunciation. The blessing of the water follows; and after the baptism there are the post-baptismal ceremonies typical of the ancient Western rite.

The Alternative Service Book brought about three important structural changes: (1) The questions on the faith are placed immediately before the baptism. (2) 'The Decision' separated the questions of the renunciation from the questions on the faith. (3) The signing of the cross, not an essential part of the sacrament, has been given an alternative – and more appropriate – position in the early part of the service. It is significant that the questions are answered by the parents and godparents 'for yourselves and for these children.' In the Prayer Book, the godparents simply answered for the children. Whereas the Book of Common Prayer required the priest to say 'Name this child', the new rites make no such requirement. The officiant is expected only to use the person's name in the act of baptizing him. This change helps to correct the belief that the name is given in baptism.

Confirmation

Turning to confirmation, Whitaker draws attention to the diverse views centring on whether or not this rite conveys the Holy Spirit. He points out that both views would be accommodated if the imposition of the hand were to follow after baptism in the case of infants and adults, as was the ancient practice recorded in the 'Apostolic Tradition'. This would mean that the hand-laying could not be reserved to the bishop, owing to his inability to attend every infant baptism. Whitaker says that 'this was the most fundamental matter discussed by the General Synod in its debate on the Ely Report, and since Synod reached no theological conclusion and declined to make any considerable change in pastoral practice, it was left to the Liturgical Commission to draft rites of baptism and confirmation which observed a theological neutrality . . .'![45]

According to the Book of Common Prayer and the Thirty Nine Articles, confirmation is not a sacrament as are baptism and the eucharist. Some see the rite as conveying spiritual strength to those who have received the Holy Spirit at baptism. This endowment is indicated in the prayer for the seven-fold gifts of the Spirit. In the revised rite of 1980, the central prayer is couched in the language of Isaiah XI.2 'Let your Holy Spirit rest upon them,' a petition which does not state which element in Christian initiation conveys this spiritual gift, whether baptism or imposition of hands.

The modern practice of some Anglican bishops of laying *both* hands on confirmation candidates is said to be traceable to the action of Peter and John in Samaria (Acts 8.17) – though this historical link is questioned – rather than to the Prayer Book, where there is a rubric which says that the Bishop 'shall lay his hand upon the head' of each confirmation candidate. There is a similar rubric, with 'hand' in the singular, in the Alternative Service Book (p. 234). The title, however, in the Prayer Book reads: 'The Order of Confirmation or Laying on of *Hands* . . .' Another debatable feature in both baptism and confirmation is the use of oil with the signing of the cross. Whitaker explains how the Liturgical Commission advised delay for further reflection before authorising this practice – advice which the General Synod did not take. It is regretted that the prayers, which would interpret the meaning of the oils, have not been included in the Alternative Service Book. With reference to the use of oil, J. D. Crichton (a Roman Catholic writer) says that 'as soon as you have to be told that this "signifies" that, you are being told at the same time that the symbol is dead.'[46]

We do well to recall David Stancliffe's chapter on 'Confirmation and its future' in the symposium 'Liturgy for a New Century'. He begins by referring to Bishop Hensley Henson's disgust in 1932 on learning that some bishops were not adhering to the canonical minimum age for confirmation – namely fourteen. He therefore wrote of 'this recklessly Romanizing trend' – possibly leading to confirmations at 12, or 10, or even 7. He sceptically suggested that 'with the easterns, we blessed oil in central cauldrons and authorized the parish priests to apply it to regenerated babies.'![47]

Presumably with the Lima text in mind, Stancliffe says that there is ecumenical consensus that baptism properly leads directly to the eucharist and argues that this must be so since one can hardly be only partly 'in Christ.'[48] While this sequence has been followed by churches as different as the Roman Catholic Church and the United Reformed Church, Stancliffe quotes Oliver Quick's description of the Anglican practice as 'intolerable' – namely the practice of infant baptism, followed by confirmation after an interval of several years, and only then admission to first communion. The underlying assumption was that confirmation conveyed an essential gift of the Holy Spirit for the completion of initiation.

The reuniting of baptism, confirmation and the eucharist can be most realistically achieved at the adult stage; and it is significant that the adult celebration is placed before the infant rite in the revised Roman Catholic liturgy and in the Anglican Alternative Service Book. As for the relationship between Baptism and Confirmation, David Stancliffe draws the conclusion, in the light of 'historical considerations', that baptism is 'a pneumatically complete rite of initiation in itself' and that confirmation has a distinct function 'not as a rite of admission to Holy Communion, nor as the passing of a test in intellectual or spiritual maturity . . . but as a rite of association with the bishop.'[49]

What would a revision of baptism and confirmation along these lines offer to the Church of England today? According to Stancliffe:-

(1) It would rule out confirmation as a pneumatic completion of baptism and provide a full unitive rite of initiation consisting of renunciation, water baptism and the seal of the Holy Spirit. 'This . . . rite would be especially welcome ecumenically.'
(2) It would end the 'agonized debate' whether or not baptism is a valid and sufficient qualification for admission to Holy Communion.
(3) It would retain an episcopal rite of confirmation, but would set it among the episcopal offices and not as part of initiation.
(4) While confirmation has had a chequered history, there now seems to be both liturgical and ecumenical convergence on an understanding of confirmation as (a) affirming our baptism, (b) making a commitment to the church and (c) having our talents recognized by the Bishop.[50]

The General Synod

The General Synod of the Church of England held in July 1991 included important debates on Christian initiation. It saw the production of three documents: (1) 'Christian Initiation and its Relation to some Patoral Offices' – a paper prepared on behalf of the Liturgical Commission by Kenneth Stevenson and David Stancliffe; (2) 'Christian Initiation – A Policy for the Church of England', a Discussion Paper by Canon Martin Reardon; (3) 'Christian Initiation Matters' – a Report by the House of Bishops.

The first document by Stevenson and Stancliffe says of confirmation that it 'often serves a number of functions beyond its earlier purpose', and lists some common interpretations of confirmation as follows: (1) It is an act of commitment, normally after instruction; (2) It conveys the Holy Spirit; (3) It should be reunited with baptism and eucharist; (4) It is a 'dismissal' of the newly-baptized; (5) It is an episcopal ratification of belonging. The Report adds that 'alongside these interpretations . . . there looms the question of admission to communion before confirmation.'[51]

While recognizing that confirmation is chiefly an episcopal rite administered to the baptized, the Report also sees the rite as appropriate (1) when receiving people from other churches, (2) when reaffirming the adult faith of baptized Christians, and (3) when the candidate is baptized.

This Report suggests that there are now no fewer than three routes to 'conscious and intelligent faith' in the Church of England, arising from present pastoral practice. The first route is traced to the Book of Common Prayer and follows the sequence of infant baptism – confirmation – holy communion. The Report admits, however, that pressure is building up for communion before Confirmation. This, we would add, may be partly due to the influence of Roman Catholic practice, which we considered earlier in this chapter. The Report goes on to say that 'pressure for early communion may be met by early confirmation.' We recall that this was the solution proposed by the Roman Catholic diocese of Salford, which sought to restore the traditional order of initiation by offering confirmation to children about seven years of age, so enabling the sacrament to fit John Paul II's expression 'the path towards the eucharist'. This Anglican Report, however, adds that administering confirmation at an earlier age might 'produce the need for yet another rite of commitment later on.'

II The second route is the 'implied norm of the Alternative

Service Book, which presupposes candidates who are old enough to answer for themselves.' It links in one service the rites of baptism, confirmation and eucharist, said to be the patristic pattern. However, there is 'pressure from certain quarters to forego the need for confirmation.' The ASB ordering of this united liturgy is seen by some people as 'exaggerating confirmation to a position of greater importance than baptism.'

III Route Three is now emerging, 'not as a result of liturgical revision, but as one of the fruits of the changing face of all the Western Churches within a pluralist society today.' Three groups of people appear, 'requiring an adapted form of Christian initiation . . . in order to ritualise reality.' (a) Those who have been baptized, even confirmed and regular communicants, but who feel the need 'to renew their faith in an impressive public rite which the church is anxious not to confuse with baptism.' (b) A second group consists of members of another church who wish to 'join the Church of England as full members.' (c) A third group includes those 'whose deepest need is a public rite of reconciliation, a solemn assurance of their spiritual wholeness in the sight of God.'

The Report believes that 'the answer to these demands, at present partly met by the renewal of baptismal promises . . . lies in a renewed and extended view of confirmation, akin to the Pastoral Offices, in which the bishop's role is the norm.'[52]

At the General Synod in February 1989, a private member's motion, proposed by Roger Godin and amended by John Packer, was approved. It read: 'This Synod calls attention both to the concern over apparent indiscriminate baptism, as expressed in 'Baptism, Eucharist and Ministry' documents, and increasingly shared by many people of differing theological persuasions in the Church of England; and also to the concern felt by others over the theological implication of rigorous baptism policies, and calls upon the Standing Committee to initiate within the lifetime of this Synod a debate based upon a suitable discussion document concerning current theological, pastoral, evangelical and ecumenical issues.'

This resolution gave rise to the 'Discussion Paper' on 'Christian Initiation – a Policy for the Church of England', drawn up by Martin Reardon, a document in which several other people have assisted, either in providing or shaping material or by contributing articles.

Early in this document, a summary statement is offered of 'the main approaches of those who advocate an open baptismal policy and those who advocate a restrictive policy.' It is pointed out that those who pursue a 'restrictive position' stress the close link in the New Testament between a personal profession of faith and the sacrament of baptism. Those who practise an 'open policy' find justification in God's prevenient grace and in Christ's statement that entry into the kingdom requires the openness of children. Traces of 'folk religion' are seen by advocates of an 'open policy' as presenting a missionary opportunity. Canon Reardon says that these two baptismal policies 'cannot be reconciled simply by looking narrowly at the act of infant baptism. If they are to be reconciled at all in a coherent policy, we shall have to take into account a whole range of issues concerning Christian initiation.'[53] We have attempted to follow this policy of comprehensiveness in this book, as the contents page indicates.

Baptismal policy: a debate

The morning of Saturday 13th July 1991 at the General Synod held in York was given up to the important debate on 'Christian Initiation: Baptismal Policy', based on the documents to which we have already referred. The Archbishop of York (Dr John Habgood) introduced the debate by quoting paragraph 92 of Martin Reardon's report: 'The solution lies not in letting one party "win" but in harnessing the energy and insights of both parties, and using them for a concerted attempt to create an initiation policy which puts baptism right at the centre of the Church's life, and sees it as an ecumenical opportunity for better pastoral care, education and evangelism.'

Dr Habgood sees 'the first area of agreement' spelled out in paragraph 45 which lists (1) a personal profession of faith; (2) immersion or pouring of water in the name of the Trinity; (3) the gift of the Holy Spirit, (4) communion and (5) reception into Church membership. With the afternoon debate in mind on the traditional sequence of baptism, confirmation and communion, the Archbishop asks: 'What is there left to do in terms of initiation once a person has been received as a communicant?' and adds that the pattern of initiation needs to be a coherent one. He also draws attention to 'some basic agreements in theology' set out in section 57[54], namely:

(a) 'The Church of England needs to restate a firm theological justification for infant baptism.'
(b) The controversy between 'open' and 'restricted' baptismal poli-

> cies should not conceal our fundamental theological agreements, such as that (1) baptism is primarily a sacrament of the grace of God; (2) it is appropriated by faith, which is God's gift; and (3) is an outward, visible and effectual sign of an inward and spiritual grace.[55]

Dr Habgood tells the Synod that 'on the understanding of covenant as sheer gift, we are baptized, whether as infants or as adults, not on the basis of our promises of faithfulness, or the promises of our parents or our godparents or of the Church, but on the basis of Christ's faithfulness.'[56] He also draws attention to Reardon's statement that baptism should be given 'more prominence as a symbolic expression and representation of God's redemption of the world through the life, death and resurrection of Christ and through the coming of the Holy Spirit.[57]

The Revd Trevor Williams, representing Oxford University, said he was secretary of a local ecumenical project – a church made up of Anglicans and Baptists who have 'anguished over baptismal policy'. They did not wish to be 'too open or too restrictive', to trivialise baptism or to encourage hypocrisy. So they drafted a new form of baptismal service, approved by the former Bishop of Oxford, Patrick Rodger. It is only after the act of baptism that the parents are asked 'to make promises which they could sincerely make'. The congregation become 'the corporate godparents or as Augustine might have said, "Mother Church is the true parent".'

Canon Michael Saward made clear that he had been 'strongly in favour' of infant baptism for 35 years and was 'not a rigorist'. However, he had many times asked sponsors whether in making the baptismal promises they were in fact perjuring themselves. He spoke of being 'greatly encouraged by the BEM challenge to us to review our practice' in view of the Anglican Church's tendency to indecision and imprecision. Saward ventured to say: 'Dolby in stereo creates precision; Dalby[58] on initiation creates confusion . . . What I fear of the excellent Reardon report is that it may produce that kind of "nothing will happen".'[59]

With reference to the canon that baptism should take place at the main church service, the Revd Dr Mark Dalby pointed out that in his church the building would be crammed to capacity, no small rooms in which to put the tiny children, regular congregations swamped, the visitors with little idea of what was happening, few people would see and there would be a vast noise! In declining to carry out this canon, Dalby quotes St Paul in support: 'Let everything be done decently and in order.'[60]

According to Mr Hugh Craig, baptism in the New Testament was available to all who desired it. Following what he believed had always been the Anglican tradition, he held that we should accept at their face value the promises made by parents and godparents.[61]

The Revd David Hawtin made a plea for further consultation with other churches. The Reardon report referred to this as 'unfinished agenda' (sections 117–126); it was, in Hawtin's view, 'a scarcely started agenda'. Initiation is into 'the Body of Christ, not just into one denomination'. What about the relation between confirmation and communion, in the light of our commitment in September 1990 to be 'Churches Together in England'?[62]

The Ven Gordon Kuhrt pointed out that we have a very serious ecumenical problem in relation to holy baptism. He quotes section 16 in the Lima document *Baptism, Eucharist and Ministry*, where we are urged to 'guard against the practice of apparently indiscriminate baptism.' He reminds the Synod that the Lambeth bishops in 1988 echoed that warning in paragraph 193 of their report: 'We accept the Lima judgment that indiscriminate infant baptism should not be practised. It obscures the purpose of baptism.' Kuhrt adds: 'There is no need for us to stand guilty before Lima or the Lambeth bishops if we practise lovingly and carefully the present canonical provision.'[63]

Reporting on this debate, the *Church Times* (19.7.91) said that 'the Synod came out clearly in favour of "controlled flexibility". The Synod commended what the Archbishop of Canterbury said afterwards was "an open system, whereby parents can bring their children, and the priest can set up his own system of nurture".' A draft canon stating that parents should be 'able', as well as willing, to make the baptismal promises, was, at the recommendation of the Archbishop of York, 'not proceeded with'.[64]

A debate on Communion before Confirmation

Reference has already been made on previous pages to the debatable issue as to whether holy communion should precede confirmation. This question exercised the minds of the House of Bishops who produced a majority report urging the General Synod to approve the following resolution: That this Synod –

(a) affirm the traditional sequence of Baptism – Confirmation – Communion as normative in the Church of England;
(b) accept that within this sequence Confirmation can take place at an early age when this is deemed appropriate by the parish priest and the bishop;
(c) agree that experiments of admission to Communion before Confirmation should be discontinued at a rate which gives due regard to the pastoral difficulties in individual dioceses and parishes;
(d) ask the Liturgical Commission to prepare a series of rites as Route Three in G S Misc 366;[65]
(e) ask the House of Bishops in consultation with the Board of Education and the Liturgical Commission to prepare a paper on patterns of nurture in the faith, including the Catechumenate.[66]

The motion was moved by the Rt Revd Michael Adie, Bishop of Guildford, who said that the bishops had been pressed to make known their views on this matter. And their conviction – though not unanimous – was that the traditional Anglican sequence should be retained. The bishops, said Michael Adie, were not convinced that there was a consensus in favour of change.

Many members of the Synod took part in the debate that followed, expressing a diversity of opinions. The Rt Revd Peter Dawes, Bishop of Derby, said he was 'keen to see the admission of children to communion before confirmation.' He said that 70% of his clergy favoured the option. He made the point that 'in many parts of the Anglican Communion this had been done for many years, as an option.' The Bishop quoted an Australian clergyman who reckoned that 80% of Anglican Churches in Australia exercised this option – for two reasons: 'First, many more people have come to believe that baptism does signify full and complete initiation.' 'The second reason is a deep hesitation about even 11-year-olds making public promises to God . . .' Peter Dawes adds that 'if confirmation is at any age, we need to push the age higher rather than lower.'[67]

The Revd John Packer, of Sheffield, told the Synod that he came from 'a Baptist/Anglican ecumenical parish.' He said that 'on Easter Day we celebrated the baptism of believers of two of our members by total immersion in the baptistery of our church. A few weeks earlier I had baptized the infant daughter of the vicar in the same church. Both of these were joyful, celebratory occasions, natural and right in our ecumenical context.' He went on to say that they also held a joint confirmation and membership service, but that here he was much less happy. 'We seem to be pretending,' he told the Synod, 'that confirmation is the equivalent of believers' baptism'. This seemed to him 'an ecumenical cul de sac'. 'As it is, we confirm 11-year-olds and the Baptist Church then unhappily receives them as members.' John Packer cherishes the prospect that in the future 'we could have a rite of adult commitment, as the Bishop of Chester suggests, which would be used alongside believers' baptism in our case, and at that point multi-membership within our local ecumenical project would make sense in a way that it just does not do now.'[68]

As producer of the Knaresborough Report in 1985, the Rt Revd John Dennis recommended the Synod to read it, as it was very pertinent to the present debate. This Report stated that in 'certain circumstances' it should be possible for communion to be given to children before their confirmation – the circumstances being (1) that the local Christian community as a whole should approve and support it and (2) that the children should be within a nurturing process.[69]

The Bishop of Whitby said that in his ministry he had found the traditional sequence of baptism – confirmation – communion to be a strength rather than a weakness. He believed that we needed to remain a church of order rather than chaos and 'to avoid an ever-increasing diversity of practice on such an important issue as Christian initiation.' The bishop severely criticised the Anglican Church's pastoral oversight when he said that 'so much of our baptismal preparation is negative and prohibitive; too much of our confirmation preparation is amateur; and our post-baptismal and post-confirmation care, of parents and young people, is minimal and ineffective.'[70]

The document issued by the House of Bishops was severely criticised by the Rt Revd Colin Buchanan. He said that 'this document has no ecumenical reference . . . no relevance to the rest of the Anglican world.' The bishops' report does not confront the Knaresborough document and is 'over-protective of the Mason-Dix position on confirmation', a rite which has 'very little root in the Scriptures and very little root in the first 200 years of the church.' Buchanan adds that 'the bishops are totally out of touch in the motion they have brought before us.'[71]

The Bishop of Chester, the Rt Revd Michael Baughen, expressed the view that 'in younger children, however serious they are, there does come a distinction between faith and commitment.' At that age, they cannot make a life commitment. He said that 'the fall-off in the church is very often over the commitment issue.' If it were generally approved, he would prefer 'to have admission to communion early on and then later confirmation.' He quoted a New Zealand bishop as saying that in his country they admitted children to communion before confirmation and that the latter rite would soon disappear. With regard to the confirmation rite in the Alternative Service Book, Michael Baughen commented that it was pre-occupied with personal faith rather than serving Christ in the world.[72]

This lengthy and vital debate ended with an amendment proposed by Mr Brian McHenry. He said, 'I beg to move as an amendment: Leave out paragraph (c) and re-letter the following paragraphs accordingly.' Paragraph (c) required that 'experiments of admission to communion before confirmation' should gradually cease. This amendment was carried by 252 to 161 – a result which meant that the main thrust of the bishops' motion was rejected by the Synod, so allowing the option of administering the eucharist to baptized but unconfirmed children to continue.

There were further embarrassing moments for some of the Bishops when Canon Peter Lock proposed that: 'This Synod request the House of Bishops to prepare draft regulations that enable children to be admitted to Holy Communion before confirmation, so that discussion can take place within the church and conditions for such admission, if any, can be considered.' The declared purpose of this motion was to pave the way for this contentious subject to be discussed in the dioceses at grass roots level. An indecisive show of hands led to a vote by houses. The vote, not surprisingly, was lost in the House of Bishops.

The Methodist Church

At the beginning of this chapter we noted John Fenwick's observation that Christians who have attended the services of other denominations have expressed surprise at finding them so similar to the ritual of their own church. Even before the impact of the ecumenical movement, the indebtedness of the Methodist Book of Offices to Anglicanism was striking. This is not surprising since Methodism began as a revivalist society within the Church of England. John Wesley (1703–1791), who was mainly responsible for shaping the early Methodist liturgy, lived and died a member of the

Anglican Church. Though he sowed the seeds of separation, it was not Wesley's wish that the Methodist movement should break away from the Established Church. The basic similarity has remained over the years, particularly with regard to the sacraments of baptism and holy communion.

At the General Synod in July 1991, the Bishop of Chester, in dealing with confirmation, said that the Anglican Church needed an 'adult commitment renewable each year like the excellent Methodist covenant service.'[73] This is the only distinctive Methodist ritual. It was drawn up by Wesley himself. We mentioned in a previous chapter that John Wesley appeared to believe in baptismal regeneration – a doctrine which his followers have not generally accepted.

As we look through the modern Methodist service for the sacrament of baptism we see elements found not only in the Anglican liturgy, but in the Roman Catholic ritual as well. The impact of ecumenism is plain. The common elements include:

(1) The proper preparation for the sacrament.
(2) The spiritual qualifications of the parents and godparents.
(3) The assurance that promises concerning the Christian upbringing of the child will be honoured.
(4) The involvement of the congregation in witnessing the baptism in church and in the spiritual nurture of the child in the future.
(5) The arrangements for emergency baptism.
(6) The pouring of water (or dipping) once or three times while saying: 'I baptize you in the name of the Father and of the Son and of the Holy Spirit.'
(7) The refusal to 're-baptize'.
(8) Conditional baptism in cases where any previous baptism is unknown.

In a document containing 'Statements of the Methodist Church on Faith and Order', it is pointed out in the Preface that 'the Conference has responsibility for interpreting the doctrinal standards of the Methodist Church.' What does it have to say about the theology of infant baptism?

A Memorandum on this question issued in 1936 states that when the sacrament is administered to infants, 'the outward sign and the inward grace are in some ways to be distinguished. The outward act anticipates the day when the child will consciously accept the inward grace.[74] Our hope and confidence is that, through the operation of the Holy Spirit, in answer to the prayers of the Church, and through the influence of Christian nurture to which the parents pledge themselves, this sacrament will be inwardly completed and made effective when the child through faith in Christ responds to the grace proclaimed and pledged by the rite.'

This Conference statement goes on to say that 'since an infant is incapable of entering into conscious fellowship with the Lord and his people, the child's membership is necessarily incomplete. By baptism the child is brought into the household of faith . . . in hope of the time when he will personally receive Jesus Christ as his Saviour and Lord.'

In a 'Statement on Holy Baptism' drawn up in 1952 it is said that 'just as Jesus welcomes the little children in the days of his flesh, so in baptism now he receives them into his company.[75] . . . In baptism Christ himself through his Church takes the children in his arms and declares what he has done and what he will do for them . . . In this sense they have entered the realm of grace.' This 'Statement' traces infant baptism to the beginnings of the Church, even 'in accordance with the mind of Christ. Not only is it sanctioned by the practice of the Church since very early times, it proclaims and offers the grace of God . . . and receives even the youngest into that realm . . .'[76]

The need of liturgical revision

The Report on Christian Initiation, written by the Faith and Order Committee and adopted by the Methodist Conference in 1987, began with the following significant statement: 'The Plymouth Conference of 1982 requested "a thorough examination at a fundamental level of the whole theology and practice of Christian initiation in the Methodist Church." The immediate cause of this resolution,' says the Report, 'was the fact that there have been a few of our ministers who feel unable in conscience to baptize infants . . . But there are other issues. The world-wide movement of renewal . . . has meant that many who have entered . . . into the experience of liberation in Christ wish . . . to seal this by the Gospel Sacrament of Baptism. If they have already been baptized as infants, they feel that this was a social custom, meaningless to them who were without conscious awareness of it. They clamour, not so much for second baptism, as for "the real thing" and various provisions for the renewal of vows they never made . . . seem a travesty . . . They feel cheated. There is some feeling that infant baptism and believers' baptism are different ordinances and should be recognised as such. There are also demands for a Service of Infant Dedication or Thanksgiving, as an alternative to Baptism.'[77]

All this, says the Report, has revived a long-standing disquiet, shared even by many who are convinced paedobaptists. It is pointed out that these problems are not peculiar to the Methodist Church and that 'opposition to indiscriminate baptism was loud in the Anglican "Parish and People Movement" in the 1950s, while all the churches which are heirs of Western Christendom are faced with the clamours, indeed the "heart-cries" of the "renewed".'[78] To the writer of this Methodist report the debate on infant baptism at the Anglican General Synod in July 1991 would have come as no surprise.

The General Synod debate concerning the administration of holy communion to baptized, but unconfirmed, children is also anticipated in this Methodist Conference Report. It speaks of 'the widely-held conviction that baptized children should not be excluded from the Lord's Table.' It states, however, that the children must show 'some serious desire and be prepared by the minister in conjunction with the appropriate youth leaders and the consent of the parents concerned.' The Report goes on to emphasise that 'baptism is the one essential rite for entry into the Church and those who have received it are entitled to their place at the Lord's Table, though it may be expedient for this to be delayed. We would not advocate communicating babes in arms as in the Orthodox Churches.'

It has not been natural in the past for Methodists to think of what they called the 'Public Reception into Full Membership' in terms of 'confirmation' – a word they have accepted from their ecumenical contacts. In this comprehensive and erudite Report on 'Christian Initiation', we have found little reference to this rite. But it does say: 'Since the second war there has been increased stress on "preparation for full membership" of those baptized in infancy. The term "confirmation" was added as an alternative title of the reception service in 1962 to give emphasis to prayer for the operation of the Holy Spirit as well as personal commitment.'[79]

The 'Public Reception into Full membership or Confirmation' is introduced by 'General Directions'. One direction says that 'those who have by baptism been admitted into the visible community of the church' should look forward to reception into full membership 'when by professing their faith in Christ they will claim for themselves the promises of God, who by his Holy Spirit will strengthen them for his service.' A second direction explains that 'when children sincerely desire to serve Jesus Christ and are receiving regular instruction in the Bible and the Faith, their names shall be brought before the Pastoral sub-committee. If they are approved, they shall be entered as "members in training"'. In other Christian circles, they might be called 'catechumens'. A further direction states that 'when those "in training" have thus been on probation for not less than three months, their names shall again be brought before the Pastoral sub-committee, which being thus satisfied, shall recommend such persons to the Church Council for admission into the membership of the Methodist Church.' The service will be conducted by the Minister and will include Holy Communion.

The Conference Report of 1987 in order to meet certain criticism offered further observations. One was that 'some revision of the 1975 rite of infant baptism . . . seems called for to meet the complex pastoral situations' in order to give 'clearer expression to the theology of grace.' Many people asked why believers' baptism cannot follow infant baptism, since some ministers and members 'cannot believe infant baptism is either scriptural or adequate to the church's mission.' In reply the Report reaffirmed 'the validity and sufficiency of infant baptism' and maintained that 'the New Testament could not countenance anything which seemed to be a repetition of baptism in the name of Jesus.' We wonder on what evidence in the New Testament the writer bases this last statement. The Report adds, however, that 'if water is administered in the name of the Father, the Son and the Holy Spirit, this is baptism and unrepeatable.' We can appreciate the difficulty people have in understanding why baptism, unlike communion, cannot be repeated.

A rite of renewal – with water?

In addition to the revision of the baptismal service, the Report recommends a 'rite of renewal' by which the new 'life in the Spirit' can be publicly celebrated and the meaning of baptism made clear. The Report then makes a proposal calculated to raise many theological eyebrows. It says that 'we have come to feel strongly that water must be included and indeed an act of immersion . . . We feel that we must learn to live with the risk of confusion for the sake of reconciling those who have such strong convictions about the need for a dramatic rite with water.' A similar proposal is put forward by

Canon Michael Cole. He is quoted by Martin Reardon, in *Christian Initiation – a Policy for the Church of England* (p.44), as 'affirming the once for all nature of baptism' and suggesting 'a recognised rite for the reaffirming of baptismal vows involving immersion' which would not be seen as 're-baptism'.

This Methodist proposal goes on to suggest that 'a certain ambiguity surrounds all rites. They mean different things to different people . . . What characterises a rite of the church is the content of the prayer which accompanies the outward sign . . . The prayer . . . will make clear that it is not baptism . . . This rite is optional . . . but thanksgiving will be paramount.' Has this Report overlooked the fact that baptism in water in the name of the Trinity is valid *without* prayer?

This Report summarised its recommendations as follows:

(1) A revision of the 1975 rite of infant baptism.
(2) The preparation of a 'Service of Thanksgiving' for the birth of a child, without baptism.
(3) A rite for the celebration of new life in the Spirit, including the use of water, but making it clear by the words used and the prayers offered that this would be neither baptism nor rebaptism.
(4) That consideration should be given to a new rite of confirmation which would by its nature be much more an act of positive commissioning . . .

The Report ended by reiterating the Conference ruling in 1975 that ministers must baptize infants whatever their personal disapproval of the practice on conscientious grounds.[80] One feels, however, that this is not the end of the matter and that in the future these deep convictions in ministerial circles may be accommodated in Methodism, as they are in the United Reformed Church.

New liturgical services

As a result of these deliberations, the Faith and Order Committee drew up two new services which were approved by the Methodist Conference in 1989. These were (1) An Act of Thanksgiving after the Birth or Adoption of a Child; and (2) A Service for the Celebration of Christian Renewal. At the Conference of 1991, the Faith and Order Committee submitted four further rites which were authorized by Conference. These four newly approved services are:

(1) A combined service for Baptism and Confirmation; (2) A Service for the Baptism of Young Children; (3) A Service for the Baptism of Young Children and Confirmation; and (4) A Service of Confirmation.

It might be thought that all this revision and new service output would last for a long time. But it will not be so! The Methodist Conference Agenda for 1991 includes this statement: 'The Faith and Order Committee originally began work on the production of these services because the Conference instructed it to do so, in response to an apparently widespread feeling that there was need for alternative services to those provided in 'The Methodist Service Book' (1975). In view of the work that has already started on a volume to replace the 1975 book, it would not be expected that the services now presented would remain in use for more than a few years.'[81]

These services, especially those for baptism and confirmation, reveal the influence of the ecumenical movement. They are strikingly similar in several places to the Alternative Service Book of the Church of England. With regard to 'An Act of Thanksgiving after the Birth or Adoption of a Child', the General Directions state that this service may be used either before or after the child has been baptized. 'The Celebration of Christian Renewal' takes place within the context of a Sunday service. It is significant – and not surprising – that the Methodist Conference of 1989 did not approve the proposal to use water. The risk of this rite with water being confused with baptism was all too apparent. Both services are brief, relevant and clearly expressed.

In the past, some parents have seemed content to accept a 'Thanksgiving Service' in place of baptism. One wonders how the 'Celebration of Christian Renewal' will relate to 'The Reception and Confirmation of Full Members'.

It is significant that adult baptism and confirmation in this Methodist liturgy are placed before the baptism of children. We recall that this was the order of priority – recognizing the adult rite as the norm – in the Roman Catholic and Anglican initiatory rites.

The United Reformed Church

One of the most remarkable features in ecumenical circles has been the amount of liturgical revision in the latter part of the twentieth century. This revisionary process has involved the United Reformed Church, a united church formed in October 1972 – after negotiations lasting 27 years – by the union of the Congregational Church and the Presbyterian Church of England. The Preface of their Service Book, issued in 1989, recalls that in 1985 'the General Assembly of the United Reformed Church decided that a Book of Services published in 1980 was in need for revision.' That was within the short space of five years!

The Preface explains that 'the demand for revision after so short a time was due to changes both in our apprehension of what is appropriate language for worship . . . and in the constitution of the URC, to whose members were added in 1981 members of the Re-formed Association of Churches of Christ in Great Britain and Ireland.'[82] Another reason for this revision is due to the impact of ecumenical contacts, 'the influence of cross-fertilization between the separated Christian traditions as they increasingly join in worship, action and study.'

It is pointed out that baptism 'derives from the saving death of Christ, but . . . takes its shape both from Jewish rites of initiation and from John the Baptist's baptism of repentance.' This Preface claims that elements in the URC's forms of service date back to Bible times and the Early Church; but 'it is to the Reformation, and perhaps especially to John Calvin, that they owe their particular shape. For Calvin, the Church was to be found wherever the Word was truly preached and the sacraments . . . administered, and this book maintains this two-fold emphasis.'

The Preface explains that the variations here introduced 'mark the changed times . . . that have made themselves felt since the previous publication.' A short service for the renewal of baptismal promises is included, designed for those who need a public reaffirmation of their membership of the body of Christ.'[83]

Under the heading of 'General Notes' in this 'Service Book', it is stated that the 'material in this book is based on historic and contemporary Reformed services, enriched with contributions from other traditions . . . Churches are free to develop their own forms, but the Reformed tradition worldwide is aware of a movement towards greater unity in worship.'[84]

As we have seen, the present ruling of the Methodist Conference is that their ministers must baptize infants even though on conscientious grounds they may believe it is unscriptural and theologically unsound. No such compulsion is laid upon ministers in the United Reformed Church. In fact, this Denomination offers a wide variety of practice, including: Thanksgiving for the Birth of a Child; Infant Baptism; Believers' Baptism; Confirmation; Renewal of Baptismal Promises and Reception of Members From Other churches.

Infant and Believers' Baptism

'The Manual' – a book dealing with the Constitution of the United Reformed Church – states that 'baptism may be administered in infancy or at an age of responsibility. Both forms of baptism shall be made available in the life of every worshipping congregation . . . When baptism is administered at an age of responsibility, upon the profession of faith, the baptized person at once enters upon the full privileges and responsibilities of membership. When baptism is administered to an infant, upon profession of the faith of his parent(s), he is placed under the nurture of the Church, . . . in due time to make his own profession of faith . . . and to enter upon the full privileges and responsibilities of membership.'[85]

This Manual goes on to say that 'the United Reformed Church includes within its membership both persons whose conviction it is that baptism can only be appropriately administered to a believer and those whose conviction it is that infant baptism also is in harmony with the mind of Christ. Both convictions are honoured by the church and both forms of baptism are understood to be used by God in the upbuilding of faith.' The Manual also adds that 'no one shall be required to administer a form or mode of baptism to which he has a conscientious objection, nor shall the form or mode of baptism used in any instance be one to which conscientious objection is taken by the person seeking baptism or by the parent requesting baptism for an infant.'[86]

It is also stated that the Gospel sacrament of baptism into Christ is a gift of God to his Church and is an appointed means of grace. Baptism is administered in water in the name of the Trinity. It is once for all and 're-baptism' is ruled out. Baptism can involve sprinkling or pouring, or by immersion. Godparents are optional.

Infant baptism is said to represent the truth that 'children of believing parents are as much part of the Church as babies are part of the families into which they are born.' As to believers' baptism, this 'represents the truth that God's saving action . . . cannot truly become effective for individuals unless they themselves respond in faith and commitment.'[87]

The Church of Scotland

As compared with the United Reformed Church, we find in the doctrine and practice of the Church of Scotland much more emphasis on infant baptism. The Panel on Doctrine issued a statement on baptismal theology in 1966 based on the work of the 'Special Commission on Baptism (1953–62) together with the considered opinions of the Presbyteries of the Church'. This official statement on baptism was in effect reaffirmed by the General Assembly in 1991. The Revd David Beckett, the secretary of the Panel of Doctrine, says that 'a proposal by the Panel to allow the exceptional baptism of infants without a communicant parent, approved by the Assembly and sent down to the Presbyteries, has now I gather been rejected by a majority of the Presbyteries. So the Law of 1963 . . . still stands.' This Act XVII 1963, which is currently in force, reads as follows:

1. Baptism may be administered to a child –
   (a) whose parents, one or both, have themselves been baptized, are in full communion with the Church, and undertake the Christian upbringing of the child;
   (b) whose parents, one or both, having been baptized but not in full communion, are such that the Kirk Session is satisfied that he or she is an adherent permanently connected with the congregation and supporting the work and worship of the church and will undertake the Christian upbringing of the child;
   (c) whose parents, one or both, have themselves been baptized, profess the Christian faith, undertake to ensure that such child grows up in the life and worship and express the desire to seek admission to full membership in the Church. In such cases the Kirk Session shall appoint the Elder of the District in which the parents reside, or some other person, to shepherd them into full communion and to exercise pastoral care of the child concerned;
   (d) who, being of unknown parentage, or otherwise separated from his or her parents, is in the view of the Kirk Session under Christian care and guardianship.
2. Baptism may be administered only by Ministers authorised by the General Assembly to dispense the Sacrament of the Lord's Supper.
3. Baptism may be administered only after the parents or guardians have received such instruction in its meaning as the Minister shall deem necessary.
4. No Minister shall baptize a child resident outwith his own

Parish, whose parents are not members or adherents of his congregation, without consent of the Minister of that Parish or of the Presbytery.

5. Without the consent of the Presbytery, no Minister may administer Baptism in a case where to his knowledge another Minister has declined to do so.
6. Baptism shall normally be administered at a Diet of public worship of the congregation of which the parents or guardians are members or adherents, or of the congregation of the Parish in which they normally reside. In exceptional circumstances Baptism may be administered elsewhere (e.g. at home, in hospitals or institutions). In every case an entry shall be made in the Register of Baptism kept by the Kirk Session of the congregation of which the parents or guardians are members or adherents, or in that of the Parish in which they normally reside, as the case may be.
7. Baptism shall be administered in the Name of the Father, and of the Son, and of the Holy Ghost, with water, by sprinkling, pouring, or immersion. Other elements may not be used.
8. In all cases a Certificate of Baptism shall be given by the Minister.
9. Nothing in this Act shall be taken to mean that the Church of Scotland rejects Baptism in the Name of the Father, and of the Son, and of the Holy Ghost duly administered in accordance with the law and discipline of other Churches.

The theology of baptism

With regard to the theology of baptism, the Statement issued by the Panel of Doctrine – which we attempt to summarize – begins by saying that 'throughout the New Testament, preaching and baptizing are closely bound together. The proclamation of the Gospel is the primary task of the church, but conjoined to it is the command of Christ to baptize . . . Proclamation of the Word can stand alone, but the administration of Baptism cannot, for it is dependent upon the promises of Christ. In administering Baptism the Church acts only as the servant of the Word of God.'

In baptism, Christ confirms his Word and seals his work of salvation. It is both an act of Christ and an act of the church – distinguishable but inseparable – an inheritance offered by the Gospel and entered into by faith. Essentially, it is 'what God in Christ has done, is doing, and will do for us.' Jesus linked his baptism with his cross and at Pentecost linked the church to himself through the baptism of the Spirit. In the One Baptism, Christ acts vicariously as Redeemer and the Church receptively as the redeemed society.

When the Church baptizes in water, Christ baptizes with his Spirit. Baptism should take place only where the Gospel is proclaimed and believed, the community in which God acts through his Word and Spirit. In baptism, we become one with Christ, sharing his righteousness and becoming 'members of the messianic people of God.' Baptism is administered in the name of the Trinity and 'our part is only to receive it, for we cannot add to Christ's finished work.'

Jesus taught that the kingdom of God 'belongs in a special way to little children . . . He received and blessed them . . . Therefore, in obedience to his example and command . . . we bring our children to him through baptism in the divine name.' This doctrinal statement goes on to say that 'in the teaching of the Apostles, children belong to the household of faith and are members of Christ in the corporate unity of the Christian family. They too participate in forgiveness and sanctification through the Spirit.' Therefore, when they reach years of understanding, they will be admitted to full communion on profession of their faith. 'The God of all grace' will establish them in his covenant and confirm them by his Spirit, so that they may serve him faithfully in his church.

The sign of the old covenant was circumcision, the seal of promise. The sign of the New Covenant is baptism, the seal of the fulfilment of the promise. 'Baptismal regeneration ex opere operato is a false doctrine since it looks for the meaning and reality of baptism in the performance of the external rite rather than in Christ, and at the same time confuses the external rite with its future fulfilment.'

'A child born of Christian parents is, through baptism, placed within the corporate union of the faithful with Christ and shares with them in the Communion of the Spirit.' This doctrinal statement makes clear that 'baptism and faith belong inseparably together.' But baptism shows that it is not upon our faith or faithfulness that we rely, but upon the faithfulness of Christ. By grace, baptism covenants us to a life of faith and obedience to God in Christ for as long as we live. 'Baptism is our initiation into a mutual relation between the act of the Spirit and the response of faith.' The Statement adds that 'baptism is administered only once, as an irrevocable seal of that finished work of Christ which sets our life on a wholly new foundation.'

On the administration of baptism, it says that the form must accord 'with its biblical institution and meaning.' The rite is performed only within the sphere of the church and includes thanksgiving for God's gift of new life; a prayer for the consecration of the water and for the preservation of the baptized; also a confession of faith in the Trinity. Only ministers of the Word and Sacraments are authorized to administer baptism. Only Christ can make baptism effective.

Baptism is administered to adults and children with the same doctrine and form. Since baptism is bound up with preaching and teaching, infants are baptized only with the assurance that they 'will be brought up in the family of God and instructed in the Christian faith.' Only children whose parents are within the life and discipline of the Church can be baptized.

This doctrinal statement ends by quoting the Westminster Confession (xxviii.5): 'Although it be a great sin to condemn or neglect this ordinance, yet grace and salvation are not so inseparably annexed unto it, as that no person can be regenerated or saved without it, or that all that are baptized are undoubtedly regenerated.'

The Baptist Church

We have left to the last our consideration of Christian initiation in the Baptist Church, not on historical grounds, for this Denomination has roots that go back to the Reformation. We are looking at it last for theological reasons. Its distinctive emphasis on believers' baptism and therefore its questioning of the validity of infant baptism sets it apart from other churches – whether Episcopal or Free. Baptist theology, however, is understood best when seen in the historical setting in which it emerged.

The modern Baptist Church is said to have its roots in seventeenth century English Separatism and possibly in the Anabaptist movement in the sixteenth century. Ernest Clipsham points out that in 1609 John Smyth's Separatist congregation, in exile in Amsterdam, was led by a study of the New Testament to accept believers' baptism as the basis of church fellowship. In 1612, a small group led by Thomas Helwys returned to England and established the first Baptist Church at Spitalfields. By the middle of the seventeenth century there were around 250 Baptist Churches in England and

Wales. It is not always realized that at first these Baptists practised affusion and only later was immersion generally accepted as the norm. From this small beginning, the Baptist denomination has become one of the largest non-episcopal churches in the world – hence the Baptist World Alliance. It has become, therefore, a force to be reckoned with in the ecumenical sphere.[88]

Baptists see Jesus as the ultimate authority in belief and practice – the Lord who makes known his will in the pages of Scripture. They stress the prophetic rather than the priestly aspects of Christianity. Their worship is characterised by freedom of form and expression. It is mainly non-liturgical, with priority being given to the preaching of the Word.

In view of their emphasis on believers' baptism, with the prerequisites of repentance and faith, they could not see their way clear to accept infant baptism. Strict Baptists regard the church as a community of believers – the ecclesia, 'called out' from the world – and tend to limit membership to those who have been baptized by immersion. 'Open' Baptist churches, as the word suggests, are prepared to receive into membership all those who make a personal confession of faith in Christ, whether or not they have been baptized.

The principles and practice of the Baptist Church present problems in interdenominational spheres. Alec Gilmore, however, refers to the insights for which Baptists have campaigned and says that 'today in ecumenical circles Baptists are listened to with more understanding than at any time since the Refomation.'

Ecumenical relationships

Further light is thrown on the relationship between the Baptist Church and other denominations by 'Guidelines for Baptismal Practice in Local Ecumenical Projects' (LEPs), drawn up in 1990 by the Advisory Committee for Church Relations and approved by the Baptist Union Council. These 'Guidelines' recalled the issuing in 1982 of the Report by the World Council of Churches on 'Baptism, Eucharist and Ministry' (BEM) and stated that the Baptist Union in its reply to BEM 'registered some reservations concerning the section on Baptism.' The Baptist Union made clear that the BEM statement that 'any practice which might be interpreted as "rebaptism" must be avoided' was wholly unacceptable.[89] But these 'Guidelines' added that Baptists in LEPs 'need to recognise the deep feelings of other denominations and be sensitive to what they regard as valid baptism'. The 'Guidelines' say that there are at least three patterns of baptismal practice possible in Local Ecumenical Projects:

(a) Baptists may choose to accept the validity of the baptismal practice of the other churches in the LEP. That would mean that Baptists would not baptize as believers those who had been baptized as infants. Baptists, however, might well press for a meaningful reaffirmation of infant baptismal vows.
(b) The churches in an LEP might agree that the baptismal rite is incomplete in the case of those people who have received infant baptism, but are not confirmed. Such people might enter the church by receiving baptism as believers.
(c) The churches may wish 'to recognise that particular understanding of baptism which finds it difficult to deny the rite of believers' baptism to those who, out of an instructed conscience and a perceived obedience, judge the infant baptism they once received not to have been true baptism.'

'The Baptist Union Council believes that Baptist participants in LEPs would wish to preserve freedom of conscience both for the individual seeking baptism and for the minister and the church asked to perform it, whichever way minister and church decide to act. Method (c) above would, we judge, usually be the most appropriate method to include in an agreement establishing a Local Ecumenical Project. Baptists in an LEP, however, need to recognise the deep feelings on this issue felt by other denominations and to be sensitive to the reactions of other Christians to what they regard as "re-baptism".'

Re-baptism

No subject threatens the ecumenical movement so much as this thorny subject of 're-baptism'. A resolution of this problem calls for charity no less than theology. In the past – and possibly in the present – some Baptists would not regard the baptism of believers, who have received the infant rite, as being 're-baptized', because they considered infant baptism as not satisfying the prerequisites of a valid sacrament. One wonders how many Baptists at the present time would go along with Neville Clark when he writes that 'the rebaptism as believers of those who have received baptism in infancy constitutes a blow at the heart of the Christian faith.'[90]

'Those Baptists in ecumenical projects', says J. F. Matthews, 'do live with the dilemma and appear to do so creatively. They act on their experience that Christ clearly blesses people on both sides . . . They ask their fellow Christians to respond with a like Christian courtesy by being careful in the administration of baptism to infants, so that the church and the parents are seen to be honest in the vows they take on behalf of the child.'[91]

Alec Gilmore, writing in 1966, drew attention to the 'British Faith and Order Conference' held two years earlier which glimpsed the possibility of a united church, recognizing the administration of both the infant rite and believers' baptism.[92] It was a worthy vision – however remote its realisation in some areas of Christendom. It was a vision which, as we have seen, was glimpsed at Lima in 1982 in the document 'Baptism, Eucharist and Ministry'. Moreover, the vision has been put into practice by the United Reformed Church after their union with the Churches of Christ.

In fact, as J. F. Matthews points out, this accommodation of both infant baptism and believers' baptism in the same Baptist Church goes back to 1780. The Church in New Road, Oxford, stated in its constitution:

> 'Whereas some of us do verily believe that the sprinkling of the infant children of believing parents in the name of the Father, the Son and the Holy Spirit, is true baptism; and others of us do believe that true Christian baptism is that which is administered to adults upon the profession of their repentance, faith and experience of the grace of God, by immersion in the name of the sacred three; yet notwithstanding this difference of sentiment, we promise to receive one another into the same affection and love.'

In contrast, however, the narrower and stricter view found expression in the articles of religion of the New Connexion of the General Baptists:

> 'We believe that it is the indispensable duty of all who repent and believe the gospel, to be baptised by immersion in water, in order to be initiated into a church state; and that no person ought to be received into the church without submitting to that ordinance.'[93]

To say that infant baptism is not a valid sacrament does not take account of Church history. To deny that the infant rite is truly baptism means that for at least a thousand years a valid baptism was not administered and is still not administered in the greater part of Christendom. If believers' baptism is an essential qualification for church membership, this means, argues Gilmore, that 'for over a thousand years the true church did not exist and that most of those who think they are church members are deluded'. Nowadays a decreasing number of Baptists, however, would accept the above premises and so would not draw the above inferences. Gilmore, a Baptist, seems reluctantly to draw the conclusion that it is better to accept the validity of infant baptism, despite its theological limitations.[94]

In his 'Discussion Paper' on 'Christian Initiation', drawn up for the Anglican General Synod in July 1991, Canon Martin Reardon says that 'perhaps the sharpest issue is that of so-called "re-baptism".' He says that what is needed to regularise the situation is (1) clearer teaching on the Anglican understanding of initiation; (2) an alternative rite which would satisfy the needs of those going outside the Church of England for 're-baptism'; and (3) an attempt to reach agreement with churches who practise only 'believers' baptism' . . . on the terms on which they would decline to offer 're-baptism'.

This practice of re-baptism, says Reardon, inevitably builds up tensions between the Church of England and those churches which practise it. 'We should, therefore, try to achieve as much agreement as is possible between churches of different denominations on this issue . . . We need to recognise that for the Baptist Union of Great Britain and Ireland this remains a great problem.' Reardon adds that 're-baptisms' are often based on two false premises:

(1) That immersion means total immersion and is necessary for baptism – a view for which, he says, there is no clear warrant in Scripture.
(2) That baptism is *primarily* a witness to the recipient's faith and total commitment to God. Reardon disagrees and says: 'It is a sign of God's prevenient grace and gift of faith, which the candidate accepts.'[95]

While recognising the general theological acceptance of this last statement by Reardon, perhaps we may be permitted to reflect for a moment on its logical consistency. If our involvement in baptism and our faith are entirely due to prevenient grace, to the initiative and gift of God, does it mean that God is entirely responsible whether or not we are baptized? If it is all of God's grace, can we claim any credit, or be liable to blame, for our being, or not being, baptized? If we accept the above premise, does it follow that only God can ultimately decide whether or not we have the faith that finds salvation in the sacrament of baptism?

This view is expressed in Harriet Auber's hymn:

'And every virtue we possess
And every conquest won
And every thought of holiness
Are *His alone*.'

The same line of thought runs through a sentence by Dr Maldwyn Hughes: 'God can be known only as he makes himself known. Man can think God's thoughts only as God kindles them within him.' Put another way: 'Revelation precedes inspiration'. Perhaps the question we have paused to ask has no logically consistent answer. Perhaps divine determinism and human freewill cannot be rationally related or logically explained. Perhaps, as Kant might say, we do not have the requisite category of thought in this life.

We have digressed somewhat. Yet, as we return to our general treatment of Christian initiation, we recall that the New Testament refers to the Gospel – which baptism expresses – as a 'mystery' (*μυστήριον*-Eph. 6.19).

'The classical Baptist case' has been summarised as follows:

(1) That in the New Testament only those who repented and confessed their faith in Christ were baptized.
(2) Only baptism by immersion adequately symbolises the burial of the believer and rising again with Christ.
(3) The church is a fellowship of believers and *only* believers.
(4) Infant baptism has no basis in Scripture. It is based on a false understanding of the nature of faith and the church.
(5) Baptism is an outward sign witnessing to an inward experience of repentance and forgiveness.[96]

Liturgical services

In 1980, the Baptist Union issued a service book called *Praise God*, with an explanatory subtitle: 'A Collection of Resource Material for Christian Worship.' The 'Introduction' to the book states that 'the formalism of the liturgical movement of the fifties has given way to a new wave of freedom, self-expression and informality . . . "Thou" has been replaced by "you" as a mode of address to the deity in a whole process of liturgical reform which has gone far wider than anything since the days of the Reformation.' This revision has involved the risk of either 'abandoning much that was good from the past or climbing on a bandwaggon that would be gone in five years time.'[97]

This book includes a service for 'Infant Dedication and Thanksgiving' and a service for 'Christian Initiation'. Both are prefaced by an explanatory note. The first says that 'Infant Dedication and Thanksgiving' admits of an infinite variety. In some cases it is a simple act of thanksgiving, in others it is an act of dedication on the part of the parents, and in others it is an occasion of infant blessing. Some people see the service as relating only to the children of Christian parents, others see it as including everybody. As part of a church service, the following order is suggested: (1) Reading of Scripture; (2) Statement about Infant Dedication; (3) Act of Dedication; (4) Blessing; (5) Prayers of Thanksgiving; (6) Lord's Prayer; (7) Hymn.[98]

The 'Introduction' to the service of 'Christian Initiation' says that among Baptists there has been a growing tendency to bring closer together the act of baptism, reception into membership and admission to communion. We have already seen a similar move towards the wholeness of Christian initiation in other denominations. Ecumenical contacts have encouraged Baptists to link baptism and communion together in one act of initiation, rather than separating baptism and reception by a shorter or longer interval of time.

This Introduction sees five essential elements in Christian initiation: (1) Reading of Scripture, stating that 'baptism bears witness to what God has done and continues to do, and that our baptism is our response to that love.'; (2) Profession of faith and commitment; (3) Prayers, including a prayer for God's action in the Spirit that those baptized may become children of God; (4) Baptism in the name of the Trinity, possibly with the laying on of hands; (5) Reception into membership and admission to communion.[99]

Reference has already been made to the work of liturgical revision over recent years. We have seen in this chapter the swift and many changes in initiatory rites in various denominations. Here is another instance. No sooner had the Baptist service book – *Praise God* – established itself than another revised liturgy was called for in the short space of eleven years. 'Praise God' was published in 1980, to be superseded in 1991 by *Patterns and Prayers for Christian Worship*.

In the Preface to this latest book, it is pointed out that 'Baptists have their roots deep within the Free Church tradition. Therefore the freedom of the Holy Spirit is a significant factor in their worship, and they do not have a fixed liturgy or approved prayer book.' Bernard Green reminds us that 'recent years have brought many changes in the approach to worship and in its language. There is now a wide variety of practice, from liturgical formality to charismatic exuberance, from reformed traditionalism to ecumenical experiment.' Green expresses the hope that 'in the contemporary ecumenical scene this book will be seen as a worthy expression of Baptist identity, which will make a useful contribution to the process of learning from one another.'[100]

The introductory section on 'Christian Worship' says that the liturgical movement has had a widespread influence on Baptist Churches through ecumenical contact. 'This has opened up for increasing numbers of Baptists an awareness of the mystical and contemplative traditions of the Church . . . The charismatic and ecumenical movements have influenced many Baptist Churches' and have led to wide diversity of practice and preference.

It is pointed out that since the nineteen-sixties there has been a perceptible shift in Baptist concepts of baptism and the Lord's Supper. 'Baptism has become far more an act of obedience in which God meets men and women as they demonstrate the reality of their repentance and identity with Christ in membership of his body, participation in his Supper, and the life of his Spirit.'[101]

The Baptism of Believers and Reception into Membership

Believers' baptism, reception into membership at the Lord's Supper and the laying on of hands, all relate to one initiation into the body of Christ. The laying on of hands does not always take place at the same point in the service. Sometimes it is in the baptistry, or before or after reception into membership. Membership 'is not, of course, always linked directly with baptism, but may follow profession of faith or transfer from another church.' That baptism can be separated from church membership seems strange to other denominations.

It will be observed that, unlike other mainstream churches, the Baptist Church, as far as we are aware, has not adopted the word 'Confirmation' as an alternative for 'Reception into membership'.

Moreover, the 'laying on of hands' does not commend itself to all Baptist ministers or churches.[102]

Infant Presentation

Under this heading, it is said that 'the form and content of a service of presentation will vary considerably . . . There is variety in the understanding of infant presentation and the circumstances of the family involved.' Elements in this Presentation can include: (1) Thanksgiving for the birth of a child; (2) Dedication of parents for the Christian upbringing of an infant; (3) The commitment of the church to support parents and to give spiritual nurture to the child.

It is pointed out that the complex situations in some home backgrounds call for 'pastoral sensitivity and careful judgment in each case.' The book includes two orders of service, designed as part of Sunday worship with all ages present. (1) The first order relates to parents who are committed Christians who will bring up their child in the life of the church. (2) 'The second order asks for a less explicitly Christian commitment, which might sometimes be more realistic.' The first pattern is called 'The Presentation of Infants'; the second pattern 'The Blessing of Infants'.[103]

As we turn from the administration of the rite to the theology of baptism, we recall Alec Gilmore's observation that there has been pressure for many years among Baptists 'to relate the material to the spiritual through the sacramental'.[104] It is clear that for some time many English Baptists have moved from a merely symbolic view of baptism to a more sacramental interpretation. Nor have they been immune to the influence of the ecumenical movement and current theology which see baptism as the gateway to membership.[105]

Professor Gunter Wagner[106] sums up the Baptist response to the ecumenical problem posed by the different forms of baptism, as follows:

(a) A growing recognition of the sacramental character of baptism.[107]
(b) A greater awareness of the need of Christian nurture before and after baptism.[108]
(c) Concern about the place of the child in the Christian community and the practice of Infant Dedication and Thanksgiving.[109]
(d) The desire to strengthen the visible unity of the rite of initiation.[110]

(e) An increasing readiness to draw practical consequences from the recognition of the reality of the faith of believers baptized in infancy.[111]

(f) An acknowledgment that 'infant baptism witnesses to valid Christian insights.'[112]

Wagner adds, however, that 'what has not come about is a straightforward acceptance of infant baptism as Christian baptism, nor is it to be expected in the future.' He says that Gilmore comes closest to it.[113] 'We have to face the fact', says Wagner, 'that in the ecumenical "infant baptism – believers' baptism debate" neither side has succeeded in convincing the other of the rightness of its position.[114]

A significant document, entitled 'Baptists and Unity', states that 'the issue facing Baptists today is whether in the total context of church relations . . . they are justified in the rigid maintenance of believers' baptism as a ground of separation from other Christian traditions. In weighing this issue they have to bear in mind (1) the widespread desire in other traditions to overcome the difficulties to which indiscriminate infant baptism has led; (2) the new theological and practical insights into the rite of Christian initiation offered by scholars of many different traditions and the very general acceptance of the validity of the basic Baptist claim; and (3) the fact that most modern schemes of union . . . provide for the recognition of both believers' and infant baptism, insisting that in the case of the latter full membership depends on a later personal profession of faith.'[115]

This document goes on to state that 'most Baptists feel an additional hesitation if it is insisted that the recognition of both current forms of baptism must exclude the baptism, on profession of faith, of anyone baptized as an infant.' It is also made clear that 'more thought must be given by Baptists to the relationship of children to the believing community . . . It remains to be seen whether any overwhelming consensus of opinion will emerge in the near future.'[116]

What of the Future?

Our study in this book has shown that all the churches in the Western world are agreed about many of the beliefs and practices relating to Baptism. They all baptize in water in the name of the Father, the Son and the Holy Spirit. Provided this basic requirement is carried out, each denomination recognizes the validity of baptism administered by all the other churches. Baptism is also associated by all denominations with entry into the Body of Christ. As a rite which the churches have in common, this sacrament is therefore cherished, among other benefits, as a valuable means of contributing to the cause of church unity. This was appreciated by the Lima Report (BEM), as we saw earlier in this chapter.

There is, however, a debit as well as a credit side. Our enquiry has also revealed the problems that beset any plans for the reunification of the separated parts of baptism and confirmation, that is, of the restoration of the original wholeness of Christian initiation. The evidence we have considered in previous chapters points to infant baptism as being the crux of the matter. We recall how 'confirmation' arose out of the circumstances caused by the introduction, or the perpetuation, of the infant rite in the Early Church. Before the 'disintegration' of this sacrament of initiation, entry into the Christian community, as we saw earlier, included baptism, confirmation and communion in one combined liturgical act, as shown in the 'Apostolic Tradition' of Hippolytus.

In our survey, we have seen some possible solutions. One was to resist the separation of the original form of initiation. This was the way the Orthodox churches went. It is still, of course, their present practice. The ritual involved the retention of infant baptism, infant 'confirmation' and infant communion. In the other extreme, as we have seen, there is the Baptist abandonment of the infant rite in post-Reformation times in favour of believers' baptism. This, they claim, is biblically based and provides the candidate for baptism with the opportunity personally to meet the prerequisites of repentance and faith. Theology apart, both the Baptists and the Orthodox churches have no problem in practice in preserving the wholeness of the sacrament.

The other churches have no such simple solution. To draw the parts of Christian initiation together by adding confirmation and communion to infant baptism is not likely to commend itself to paedobaptists. The apparent passivity of the baby in baptism does not encourage the addition of two further rites in which the infant would not be rationally involved.

Another way of restoring the desirable wholeness of initiation would be to adopt the Baptist practice of baptizing people at an age when they can personally and wittingly participate. But our study has shown that this displacing of the infant rite in favour of believers' baptism would be resisted by many Christians. The current resistance to such a baptismal change, however, is more difficult to justify in these modern times than it was centuries ago. Earlier chapters in this book have shown the tenacious way with which people have clung, and still cling, to the administration of infant baptism.

Yet there was much recognition in the past of the normative status of adult baptism. We saw on previous pages how little liturgical provision there was in the early centuries for the baptism of infants. The adult rite had to suffice. Moreover at the present time the Baptists are not the only Christians who favour – in theory if not in practice – the baptism of believers. In our study of initiation in the mainstream churches, we saw how increasingly adult baptism has been regarded as the norm and has been placed first before the infant rite in the order of services.

The demand for emergency baptism for a premature or sickly baby is perhaps traceable, as we suggested in a previous chapter, to a subconscious fear relating to some 'original sin' which might threaten the infant's spiritual welfare in the world to come. A seemingly related concern was dealt with in chapter nine in which we considered the question whether baptismal grace was essential to ensure eternal salvation. It is suggested that here we have an undesirable element of Augustinian doctrine that should be laid to rest.

If it can be shown that infant baptism is not essential to 'ultimate salvation' – as the Anglican 'Alternative Service Book' makes plain – then the way is clear for parents to consider either 'Infant' or 'Believers Baptism' without any kind of theological necessity pressing upon them. Moreover, if parents can be persuaded that having a baby baptized need not necessarily be 'the thing to do', then they could decide, uninfluenced by undesirable pressure, whether to postpone baptism till the child is old enough to participate. They might consider, in place of infant baptism, to have a 'Thanksgiving' or 'Dedication' service – a service to which much attention is being given in the ecumenical sphere, as our study of the churches has shown.

In the event of there being an appreciable movement from the infant stage to the level at which a person can make a profession of the Christian faith, then baptism of believers would come to be recognized as normative in practice as well as being, as it is already, normative in theory. If Scriptural warrant be sought, we recall that in chapter three we looked in vain for any direct evidence of infant baptism in the New Testament. This, as we saw, is a debatable question. But what is not in doubt is that adults were baptized in large numbers. If we may allow ourselves free rein and conjure up a situation in the future in which baptism had become for believers only, then one of the most difficult and contentious issues of the present time would have been resolved, namely the troublesome question of the 'indiscriminate baptism' of infants. It is not surprising that people are disturbed by a situation in which most of the infants baptized never fulfil in later life the baptismal vows made on their behalf by parents and godparents. The disparity between the Baptismal register and the Confirmation register speaks for itself.

Perhaps the solution lies in a via media. Speaking as a Baptist, Alec Gilmore says that 'the very inconclusiveness of the arguments for and against both forms of baptism ought to make us stop and think, and ought to deliver us from a dogmatism that ill-becomes the scholar searching for the truth.' Looking realistically to the future, Gilmore hopes for harmony and co-operation in the ecumenical sphere by supporting, not infant baptism or believers' baptism, but both. He asks: 'Is there not room in the providence of God for both forms of baptism to co-exist? And might not this inconclusiveness be one means by which God is seeking to lead His Church into something richer than our forefathers ever dreamed of?'[117]

These sentiments have been exemplified, as we have seen, in the 'Scheme of Church Union in North India and Pakistan' (1965) and in the 'Negotiations between the Churches of Christ and the United Reformed Church' (1975). This latter Report gives us pause for thought when it makes the significant comment that 'what is theologically wrong cannot be pastorally right.'[118]

In his 'Discussion Paper' submitted to the Anglican General Synod in July 1991, Canon Martin Reardon writes: 'It is therefore strongly to be recommended that a review of the Church of England's policy on Christian initiation should be done in consultation with representatives of other churches, so that as far as possible our policies coincide, and where they cannot that all unnecessary friction and rivalry be removed.'[119]

In his scholarly book on *The Biblical Doctrine of Initiation*, Reginald White says that the uneasiness of the modern church is due largely to baptismal inadequacies. The recovery of a true apostolic baptism that gives due place to what God does in baptism and to the intimate relation of baptism to the Spirit, to the church and to Christian experience, would go far to restore ethical and spiritual realism to the church's evangelism and baptismal practice.

In conclusion, we would observe that in the sphere of religion the future is inseparably connected with the present and the present with the past. This partly explains the comprehensiveness of this study. Our survey of the evidence relevant to the question of infant baptism in the Bible, in the history of the church and in the contemporary ecumenical sphere is designed to provide a focus for the future. As we said at the beginning, we have attempted an objective study, with no personal axe to grind and representing no one particular denominational position. It is hoped that the account of our enquiry in these pages will contribute towards the shaping of a baptismal theology and practice which will commend itself in these ecumenical days to all the churches.

Postscript

Three important events in the sphere of Christian Initiation have taken place after the typescript of this book had been sent to the publisher. They are significant and relevant to this study. The first event is called:

(1) *'A major new venture of unity and mission.'*

The Bishop of Oxford, in a BBC 'Thought for the Day', drew attention to a notable development in connection with the local ecumenical project (LEP) at Milton Keynes. It was the dedication in March 1992, of the 'Church of Christ the Corner Stone' in the presence of the Queen and the Duke of Edinburgh. Taking part in the service were the Archbishop of Canterbury, Cardinal Basil Hume, the Revd Dr John Newton and the Revd Desmond Pemberton. Thus were represented the Church of England, the Roman Catholic Church and the Free Churches. The attractively printed Order of Service says: 'The dedication of the Church by the four Presidents of Churches Together in England in the presence of Her Majesty the Queen is an indication of the significance of the project as a major new venture in unity and mission.'

Canon David Goldie, a member of this ecumenical team ministry, has provided information regarding the arrangements made for infant baptism, believers' baptism and confirmation. The baptismal policy has been 'to meet people where they are' as far as parishioners are concerned and to respond positively (with preparation and follow up) to requests from outside the ecumenical congregation. The need was felt to have an ecumenical baptismal liturgy and after much planning and consultation permission was given by the sponsoring body to use a special order of service for baptism partly based on the service used in the Blackbird Leys LEP in Oxford, in which the promises come as a response to the sacrament and not as a precondition of it.

The Sponsoring Body endorsed the following 'Interim Policy on Baptism':

(a) Where parents ask for a Service of Thanksgiving or for Infant Baptism for their children, we will consider their requests, making sure that they have considered the full implications of both.
(b) Adult converts not baptized in infancy will be offered the choice of Baptism-with-Confirmation or Believers' Baptism.
(c) To those who have been baptized in infancy and confirmed, or who have been baptized as believers, but who subsequently have a conversion experience, we will offer a Service of Renewal of Baptismal Vows.
(d) Converts who have been baptized in infancy but not confirmed will be offered Confirmation, preferably according to an Ecumenical Rite. However, if they ask for Believers' Baptism that request is open to agreement in the usual way by the Baptist Membership.

David Goldie says that confirmations have been ecumenical because it has seemed wrong to make confirmands choose a particular denominational door to enter into the communicant life of the church. This means that at confirmation they become adult members of the Church of England, the United Reformed Church, the Methodist Church or the Baptist Church. Hands are laid on each candidate by four ministers – the Anglican Bishop being the only one 'from outside'.

(2) *'Confirmation and Re-affirmation of Baptismal Faith'*

To meet the liturgical needs of such local ecumenical projects as the one at Milton Keynes, a new ecumenical initiation service has been published recently by The Canterbury Press Norwich with the title *Confirmation and Re-affirmation of Baptismal Faith*. It has been drawn up by the Joint Liturgical Group, with a Foreword by the chairman, Donald Gray, and a Commendation by Martin Reardon, the General Secretary of 'Churches Together in England'.

The Foreword points out that the Joint Liturgical Group 'has played a significant part in helping the churches in Britain to find common forms of worship'. This Group was asked to look into the question of joint confirmation services for use in local ecumenical projects. This new rite was the result – a 'product of careful study and reflection, based upon active experience in current ecumenical situations'.

Canon Donald Gray adds that 'joint confirmation services . . . is a concept with which not everyone is entirely happy. It is perhaps best seen as an interim stage in a new engagement with baptism on the part of the Churches. In the present state of ecumenical relationships we believe that "Confirmation and Re-affirmation of Baptismal Faith" provides an order that is both theologically responsible and liturgically vivid.'

The 'Introduction' to this new rite says that 'for some, God's call involves public identification with their earlier baptism; for some, returning to faith and discipleship; for some, accepting new or wider responsibilities within the body of Christ. . . . For all, it depends on the activity of the Holy Spirit, who seals, unites and strengthens the people of God and who brings a foretaste of the world to come.'

(3) '*Communion Before Confirmation*'

In the 'Preface' to the above new liturgy, linking confirmation to baptism, a reference is made to the 'unresolved discussion as to how confirmation relates to admission to communion'. On previous pages, we considered the discussion that has taken place in some Denominations on the question whether baptized children should be admitted to the Eucharist prior to 'Confirmation' or 'Reception into Church Membership'. The Church of Scotland, after several years' hesitation, has reached a definite decision in favour of baptism, followed by instruction, being sufficient qualification for receiving Holy Communion.

We are indebted to the Revd David Hamilton, of the Church of Scotland's Department of Education, for an explanation as to how this important decision was reached. A Report, issued by the Youth Education Committee, dealing with children and communion, was approved by the General Assembly of the Church of Scotland in 1991 and subsequently by the Presbyteries during 1991-92. It was eventually converted into a standing Act in May 1992. Under the terms of this Act, Kirk Sessions are now free to declare themselves ready to permit baptized children to receive Holy Communion.

The above Report states that the conditions of access to the Lord's Table 'require that the individuals concerned should be baptized, should have received appropriate instruction in the fundamentals of the faith and should, in the view of the Kirk Session, be of Christian character.' The Working Party set up by the Board of Education, under the Rt Revd Professor Robert Davidson, found 'no substantive theological obstacle to the participation of baptized children in the sacrament of the Lord's Supper' and stands firm on 'the primacy of divine grace', which is 'unconditional and unconditioned and, whatever practical difficulties and expediences may be imagined as barriers to the opening of the Lord's Table to children . . . the invitation is of Christ who summons us to gather at His Table.'

This Report also raises the question as to how and to what extent the Lord's Table is truly open. 'Does the principle of unconditional grace override the need for the response of faith? If not, how might this faith be expressed or appraised without resorting to some form of fencing the Table?'

The 'Church of Scotland Education' have published two books, edited by D. G. Hamilton and F. A. J. Macdonald, on the subject of administering Holy Communion to baptized children. One book is entitled *Too Young to Matter?* (1991). This includes the Report approved by the General Assembly and explains the reasons for the adoption of the proposals. The other book, *Children at the Table* (1985), contains essays which consider more deeply the theological, historical and educational issues which underlie the new legislation.

Notes

Chapter One

1 E. Hoskyns & N. Davey, The Riddle of the New Testament p. 10
2 A. Gilmore: Baptism and Christian Unity p.8
3 The Divine Human Encounter, p.181
4 Reconstruction of Belief, p.750

Chapter Two

1 Christian Baptism ed. A. Gilmore pp. 46, 48
2 Documents p.116; Theology, Church and Ministry p. 36
3 The Shape of the Liturgy p. 3
4 Scripture and Tradition p. 14
5 Early Christian Creeds p. 8
6 Early Christian Doctrines p. 44
7 Fathers and Heretics pp. 2 f.
8 Theology, Church and Ministry p. 45
9 Tradition and the Spirit p. 29
10 See Kelly: Early Christian Doctrines p. 50
11 Fid. orth. 1.1
12 haer. 4,26.2
13 op. cit. p. 16
14 de praescript 15.17
15 de Spir. Sanct. 66, 67
16 The Seal of the Spirit pp. 33 f.
17 Commonitorium II, 2, 3
18 Principles of Christian Theology p. 11
19 op. cit. p. 12
20 The Doctrine of Assurance pp. 163 ff.
21 Domestic State Papers – Edward VI, Vol. XV, No. 15; See Scripture and Tradition, ed. Dillistone, p. 100
22 Scripture, Tradition and Reason p. 229
23 A New Dictionary of Christian Theology p. 575
24 Tradition and the Spirit pp. 19, 21
25 Principles of Christian Theology p. 31
26 op. cit. p. 412
27 op. cit., p. 342

28 Prestige: Fathers and Heretics p. 21
29 D. E. W. Harrison: Scripture and Tradition: Dillistone (ed) p. 138
30 H. Cunliffe-Jones and B. Drewery (eds) A History of Christian Doctrine p. 405
31 The Church and the Reality of Christ p. 29. Quoted by J. Macquarrie: Theology, Church and Ministry p. 46 f.
32 Scripture and Tradition p. 140
33 Early Christian Fathers p. 87
34 Letters of John Wesley Vol. 3. p. 159; A. S. Yates: The Search for Certainty p. 46

Chapter Three

1 Confirmation: Its Place in the Baptismal Mystery, p. 150
2 Reasonable Belief, p. 226
3 The New Testament Doctrine of Baptism, p. 124
4 Ign. Smyrna 13.1
5 op. cit. p. 20
6 ibid
7 New Testament Theology, p. 153
8 op. cit. p. 21
9 Baptism in the New Testament, p. 315
10 Die Taufe im Neuen Testament, p. 37
11 Christian Baptism, ed. A. Gilmore, p. 123f
12 op. cit. pp. 22, 28
13 op. cit. p. 88 note 1
14 The Theology of St Paul, p. 174
15 op. cit. p. 88
16 op. cit. p. 16
17 op. cit. p. 91
18 The Origins of Infant Baptism, p. 15
19 Baptism in the New Testament, p. 314f
20 op. cit. p. 315
21 op. cit. Vol. 1, pp 340ff; Williams, Commentary on the Acts of the Apostles, p. 138
22 The New Testament Doctrine of Baptism, p. 122
23 op. cit. p. 89
24 Bruce Metzger: A Textual Commentary on the Greek New Testament, p. 447
25 op. cit. p. 15
26 op. cit. p. 91
27 Infant Baptism in the First Four Centuries, p. 23
28 Origins of Infant Baptism, p. 25
29 op. cit. p. 94
30 op. cit. p. 131f
31 Infant Baptism in the First Four Centuries, p. 40

32 Zum Problem der Kindertaufe im Urchristentum, p. 123
33 op. cit. p. 41
34 op. cit. p. 72
35 op. cit. p. 85
36 The Origins of Infant Baptism, p. 61
37 op. cit. p. 86
38 op. cit. p. 26
39 op. cit. p. 26
40 op. cit. p. 27
41 Baptism in the New Testament, p. 342
42 What Baptists Stand For, p. 224
43 op. cit. pp. 46f
44 Aland. op. cit. p. 81f
45 op. cit. p. 48
46 Mark 10. 13–16; Matthew 19. 13–15; Luke 18. 15–17
47 op. cit. p. 49
48 See I. H. Marshall: The Gospel of Luke. A Commentary on the Greek Text, p. 682
49 Baptism in the New Testament p. 75
50 op. cit. pp. 77f
51 op. cit. p. 78
52 What Baptists Stand For, p. 236f
53 The One Church, p. 68; quoted by Beasley-Murray: op cit. p. 325
54 op. cit. p. 54
55 The Gospel of Luke, p. 682
56 Baptism in the New Testament p. 322
57 op. cit. p. 55
58 Commentary on a Harmony of the Evangelists, Vol. 2. p. 391
59 See Christian Baptism, ed. A. Gilmore. p. 169
60 The Unity of the Bible p. 167
61 E.R.E. Vol. 2 pp. 38f
62 Sacraments in the New Testament pp. 9ff; Christian Baptism, ed. A. Gilmore p. 82
63 Hastings: Dictionary of the Apostolic Church p. 130
64 Liturgy and Worship p. 417
65 F. C. Conybeare: The Eusebian Form of the Text Mt. 28.19 p. 282f
66 The Making of the Church p. 149
67 Essays Catholic and Critical p. 417f
68 A History of the Expansion of Christianity. Vol. I p. 118
69 The New Testament Doctrine of Baptism p. 130
70 op. cit. Vol. 1 p. 352

Chapter Four

1 Infant Baptism in the First Four Centuries p. 66
2 The Christian Platonists of Alexandria p. 246

3 History of Dogma, Vol. 2 p. 365
4 The Ideas of the Fall and Original Sin p. 219f
5 A. Gilmore ed., Christian Baptism p. 205
6 op. cit. p. 70
7 op. cit. p. 69
8 op. cit. p. 15.11
9 op. cit. p. 71
10 Papyrus 2486 in the British Museum
11 Against Heresies ii, 22.4
12 op. cit. p. 73
13 Adv. haer. 1.21.1; 3.17.1
14 Christian Baptism, A. Gilmore, edit. p. 198
15 Adv. haer. 4.23.2
16 op. cit. 1.9.4
17 Demonstration of the Apostolic Preaching p. 41
18 Did the Early Church Baptize Infants? p. 59
19 Mark 10.13ff and parallels
20 Preface to The Apostolic Tradition
21 op. cit. 42.1; 43.2
22 op. cit. 46.4
23 op. cit. p. 51
24 For relevant quotations on Baptism from Tertullian's writings, see A New Eusebius, edited by J. Stevenson, pp. 183ff and E. C. Whitaker: Documents of the Baptismal Liturgy pp. 7ff.
25 History of the Christian Church p. 125
26 See H. Chadwick, The Early Church, p. 90
27 Article on Tertullian in The New International Dictionary of the Christian Church, J. D. Douglas, ed. p. 960
28 Enthusiasm p. 33
29 Infant Baptism in the First Four Centuries p. 81
30 op. cit. p. 85
31 De Baptismo 18.5
32 op. cit. 18.4
33 ibid 18.6
34 The New Testament Doctrine of Baptism p. 133
35 Pilate to Constantine p. 237
36 De Baptismo, chap. 20
37 op. cit. 3.2,3
38 De Anima 38.2
39 See Aland op. cit. p. 69
40 Encyclopedia of Religion Vol. 2. p. 62
41 Pilate to Constantine p. 235
42 See Study of Liturgy, edited by Jones, Wainwright and Yarnold, p. 88
43 See A New Eusebius, J. Stevenson (ed) p. 126
44 Did. 7.1,2
45 op. cit. 9.5
46 For evidence in support of affusion in the Early Church, see C. F.

Rogers: Baptism and Christian Archaeology; J. G. Davies: The Making of the Church
47 Vision III.7.5
48 Sim. 9.16,3f
49 Augustus to Constantine p. 327
50 61.2f
51 65.1ff; E. C. Whitaker: Documents of the Baptismal Liturgy pp. 1ff
52 Apol. 1.15
53 The New Testament Doctrine of Baptism p. 132
54 op. cit. p. 132
55 Justin. Apol. 1.15.6
56 Apology 1.61,2; 65.1; Christian Baptism, A. Gilmore ed. p. 196
57 Church, Sacraments and Ministry p. 45
58 The Christian Fathers pp.87f
59 The Origins of Infant Baptism p. 75
60 Article on Baptism in Encyclopedia of Theology Karl Rahner (ed) p. 69
61 Infant Baptism in the First Four Centuries p. 59
62 Martyrium Polycarpi 18.3 states that this was a contemporary account (Church of Smyrna). It also appears in Eus. Hist. Eccl. 15.20
63 See Lightfoot: Apostolic Fathers, Vol. 1 pp. 437ff
64 Dictionary of the Apostolic Church, J. Hastings (ed) p. 136
65 See chapter eleven
66 The Theology of Confirmation in Relation to Baptism p. 37
67 Adv. Haer. iii 3.4
68 op. cit. p. 63
69 op. cit. pp. 64, 67, 82
70 op. cit. p. 64
71 Pliny. Epist. 10.96; Hippolytus: Church Order can. 45f; A History of the Early Church p. 130
72 Eusebius Hist. Eccl. V. 24.7
73 op. cit. p. 69
74 op. cit. p. 73
75 1 Clem. 46.5
76 op. cit. 9.4; cf. 1 Pet. 3.20f
77 op. cit. 36.2 See A. Gilmore, ed. Christian Baptism p. 192
78 1 Clem. 65.1
79 ibid. 63.3
80 op. cit. p. 85
81 op. cit. p. 78f
82 op. cit. 86
83 History of Primitive Christianity p. 50
84 New International Dictionary of the Christian Church p. 100
85 Baptism in the New Testament p. 329
86 Heresies 2.22.4; A History of the Christian Church p. 87
87 The Baptist Liturgy p. 29

Chapter Five

1 Dictionary of Christian Theology, p. 171
2 The Christian Fathers p. 119
3 E.R.E. Vol. 2 p. 393
4 op. cit. p. 27
5 Augustus to Constantine pp. 70,123f
6 op. cit. p. 334f
7 Origins of Infant Baptism p. 73
8 Ideas of the Fall and of Original Sin p. 223
9 Christian Baptism, A. Gilmore (ed.) p. 189
10 Hom. VIII and XII in 1 Cor.
11 De Prin. iii.5
12 Baptism Today and Tomorrow p. 163f
13 Baptism in the New Testament p. 352
14 Zum Problem der Kindertaufe im Urchristentum, p. 142
15 Urchristentum und Kindertaufe Z.N.W. Vol. 29 p. 100
16 op. cit. p. 354
17 Det. Kristna Dopet p. 92; Beasley-Murray op. cit. p. 354
18 The Seal of the Spirit pp.97f
19 op. cit. p. 355
20 Infant Baptism in the First Four Centuries p. 95
21 See chapter nine on 'Grace'
22 op. cit. pp. 102, 150
23 op. cit. p. 355
24 op. cit. p. 356f
25 op. cit. p. 357
26 The Study of the Liturgy, edited by C. Jones, G. Wainwright, and E. J. Yarnold. p. 109. cf. Dom Gregory Dix: The Shape of the Liturgy
27 See also Lampe: Seal of the Spirit p. 93
28 We shall consider the implications of this statement in chapter nine.
29 op. cit. pp. 358f
30 op. cit. p. 359
31 A History of the Christian Church p. 87f
32 Epistle 59
33 Catechetical Lectures of Cyril of Jerusalem p. 9
34 The Water that Divides p. 80
35 Orat., xl In Sanctum Baptisma, 28
36 Orat., xl, 6–7
37 See N. P. Williams: The Ideas of the Fall and Original Sin, p. 290; Christian Baptism, A. Gilmore (ed) p. 210
38 Hom. 5.3 in 2 Tim; Hom. 2.2 in Eph; Hom. 3.4 in Phil; Christian Baptism, A. Gilmore (ed) p. 212
39 Hom. 40 in Gen.
40 Conf. i, 11, 17

41 The New International Dictionary of the Christian Church, J. D. Douglas (ed.) p. 100
42 What Baptists Stand For p. 219
43 De nupt. et. conc. i. 29
44 Bapt. iii, 17, 22
45 Session 7, Canons on the Sacrament of Baptism, 1–14, D.857–870.
46 D.797
47 ad. Marc. 1.20 and Sermo. 294
48 Study of Liturgy, edit. Jones, Wainwright & Yarnold pp. 95f
49 Conf. 1.18
50 op. cit. p. 96
51 The New International Dictionary of the Christian Church p. 755
52 The Key of Truth p. 118
53 The Study of Liturgy pp. iiif
54 Christian Initiation: Baptism in the Medieval Church p. 3
55 The Study of Liturgy, eds. Jones, Wainwright and Yarnold p. 118
56 Verduin, The Reformers and Their Stepchildren p. 153
57 A New International Dictionary of the Christian Church p. 1026
58 Neander: Church History viii, p. 339; W. H. Robinson: Baptist Principles, p. 63
59 See Article by Gregory Baum in Encyclopedia of Theology ed. Karl Rahner
60 See Mark 7.34 Ephphatha (Εφφαθα), only here in the New Testament
61 A History of the Church in England pp. 123f

Chapter Six

1 Church, Sacraments and Ministry p. 49
2 Adult Baptism Grove Worship Series No. 91. p. 7
3 Study of Liturgy p. 120f
4 See chapters three and seven
5 L. Enders: Dr Martin Luther's Briefwechsel iii, 276; Christian Baptism, A. Gilmore (ed.) p. 234
6 See chapter nine.
7 Religious Thought in the Reformation p. 77
8 Primary Works, ed. H. Wace and C. A. Buckhein p. 138
9 Christian Initiation: The Reformation Period p. 5
10 Knaake (ed), Works of Martin Luther Vol. 30 p. 448
11 See J. D. C. Fisher, op. cit. p. 46
12 Verduin, The Reformers and their Stepchildren p. 198
13 See chapter three where we discussed whether Christ instituted Baptism.
14 Queller zur Geschichte der Taufer in der Schweiz. p. 186; See D. Bridge The Water that Divides p. 103.
15 See chapters nine and ten.
16 See Christian Baptism, A. Gilmore (ed.) p. 234

17 See next chapter.
18 B. Reardon: op. cit. pp. 104f
19 See chapter ten.
20 Christian Baptism, A. Gilmore (ed.), p. 233
21 The Encyclopedia of Religion, Vol. 2, p. 241
22 op. cit. Vol. 13 pp.324f
23 op. cit. p. 200
24 Institutes of the Christian Religion, IV, XV, 20
25 op. cit. IV, 16, 19
26 See chapter ten.
27 op. cit. IV. 16.0
28 See J. D. C. Fisher, Christian Initiation: The Reformation Period pp.116f; W. D. Maxwell: The Liturgical Portions of the Genevan Service Book, 70.
29 B. J. Kidd, Documents illustrative of the Continental Reformation p. 650; J. D. C. Fisher: op. cit. p. 112.
30 The Water that Divides p. 124
31 Works 1 (1846) The History of the Reformation in Scotland p. 197.
32 See J. D. C. Fisher: op. cit. pp. 118f
33 An abbreviated title for The Institution of a Christian Man
34 T. A. Lacey, The King's Book pp. 41ff; See J. D. C. Fisher: op. cit. pp. 76f, to whose books on Christian Initiation I am much indebted.
35 See J. R. Green, A Short History of the English People pp. 463ff.
36 Christian England, p. 145
37 Offor (ed.) The Works of John Bunyan Vol. 2 p. 604
38 W. J. McGlothlin, Baptist Confession of Faith, Clause X; Christian Baptism, A. Gilmore (ed.) p. 277
39 Short History of the Anabaptists (1647)
40 Plain Scripture Proof of Infants, Church membership and baptism; See Christian Baptism pp. 279f.
41 The Golden Chaine, Works (1635), p. 73
42 See A. Gilmore (ed.) op. cit. p. 281
43 The New International Dictionary of the Christian Church p. 100.
44 A. S. Yates: The Search for Certainty
45 History of England in the Eighteenth Century, Vols. 2 and 3
46 In our view wrongly called his 'conversion'. See The Search for Certainty, chapter 2.
47 Journal of John Wesley, Vol. 1 p. 475
48 Christian Baptism, A. Gilmore (ed.) p. 305

Chapter Seven

1 The Interpreter's Dictionary of the Bible, Vol. 1. p. 629
2 op. cit. 15.26
3 The Interpreter's Dictionary of the Bible, Vol. 1. p. 629

4 The Teaching of the Church Regarding Baptism; Grove Booklet on Ministry and Worship No. 24. p. 9
5 Infant Baptism in First Four Centuries, p. 29
6 Encyclopedia of Religion, p. 60
7 op. cit. p. 28
8 Grove No. 20. p. 13
9 Similitudes 9.16; The Theology of St Paul p. 175
10 It is pointed out that Justin Martyr, in his Dialogue with the Jew Trypho, describes baptism as a 'spiritual circumcision' in contrast to 'the circumcision of the flesh' which was characteristic of the old covenant.
11 Dial. cum Tryph. 43; Flemington The New Testament Doctrine of Baptism p. 131
12 Quoted by Dr Henry Cooke: What Baptists Stand For p. 224
13 The Church in the Power of the Spirit p. 232f
14 Die Taufe in Neuen Testament p. 21
15 See Beasley-Murray: Baptism in the New Testament p. 329
16 op. cit. p. 334
17 op. cit. p. 151
18 op. cit. p. 199
19 op. cit. p. 155f
20 Seal of the Spirit p. 5
21 op. cit. p. 40
22 Dictionary of the Bible, 2nd edition. p. 89 edited by F. C. Grant and H. H. Rowley
23 The Theology of St Paul p. 170
24 See Christian Baptism: A. Gilmore (ed.) p. 139f
25 See our consideration of this verse in chapter three.
26 1955 p. 21
27 Die Apostelgeschichte p. 542; Did the Early Church Baptize Infants, p. 82
28 Aland op. cit. p. 84
29 Pilate to Constantine p. 236f
30 Prof. Henry Chadwick suggests that the least unlikely date is about AD 70–100. 'It may be odd there', he says, 'but it is odder anywhere else'! The Early Church p. 47
31 Barn. 11.11; 16.8; 4.8; Grant: Augustus to Constantine p. 323
32 Dial. cum Tryph 19.2; 43.2
33 Hom. 3.7 in 2 Cor.
34 Hom. 40 in Gen; Christian Baptism p. 212
35 Op. imp. c. Julian. 6.18; Ep. 187.11.34; Ep. 265.4; Christian Baptism p. 215
36 Aug. De Bapt. contra Donatistas iv 24; Flemington op. cit. p. 131
37 Religious Thought in the Reformation p. 104
38 op. cit. p. 105
39 See J. D. C. Fisher: Christian Initiation in the Reformation Period pp. 46, 68.

40 See our consideration of these texts in chapter three.
41 E.R.E. Vol. 3. p. 405
42 Religious Thought in the Reformation p. 201
43 See Donald Bridge: The Water that Divides p. 122f
44 W. D. Maxwell: The Liturgical Portions of the Genevan Service Book, p. 71; J. D. C. Fisher: Christian Initiation, The Reformation Period p. 115
45 See our discussion of Scripture and Tradition in chapter two.
46 Works (Parker Society) Vol. 2. pp. 56ff; J. D. C. Fisher op. cit. p. 88.
47 Infant Baptism under Cross-examination p. 10
48 Christian Baptism (ed) A. Gilmore p. 316

Chapter Eight

1 Theology of St Paul, p. 46
2 Principles of Theology, p. 242
3 The Sacramental Society, p. 130
4 A New Dictionary of Christian Theology, p. 420f.
5 Mand. II.1
6 Sim. IX. 29.1
7 Augustus to Constantine, p. 334f.
8 De Baptismo 39.4; 40.1.
9 E.R.E. Vol. 9. p. 560
10 De Anima 39.3ff
11 Encyclopedia of religion Vol. 7, p. 282
12 De Princ. 2.9.1–6; 1.8.1.
13 De Princ. iii 2,2; 5,4
14 Oxford Dictionary of the Christian Church, F. L. Cross (ed.) p. 994
15 New International Dictionary of the Christian Church, p. 32f.
16 De myst. 32; enarr. in ps. 48.8
17 See The Study of Liturgy, ed. by C. Jones, G. Wainwright and E. J. Yarnold, P. 104.
18 The Baptismal Liturgy, p. 49
19 J. N. D. Kelly: op. cit. p. 255
20 op. cit. p. 350
21 See Christian Baptism, ed. A. Gilmore, p. 211
22 De civ. dei 22, 24.2; Kelly op. cit. p. 364
23 Enchir. 93; Kelly: op. cit. p. 366
24 The Early Church, p. 228
25 Encyclopedia of Religion, Vol. 13, p. 330
26 David Ayerst and A. S. T. Fisher: Records of Christianity Vol. 1. p. 283
27 A History of Christian Doctrine (ed.) H. Cunliffe-Jones p. 162
28 ibid. p. 161
29 New International Dictionary of the Christian Church, ed. J. D. Douglas, p. 555

30 Unfinished Work 3,67; 1.48; D. Ayerst and A. S. T. Fisher: Records of Christianity, Vol. 1. p. 284
31 See Oxford Dictionary of the Christian Church, p. 1011
32 History of Christian Doctrine, p. 274
33 Christian Initiation: Baptism in the Medieval West, p. 112f
34 A History of Christian Doctrine, p. 406
35 B. M. G. Reardon: op. cit. p. 100ff.
36 See J. D. Fisher: Christian Initiation: The Reformation Period, pp. 58, 68
37 Commentary on a Harmony of the Evangelists, Vol. 2, p. 390f; Quoted by Dr Beasley-Murray: Baptism in the New Testament p. 321, note 3.
38 J. D. C. Fisher: Christian Initiation: The Reformation Period, p. 115f.
39 J. C. Wenger (ed.): Menno Simons: The Complete Writings p. 669
40 op. cit. p. 222
41 Baptism in the New Testament. p. 366
42 The Baptismal Liturgy, p. 64
43 What Baptists Stand For, p. 218
44 New Testament Doctrine of Baptism, p. 139f.
45 A New Dictionary of Christian Theology, p. 209
46 E. J. Bicknell: The 39 Articles, p. 232
47 ibid.
48 F. R. Tennant: Origin of Sin, p. 31
49 E.R. E. Vol. 9, p. 563

Chapter Nine

1 Oxford Dictionary of the Christian Church, p. 586
2 Spirit, Church and Sacraments, p. 86
3 De corrept. et grat., 10, 38, 45
4 The Teaching of the Church regarding Baptism, p. 9
5 Schmemann: Of Water and the Spirit, p. 58
6 Burnish: The Meaning of Baptism, p. 103
7 Expositio in Ephesios 5.1
8 A History of Christian Doctrine, ed. H. Cunliffe-Jones p. 159f.
9 See H. Chadwick: The Early Church, p. 228
10 Summa Theologiae Part 3, Questions 66–69; Christian Baptism, ed. A. Gilmore p. 218.
11 The Doctrine of Grace in the Apostolic Fathers, p.v.
12 op. cit. p. 133
13 op. cit. p. 140
14 op. cit. p. 141
15 The Christian Fathers, pp. 133f.
16 op. cit. p. 110
17 Dictionary of the Apostolic Church, Vol. 1. p. 513
18 The Theology of St Paul, p. 172
19 The Theology of the New Testament, Vol. 1. p. 135

20 Essays and Addresses p. 241
21 E.R.E. Vol. 2, p. 397
22 The Sacramental Society, p. 126f
23 Of Water and Spirit, pp. 53ff; Burnish: The Meaning of Baptism, pp. 100ff.
24 Cat. 3.4
25 Cat. 1.6; 2.9; 3.2ff.
26 Cat. 1.4; 17.37
27 Burnish: The Meaning of Baptism pp. 8, 84
28 McGiffert: History of Christian Thought, Vol. 1. p. 241
29 op. cit. p. 130
30 Seventeenth Sunday After Trinity
31 See McGiffert: op. cit. Vol. 2. p. 112
32 A History of Christian Doctrine, p. 167 ed. H. Cunliffe-Jones
33 Inst. IV, xiv. 14
34 We shall consider emergency baptisms in a later chapter.
35 Eccl. Pol. V. 60, 64
36 op. cit. p. 236
37 Laud. 37
38 ap. Eus., V. Const., 4.62; Lampe op. cit. p. 239
39 See Lampe, op. cit. pp. 244, 246
40 op. cit. p. 180
41 ibid. p. 187
42 The Faith of the Christian Church, p. 333
43 Early Christian Doctrines, p. 193
44 Grove Worship Series No. 91, p. 8
45 Walker: A History of the Christian Church, p. 247
46 Baptism Today and Tomorrow, p. 13
47 See Henry Chadwick: The Early Church, pp. 119f, 220.
48 Aug. de Bapt. contra Don. vi. 25
49 Contra Ep. Parm. ii. 13
50 History of Christian Thought, p. 318
51 W. Walker: A History of the Christian Church, p. 247
52 The Faith of the Christian Church, pp. 340, 331
53 Institutes IV, xv. 14
54 Harnack: Grundriss der Dogmengeschichte 1891, p. 366; E.R.E. Vol. 6, p. 366
55 J. D. C. Fisher: op. cit. p. 69
56 History of the Christian Church, p. 425
57 The Faith of the Christian Church, p. 332
58 History of Dogma, viii, p. 216
59 Inst. IV, xiv, 14
60 E.R.E. Vol. 2. p. 40f; A History of Christian Doctrine, ed. H. Cunliffe-Jones, p. 444f
61 The New Testament Doctrine of Baptism, p. 116
62 Libri quattuor sententiarum iv. 1

63 Summa Theologiae Vol. 2. 112.4; McGiffert: History of Christian Thought, Vol. II, pp. 283, 314f.
64 Von der Taufe, von der Widertaufe, von der Kindertaufe C.R. 91, p. 245
65 J. D. C. Fisher, op. cit. p. 129
66 Institutes, Vol. iv, 14.1
67 B. M. G. Reardon: Religious Thought in the Reformation pp. 104, 200
68 Hooker: Sermon on Justification 5.50.1,3; 5.57. 1–5; A History of Christian Doctrine, ed. H. Cunliffe-Jones, pp. 422ff.
69 The Theology of Baptism in Baptist History, Baptist Quarterly, Vol. XV, p. 100
70 Baptism Today and Tomorrow, p. 26
71 Religious Values in the Sacraments, p. 60
72 op. cit. p. 32f.
73 Christian Baptism, ed. A. Gilmore, p. 323
74 A History of English Baptists, p. 269; R. Burnish: Meaning of Baptism, p. 148
75 The Faith of the People of God, p. 75
76 The One Church in the Light of the New Testament, p. 77
77 Denzinger: Enchiridion, p. 341f
78 A Dictionary of Christian Theology (ed.) A. Richardson, p. 123
79 The Faith of the Christian Church, p. 334 Christian Baptism (ed.) A. Gilmore, p. 221
80 Sess. 7. Canons on the Sacrament of Baptism 1–14 D. 857–70
81 See New International Dictionary of the Christian Church, p. 100
82 Harnack: History of Dogma, Vol. vii, p. 217
83 Harnack: op. cit. Vol. vii, p. 250
84 Calvin: Tracts, Vol. ii, p. 217
85 E.R.E. Vol. 2, p. 401
86 A History of Christian Doctrine, p. 276
87 The Church in the Power of the Spirit, p. 240
88 Eph. 18.2; R. M. Grant: Augustine to Constantine, p. 325
89 Ante-Nicene Fathers ed. A. Roberts and J. Donaldson, Vol. viii, p. 44
90 Christian Baptism, ed. A. Gilmore p. 193f
91 Adv. Jud. 8; De Bapt. 9
92 Eclogae 7
93 Exp. Ev. Luc. 2,83
94 De Bap. 1,2
95 Ep. 70.1
96 See Bethune-Baker: An Introduction to the Early History of the Christian Church, p. 381
97 See Didachi, vii. 1
98 Baptism in the New Testament p. 4; Christian Initiation: Baptism in the Medieval Church, p. 14
99 Gelasianum p. 477; Fisher: op. cit. p. 1
100 De Spiritu Sancto, Vol. 1. 6.77

101 Cat. 3.3
102 Documents of the Baptismal Liturgy pp. 4, 7.11
103 op. cit. pp. 119, 138, 160, 186
104 E. C. Whitaker: The Baptismal Liturgy, pp. 4f, 47
105 Ambrose, de Sac. 1.15; The Study of Liturgy, ed. C. Jones, G. Wainwright and E. Yarnold (1978) p. 102
106 In Act. hom. 1, 5
107 Eusebius: Life of Constantine iv. 61
108 The Study of Liturgy, p. 111
109 The Study of Liturgy, p. 125
110 See Christian Baptism, A. Gilmore (ed) p. 100
111 Cat. Lect. xx. 6
112 History of Primitive Christianity p. 150
113 Christian Baptism, p. 274
114 See Dr J. G. Davies: The Making of the Church, p. 152
115 The Seal of the Spirit, p. 167
116 op. cit. p. 168
117 Baillie: The Theology of the Sacraments, p. 51; Hanson: Church, Sacraments and Ministry, p. 36f.
118 Outward and Inward in Biblical Theology, pp. 196ff.
119 The Theology of St Paul, pp. 171f.
120 Gilmore: Baptism and Christian Unity, p. 41
121 op. cit. pp. 40ff.
122 Science and Christian Belief, pp. 43ff., 54ff.
123 Gilmore, op. cit. p. 45
124 Wiles: The Christian Fathers, p. 122
125 The Faith of the Christian Church, pp. 339ff.
126 Knaake (ed.) Works of Martin Luther, Vol. 30, p. 476; D. Bridge and D. Phypers: The Water that Divides, p. 109
127 See Christian Initiation: The Reformation Period, p. 5
128 Commentary on a Harmony of the Evangelists Vol. 2, p. 390
129 Principles of Christian Theology, p. 411
130 De Civitate xxii 30; An Introduction to the Early History of Christian Doctrine, p. 310
131 The New Testament Doctrine of Baptism, p. 138f.
132 Barth: The Teaching of the Church regarding Baptism; Moltmann: The Church in the Power of the Spirit, p. 238f.
133 Die Zeit der Kirche, p. 107ff
134 Christian Baptism, ed. A. Gilmore, p. 101
135 The church and the Sacraments, p. 198
136 op. cit. p. 91

Chapter Ten

1 No. 111 p. 4
2 Baptism Today and Tomorrow, pp. 27f, 37

3 The Church and the Sacraments, pp. 92, 13
4 Ideas of the Fall and of Original Sin, p. 550
5 New Testament Doctrine of Baptism, p. 124
6 Baptism in the New Testament, p. 347
7 Baptism Today and Tomorrow, p. 142
8 Christian Baptism, ed. A. Gilmore, p. 114
9 op. cit. p. 101
10 The Seal of the Spirit, p. 149
11 Study of Liturgy, ed. C. Jones, G. Wainwright, E. Yarnold, p. 84
12 D. Bridge and D. Phypers: The Water that Divides, p. 21
13 Principles of Christian Theology, p. 407
14 op. cit. p. 49
15 The Pauline Idea of Faith in its Relation to Jewish and Hellenistic Religions, p. 43
16 Christian Baptism, ed. A. Gilmore, pp. 134, 141
17 The Doctrine of Confirmation. Theology, Vol. 48, p. 201
18 Vis. III.iii 5
19 F. C. Grant and H. H. Rowley, eds. Dictionary of the Bible, p. 89
20 The Way of Christ pp. 8f; Burnish: The Meaning of Baptism, p. 153
21 Christian Baptism, p. 198
22 Documents of the Baptismal Liturgy, p. xiii
23 De Spiritu Sancto, 26–28
24 The Meaning of Baptism, p. 190
25 E.R.E. Vol. 2, p. 395
26 Cat. Lect. 17.36
27 op. cit. pp. 113, 121f
28 Key of Truth, p. 117
29 Religious Thought in the Reformation, p. 214
30 The Church in the Power of the Spirit, p. 228
31 The Faith of the Christian Church, p. 341
32 See A. Gilmore: Baptism and Christian Unity, p. 19
33 Reformation Writings of Martin Luther, trans. B. L. Woolf, p. 261
34 Woolf: op. cit. p. 264; J. D. C. Fisher: Christian Initiation: The Reformation Period pp.3ff
35 See A. Gilmore: op. cit. pp. 19f
36 Luther's Primary Works: eds. H. Wace and C. Buckheim pp. 324ff
37 See Christian Baptism: ed. A. Gilmore, p. 234
38 Institutes III ii 35
39 See Gilmore: Baptism and Christian Unity, p. 21
40 F. L. Cross ed. The Oxford Dictionary of the Christian Church, p. 127
41 J. C. Wenger, ed. Menno Simons: The Complete Works, p. 120
42 op. cit. pp. 238ff; Reardon: op. cit. pp. 221f
43 Baptism in the New Testament, pp. 54ff
44 See Christian Baptism: A. Gilmore, ed. p. 95
45 See chapter three.
46 Cullmann: op. cit. p. 52

47 The Church and the Sacraments, p. 214
48 Tradition and the Spirit, p. 103
49 Encyclopedia of Theology, edited by Karl Rahner, pp. 72, 75
50 op. cit. pp. 180f
51 The Proposed Services of Baptism and Confirmation Reconsidered, p. 18
52 Reformation Writings of Martin Luther trans. B. L. Woolf, p. 271; J. D. C. Fisher: Christian Initiation: The Reformation Period, pp.3f
53 D. L. Weatherhead: Psychology, Religion and Healing
54 Baptismal Discipline, p. 13
55 Expositor Vol. 13 p. 197
56 Church and Sacraments, p. 2
57 E.R.E. Vol. 2 p. 394
58 op. cit. p. 170
59 The Faith of the People of God, pp. 77f
60 The New Testament Doctrine of Baptism, p. 127
61 The Baptismal Interrogations. Theology Vol 59, p. 104
62 Baptism in the New Testament, p. 349f
63 Christian Initiation: Baptism in the Medieval West, p. 47
64 op. cit. pp. 211f
65 op. cit. p. 12
66 A Dictionary of Christian Theology, p. 172
67 op. cit. p. 4
68 The Water that Divides, p. 48f
69 De Baptismo 18
70 The Faith of the Christian Church, p. 341
71 op. cit. p. 137
72 B. Manning: Why Not Abandon the Church, pp. 47f
73 J. Hastings: Dictionary of the Apostolic Church, p. 136
74 The Sacramental Society, p. 132f

Chapter Eleven

1 A. P. Milner: The Theology of Confirmation p. 6
2 op. cit. p. 7
3 The Ministry, Rites and Organisation of the Apostolic Church p. 43
4 The Theology of Confirmation in Relation to Baptism pp.5 ff.
5 Principles of Christian Theology p. 414
6 Christian Baptism, A. Gilmore (ed) p. 118
7 The Seal of the Spirit p. 72
8 B. M. Metzger, A Textual Commentary on the Greek New Testament pp. 360f
9 See C. S. C. Williams, The Acts of the Apostles p. 120
10 op. cit. p. 18
11 See Clarke and Harris, Liturgy and Worship p. 445
12 The New Testament Doctrine of Baptism pp. 150 ff.

13 op. cit. p. 65
14 M. Barth, Die Taufe-ein Sankrament pp. 169ff
15 A. Gilmore (ed), Christian Baptism pp. 120f
16 op. cit. p. 446
17 Augustine, De Bapt. iii. 16; Caird, The Apostolic Age pp. 69f
18 op. cit. pp. 149f
19 op. cit. p. 78
20 The Thirty Nine Articles p. 477
21 Thornton, Confirmation, its Place in the Baptismal Mystery p. 21; Dix, Confirmation or Laying on of Hands p. 10
22 Baptismal Anointing p. 17
23 op. cit. pp. 7f
24 Simil. XI. xvi. 4; op. cit. p. 150
25 See J. D. C. Fisher, Christian Initiation: The Reformation Period pp. 206f.
26 The Seal of the Spirit p. 82
27 The Theology of Confirmation in Relation to Baptism pp. 10ff.
28 Pilate to Constantine p. 243
29 Early Christian Doctrines p. 194
30 See J. Bulloch, op. cit. p. 240
31 Study of Liturgy p. 89
32 Documents of the Baptismal Liturgy p. xiv
33 De Bapt. Chs. 3, 4, 6–8; Noakes, Study of Liturgy p. 92
34 De Bapt. 1.18| 6.; Early Christian Doctrines p. 209
35 op. cit. p. 162
36 G. Dix, Apostolic Tradition pp. 38ff.
37 The Baptismal Liturgy p. 11
38 The Seal of the Spirit pp. 135ff
39 op. cit. p. 207
40 See Lampe, op. cit. pp. 152f
41 The Early Church pp. 102f
42 A History of the Early Church p. 98
43 op. cit. p. 48
44 op. cit. p. 24
45 op. cit. p. viii
46 The Christian Fathers pp. 116f
47 Confirmation: Its Place in the Baptismal Mystery p. 192
48 Article: The Significance of the Pre-baptismal Seal in St John Chrysostom – Studia Patristica Vol. VI p. 90
49 op. cit. pp. 31 f
50 Documents of the Baptismal Liturgy pp. XVIff
51 op. cit. pp. 82, 85
52 The Theology of Confirmation p. 47
53 See The Study of Liturgy, edit. by C. Jones, G. Wainwright and E. Yarnold pp. 115f.
54 Chronicle of Convocation 1945, I. pp. 53–69; Dix, op. cit. p. 30
55 See Fisher, op. cit. p. 160

56 The Theology of Confirmation in Relation to Baptism p. 29
57 op. cit. p. 229
58 De Inst. Cleric. I xxviii
59 Dix, op. cit. p. 27
60 J. D. C. Fisher, op. cit. pp. 29ff
61 See J. Bulloch, Pilate to Constantine p. 243
62 Conc. Lamb, cap. iv. ap Mansi, Acta Conc. viii. 863; quoted by Dix, op. cit. p. 33
63 Synod. Exon. can. iii ibid 1076
64 op. cit. pp. 21ff
65 M. Deanesly, A History of the Medieval Church p. 207
66 Church, Sacraments and Ministry p. 48
67 The Sacrament of Confirmation in the Early-Middle Scholastic Period p. 5
68 Fisher op. cit. p. 129
69 See E. C. Whitaker: Baptismal Liturgy
70 op. cit. p. 69
71 Study of Liturgy, eds. Jones, Wainwright and Yarnold p. 128
72 A remarkable statement!
73 Von ehelichen leben p. 281
74 See J. D. C. Fisher, Christian Initiation: The Reformation Period – a book to which we are much indebted.
75 De Vera et Falsa Religione pp. 201f; 302
76 Institutes IV. 19, 13
77 op. cit. IV. 19.4
78 op. cit. pp. 258f
79 Institutes IV. 19. 5,7
80 op. cit. p. 255
81 Antidote to the Canons on Confirmation p. 184. Calvin could have quoted Acts 20, verses 17 & 28 where the same people are referred to as 'elders' (πρεσβυτέροι) and 'bishops' (ἐπισκόποι)
82 Institutes IV 19, 11
83 Fisher, op. cit. p. 203
84 op. cit. p. 62
85 See Hippolytus Apostolic Tradition 21 ed. B. Botte pp. 44 ff; Whitaker op. cit. pp. 2 ff
86 Fisher, op. cit. p. 239
87 Whitaker op. cit. p. 178
88 Bucer: Works V. p. 489
89 Fisher, op. cit. pp. 252 f

Chapter Twelve

1 Liturgy For a New Century pp. 45ff
2 BEM 1982–1990. p. vii
3 BEM p. 3

4 BEM p. 4
5 BEM p. 5
6 BEM 1982–1990 pp. 109f
7 BEM p. 6
8 BEM 1982–1990. p. 39
9 op. cit. p. 52
10 op. cit. p. 53
11 op. cit. pp. 54f
12 op. cit. p. 108f
13 op. cit. p. 112
14 Why It Matters p. 22
15 ibid
16 Ecumenical Perspectives on Baptism, Eucharist and Ministry. p. 34
17 BEM p. 4
18 op. cit. p. 38
19 op. cit. p. 38f
20 British and Irish Churches Respond to BEM pp. 12f
21 op. cit. p. 13
22 op. cit. pp. 14f
23 op. cit. p. 16
24 op. cit. p. 18
25 op. cit. p. 19
26 Christening: The Making of Christians. p. v
27 op. cit. pp. 18f
28 op. cit. p. 107
29 The Rites of the Catholic Church p. vii
30 op. cit. pp. 188ff
31 See chapter 10 on relating faith to infant baptism
32 See chapters 9 and 11
33 See chapter 8 on 'Original Sin and Infant Baptism'
34 The Rites of the Catholic Church as Revised by the Second Vatican Ecumenical Council. p. 309
35 See Second Vatican Council, Constitution, Sancrosanctum Concilium, No. 71
36 Tertullian, De resurrectione mortuorum viii, 3
37 The Rites of the Catholic Church pp. 310ff
38 Christening: the Making of Christians pp. 153ff
39 New Liturgy Autumn 1990 No. 66
40 Liturgy Constitution 71
41 The Baptismal Liturgy p. 70
42 See chapter 8.
43 op. cit. p. 74
44 See chapter 2
45 op. cit. pp. 79f
46 Christian Celebration: The Sacraments p. 22; quoted by Whitaker op. cit. p. 82
47 Selected Letters ed. Brayley

48 See BEM (1982) Commentary (14) p. 5
49 Liturgy for a New Century pp. 77f
50 op. cit. pp. 78ff
51 op. cit. p. 4
52 op. cit. pp. 5ff
53 op. cit. p. 2
54 Christian Initiation – A Policy for the Church of England p. 21
55 The Catechism and Article 25
56 General Synod 1991 Report of Proceedings Vol. 22, No. 2. p. 275
57 op. cit. p. 276
58 The author of a book on 'Open Baptism'.
59 op. cit. p. 281
60 op. cit. p. 283
61 op. cit. p. 286
62 op. cit. p. 289
63 op. cit. p. 299
64 op. cit. p. 297
65 Christian Initiation and its Relation to some Pastoral Offices
66 op. cit. p. 305
67 op. cit. pp. 310f
68 op. cit. pp. 312f
69 op. cit. p. 315
70 op. cit. pp. 318f
71 op. cit. p. 326
72 op. cit. p. 329
73 Report of Proceedings Vol. 22. No. 2. p. 329
74 See chapter 9 on 'The Essence and Effectiveness of Grace'.
75 In chapter 3 the relevance of Mark 10. 13–16 to baptism was questioned.
76 'Statements of the Methodist Church on Faith and Order' pp. 48f
77 Methodist Conference, Portsmouth, 1987. Agenda pp. 602f
78 op. cit. p. 603
79 op. cit. p. 624
80 Methodist Conference, Portsmaouth, 1987. Agenda p. 646
81 op. cit. p. 153
82 See 'Proposals for Unification' published in 1976 by the Churches of Christ and the United Reformed Church.
83 Service Book (1989) United Reformed Church pp. vif
84 op. cit. p. ix
85 The Manual: United Reformed Church pp. 3f
86 op. cit. p. 4
87 URC: Baptism, Infant or Believers? p. 4
88 See New International Dictionary of the Christian Church pp. 101f
89 BEM para. 13 p. 4; Report on the Process and Responses p. 48
90 Christian Baptism, ed. A. Gilmore pp. 325f
91 Baptism: A Baptist View p. 26
92 Baptism and Christian Unity p. 14

93 op. cit. pp. 14f
94 op. cit. p. 81
95 Christian Initiation – A Policy for the Church of England pp. 4ff
96 cf. J. F. Matthews, op. cit. pp. 16f
97 Praise God: A Collection of Resource Material for Christian Worship pp. xiff
98 op. cit. pp. 129ff
99 op. cit. pp. 137ff
100 Patterns and Prayers for Christian Worship pp. vff
101 op. cit. pp. 3ff
102 op. cit. p. 93ff
103 op. cit. pp. 109ff
104 See chapter 9 above on 'The Essence and Effectiveness of Grace'
105 Baptism and Christian Unity pp. 12f
106 Professor of New Testament in the Baptist Theological Seminary of Ruschlikon
107 Faith and Order Paper No. 97, pp. 104f
108 Christian Baptism, ed. A. Gilmore p. 326
109 The Child and the Church: a Baptist Discussion
110 G. R. Beasley-Murray, Baptism in the New Testament pp. 393ff
111 G. R. Beasley-Murray, Baptism Today and Tomorrow pp. 167ff
112 Faith and Order Paper No. 97 pp. 101, 104
113 Baptism and Christian Unity p. 81
114 Ecumenical Perspectives on Baptism, Eucharist and Ministry p. 26
115 Baptist Union Documents pp. 167f
116 op. cit. p. 168
117 Baptism and Christian Unity pp. 82f
118 op. cit. p. 3
119 Christian Initiation: A Policy for the Church of England p. 47

Bibliography

K. Aland. *Did the Early Church Baptize Infants?* SCM. 1963

D. Ayerst and A. S. T. Fisher. *Records of Christianity. Vol. I.* Blackwell 1971

G. Aulen. *The Faith of the Christian Church.* SCM 1961

Alternative Service Book: Commentary by the Liturgical Commission. Baptism and Confirmation (pp. 105–119) Church Information Office. 1980

Anglican Worship Today. Initiation Services. pp. 152–182. Collins Liturgical Publications. 1980

Baptism, Eucharist and Ministry. Faith and Order Paper No. 111. World Council of Churches. 1982

Baptism, Eucharist and Ministry 1982–1990. Report on the Process and Responses. Faith and Order Paper No. 149. World Council of Churches. 1990

British and Irish Churches Respond to B.E.M. BCC. 1988

K. Barth. *The Teaching of the Church Regarding Baptism.* SCM. 1948

Baptist Union Documents 1948–1977. Baptist Historical Society. 1980

D. S. Bailey. *Sponsors at Baptism and Confirmation.* SPCK. 1952

C. K. Barrett. *Church, Ministry and Sacraments in the New Testament.* Paternoster. 1985

R. Bauckham and B. Drewery (Eds). *Scripture, Tradition and Reason.* T. & T. Clark. 1988

G. R. Beasley-Murray. *Baptism Today and Tomorrow.* Macmillan. 1966

G. R. Beasley-Murray. *Baptism in the New Testament.* Paternoster. 1972

J. F. Bethune-Baker. *An Introduction to the Early History of Christian Doctrine.* Methuen. 1923

Biblical Doctrine of Baptism: Church of Scotland Commission. St Andrew's Press. 1958

E. J. Bicknell. *The Thirty Nine Articles of the Church of England.* Longmans. 1946

C. Brown (Ed). *New International Dictionary of New Testament Theology.* Paternoster. 1975

G. W. Bromiley. *Baptism and the Anglican Reformers.* Lutterworth. 1953

D. Bridge and D. Phypers. *The Water That Divides.* IVP 1977

C. Buchanan. *A Case for Infant Baptism.* Grove Books. 1973

C. Buchanan. *Infant Baptism in the Church of England.* Grove Books. 1992

R. Bultmann. *Theology of the New Testament*. SCM. 1952
J. Bullock. *Pilate to Constantine*. St Andrew's Press. 1981
R. Burnish. *The Meaning of Baptism*. SPCK. 1985
G. A. Butterick. (Ed). *The Interpreter's Dictionary of the Bible*. 4 Vols. Abingdon Press. 1962
G. B. Caird. *The Apostolic Age*. Duckworth. 1975
J. Calvin. *Institutes of the Christian Religion*. SCM. 1961
Canons of the Church of England. SPCK. 1990
W. Carr. *The Priority of Grace*, Chapter 4 in Brief Encounters. SPCK. 1985
H. Chadwick. *The Early Church*. Hodder. 1968
Christian Initiation and Church Membership. BCC. 1988
Christian Initiation Matters – a Report by the House of Bishops. General Synod. 1991
N. Clark and R. Jasper. *Initiation and Eucharist*. SPCK. 1972
W. Clark (Ed). *Liturgy and Worship*. SPCK. 1964. The chapter on Baptism quotes early church documents
H. Conzelmann. *History of Primitive Christianity*. DLT. 1973
H. Cook. *What Baptists Stand For*. Carey Kingsgate Press. 1947
J. D. Crichton. *Christian Celebrations: The Sacraments*. Chapman 1973
F. L. Cross and E. A. Livingstone (Eds): *The Oxford Dictionary of the Christian Church*. 2nd Edit. Oxford. 1977
F. L. Cross. *The Early Christian Fathers*. Duckworth. 1960
P. Crowe. *Christian Baptism*. Mowbray. 1980
O. Cullmann. *Baptism in the New Testament*. SCM. 1950
H. Cunliffe-Jones (Ed). *History of Christian Doctrine*. T. & T. Clark. 1980
M. Dalby. *Open Baptism*. SPCK. 1989
E. H. Davenport. *The False Decretals*. Oxford. 1916
J. G. Davies (Ed). *A Dictionary of Liturgy and Worship*. SCM. 1984
J. G. Davies. *Spirit, Church and Sacraments*. Morehouse-Gorham. 1954
M. Deanesly. *A History of the Medieval Church*. Methuen. 1965
F. W. Dillistone (Ed). *Scripture and Tradition*. Lutterworth. 1955
G. Dix. *The Shape of the Liturgy*. A. & C. Black. 1964
G. Dix. *The Apostolic Tradition of Hippolytus*. SPCK. 1968
G. Dix. *The Theology of Confirmation in Relation to Baptism*. A. & C. Black. 1953
N. Dixon. *Troubled Waters*. Epworth. 1979
J. D. Douglas (Ed). *The New International Dictionary of the Christian Church*. Paternoster. 1978
J. D. Dunn. *Baptism in the Holy Spirit*. SCM. 1970
Encyclopedia of Religion. Macmillan and Free Press. 1987
D. L. Edwards. *Christian England. Vol. 2*. Collins. 1983
Ely Report: Christian Initiation. Church Information Office. 1971
J. D. Fisher. *Christian Initiation: Baptism in the Medieval West*. SPCK. 1965
J. D. Fisher. *Christian Initiation: The Reformation Period*. SPCK. 1982
W. F. Flemington. *The New Testament Doctrine of Baptism*. SPCK. 1953
Folk Religion: Friend or Foe? (M. Silversides) Grove Books. 1986
W. H. Frend. *The Early Church*. SCM. 1982

F. Gavin. *The Jewish Antecedents of the Christian Sacraments*. SPCK. 1928
General Synod of the Church of England (1991). *Report of Proceedings. Vol. 22. No. 2*
A. Gilmore (Ed). *Christian Baptism*. Lutterworth. 1959
A. Gilmore. *Baptism and Christian Unity*. Lutterworth. 1966
C. Gore. *Reconstruction of Belief*. John Murray. 1926
R. M. Grant. *Augustus to Constantine*. Collins. 1971
Greek New Testament. United Bible Societies. 2nd Edit. 1968
M. Green. *Baptism: Its Purpose, Practice and Power*. Hodder. 1987
D. G. Hamilton. *Too Young to Matter?* Church of Scotland Education. 1991
D. G. Hamilton (Ed). *Children at the Table*. Church of Scotland Education. 1982
A. Hanson. *Church, Sacraments and Ministry*. Mowbray. 1975
A. T. Hanson. *Reasonable Belief*. Oxford. 1980
J. Hastings (Ed). *Encyclopedia of Religion and Ethics* (E.R.E.) 13 Vols. Relevant Articles. T. & T. Clark. 1912/1937
J. Hastings. *Dictionary of the Apostolic Church*. T. & T. Clark. 1915
P. C. Hodson and R. H. King. *Christian Theology, an Introduction to its Traditions and Tasks*. SPCK. 1983
D. R. Holeton (Ed). *Christian Initiation in the Anglican Communion*. International Anglican Liturgical Consultation, Toronto. 1991. Grove. No. 118.
J. Jeremias. *Infant Baptism in the First Four Centuries*. SCM. 1960
J. Jeremias. *The Origins of Infant Baptism*. SCM. 1963
P. K. Jewett. *Infant Baptism and the Covenant of Grace*. Eerdmans. 1978
D. Jenkins,. *Tradition and the Spirit*. Faber and Faber. 1951
C. Jones, G. Wainwright and E. Yarnold (Eds). *The Study of Liturgy*. SPCK. 1978
J. N. Kelly. *Early Christian Doctrines*. Black. 1977
J. N. Kelly. *Early Christian Creeds*. Longmans. 1979
H. C. Kee. *Christian Origins in Sociological Perspective*. SCM. 1980
M. Kinnamon. *Why It Matters*. World Council of Churches. 1985
Kittel and Friedrich. *Theological Dictionary of the New Testament*. Abridged by G. W. Bromily. Paternoster. 1988
G. Kuhrt. *Believing in Baptism*. Mowbray. 1987
Knaresborough Report: Communion Before Confirmation. Church Information Office. 1985
G. W. Lampe. *The Seal of the Spirit*. SPCK. 1967
K. S. Latourette. *The First Five Centuries in A History of the Expansion of Christianity. Vol. 1*. Eyre and Spottiswoode. 1938
H. Lietzmann. *A History of the Early Church*. Lutterworth. 1961
J. Macquarrie. *Principles of Christian Theology*. SCM. 1966
J. Macquarrie. *The Faith of the People of God*. SCM. 1972
J. Macquarrie. *Tradition, Truth and Christology*, chapter 5 in Theology, Church and Ministry. SCM. 1986
A. C. McGiffert. *A History of Christian Thought. Vols. 1 and 2*. Scribners. 1932

P. Marcel. *The Biblical Doctrine of Infant Baptism*. James Clarke. 1953
J. F. Matthews. *Baptism – A Baptist View*. Baptist Publications. 1976
Methodist Conference (1987) Agenda. *Christian Initiation*. pp. 602–650
Methodist Conference (1991) Agenda. *Faith and Order Report* pp. 153–180
Methodist Statements of Faith and Order. 1933–1983. Methodist Publishing House. 1984
B. M. Metzger. *A textual Commentary on the Greek New Testament*. United Bible Societies. 1975
A. P. Milner. *The Theology of Confirmation*. Mercier Press. 1972
L. L. Mitchell. *Baptismal Anointing*. SPCK. 1966
J. Moltmann. *The Church in the Power of the Spirit*. SCM. 1977
J. R. Moorman. *History of the Church in England*. Black. 1976
O. O'Donovan. *On the Thirty Nine Articles*. Paternoster. 1986
One Lord, One Baptism. W.C.C. Commission on Faith and Order. SCM. 1960
R. R. Osborn. *Forbid Them Not*. SPCK. 1972
C. Owen (Ed). *Reforming Infant Baptism*. Hodder. 1990
J. D. Pawson and C. Buchanan. *Infant Baptism Under Gross-Examination*. Grove Books. 1974
J. D. Pawson. *The Normal Christian Birth*. Hodder. 1989
M. Perham (Ed). *Liturgy For a New Century*. SPCK. 1991
M. Perry (Ed). *Crisis For Confirmation*. SCM. 1967
G. L. Prestige. *Fathers and Heretics*. SPCK. 1958
'Proposals for Unification' between the United Reformed Church and the Churches of Christ. 1976
O. C. Quick. *Doctrines of the Creed*. Collins. 1963
K. Rahner (Ed). *Encyclopedia of Theology*. Burns and Oates. 1977
A. M. Ramsey. *The Doctrine of Confirmation* (*Theology* XLVIII 1945)
B. M. Reardon. *Religious Thought in the Reformation*. Longmans. 1981
M. Reardon. *Christian Initiation – A Policy for the Church of England*. Church House Publishing. 1991
A. Richardson and J. Bowden (Eds). *A New Dictionary of Christian Theology*. SCM. 1983
A. Roberts and J. Donaldson (Eds). *Ante-Nicene Fathers. Vols. 2*, 7 and *8*. T. & T. Clark. 1867–97
Rite of Christian Initiation of Adults. A Study Book. St Thomas More Centre. 1988
A. Schmemann. *Of Water and the Spirit*. SPCK. 1976. (A valuable theological commentary on the baptismal liturgy of the Eastern Orthodox Church.)
M. Searle. *Christening: The Making of Christians*. The Liturgical Press. 1941.
C. R. Smith. *The Sacramental Society*. Epworth Press. 1927
J. Stevenson (Ed). *A New Eusebius*. SPCK. 1980
J. Stevenson (Ed). *Creeds, Councils and Controversies*. SPCK. 1978
K. Stevenson and D. Stancliffe. *Christian Initiation and its Relation to Some Pastoral Offices*. (Article in *Theology*. July 1991)

L. S. Thornton. *Confirmation: Its Place in the Baptismal Mystery*. A. & C. Black. 1954
M. Thurian (Ed). *Ecumenical Perspectives on Baptism, Eucharist and Ministry*. World Council of Churches. 1983
M. Thurian and G. Wainwright (Eds). *Baptism and Eucharist: Ecumenical Convergence in Celebration*. World Council of Churches. 1983
T. F. Torrance. *The Doctrine of Grace in the Apostolic Fathers*. Oliver and Boyd. 1948
United Reformed Church. *Service Book*. Oxford University Press. 1989
United Reformed Church. *Orders of service for Baptism, Confirmation, Thanksgiving and Renewal of Baptismal Promises*. Oxford University Press. 1989
United Reformed Church. *The Manual*. 2nd Edit., N. D. but after 1981
L. Verduin. *The Reformers and Their Stepchildren*. Paternoster. 1964
G. Wainwright. *Christian Initiation*. Lutterworth. 1969
W. Walker. *A History of the Christian Church*. T. & T. Clark. 1959
J. W. Wand. *A History of the Early Church*. Methuen. 1975
E. C. Whitaker. *Documents of the Baptismal Liturgy*. SPCK. 1970
E. C. Whitaker. *The Baptismal Liturgy*. SPCK. 1981
E. C. Whitaker. *A Case for Exorcism in Baptism* (*Theology*. Vol. LX. 1957)
E. C. Whitaker. *Sacramental Initiation Complete in Baptism*. Grove Liturgical Studies. No. 1. 1975. See also his Introduction to *Documents of the Baptismal Liturgy*.
D. E. Whiteley. *The Theology of St Paul*. Blackwell. 1964
R. E. White. *Biblical Doctrine of Initiation*. Eerdmans. 1960
A. R. Whitham. *A History of the Christian Church*. Rivingtons. 1954
M. Wiles. *The Christian Fathers*. SCM. 1981
M. Wiles and M. Santer. *Documents in Early Christian Thought*. Oxford University Press. 1976
C. S. Williams. *Acts of the Apostles*. A. & C. Black. 1964
N. P. Williams. *Ideas of the Fall and of Original Sin*. Longmans 1927
B. L. Woolf. *Reformation Writings of Martin Luther*. Lutterworth. 1952

Index of Subjects

Index of People

Index of Scripture references